History Comes to Life

Collecting Historical Letters and Documents

by Kenneth W. Rendell

NORMAN AND LONDON: UNIVERSITY OF OKLAHOMA PRESS ❧ 1995

Library of Congress Cataloging-in-Publication Data

Rendell, Kenneth W.
    History comes to life : collecting historical letters and
documents / Kenneth W. Rendell.
       p.   cm.
    Includes bibliographical references and index.
    ISBN 0–8061–2764–3
    1. Manuscripts—Collectors and collecting—United States.
I. Title.
Z997.2.U6R45 1995
091'.075—dc20   95–1984
                                                 CIP

The paper in the book meets the guidelines for permanence and durability
of the Committee on Production Guidelines for Book Longevity
of the Council on Library Resources, Inc.

1 2 3 4 5 6 7 8 9 10

CONTENTS

ARTS AND LETTERS

OTHER AREAS

DEDICATION

This book is written for the hundreds, actually thousands, of people with whom I have had the immense pleasure of sharing the field of collecting historical letters and documents since 1959. The substance of this work is the result of our conversations—conversations that have frequently been as interesting and meaningful as the historical autographs themselves.

Collecting historical letters and documents is based on an interest in people and events beyond one's self, but one's self is an integral—indeed, the crucial—element. People collect material that touches feelings, events, and thoughts in their lives, pieces that give the feeling of the "presence" of the personality and time.

People have to have the spark—the interest—the thrill—and I trust the information in this book will then fan that spark into the flames that make historical letters and documents bring history alive.

SPECIAL THANKS

The original draft of this book was reviewed by Terry Belanger, Roy Davids, Rosalie Fawcett, and Shirley McNerney, whose comments and advice have greatly improved the final version.

PREFACE

In 1959, I traded my collection of English medieval coins to a friend in exchange for his collection of presidential letters and immediately became enthralled by the feeling of intimacy with history that these letters gave me. At the time I was a specialist dealer in American colonial coinage, but within a matter of a few months I knew that my life was rapidly heading toward a different path in my pursuit of history. Carried away by my new passion at a New Hampshire auction of the estate of an autograph dealer, I bought most of what was offered and instantly became a dealer to pay for my purchases.

I have loved every—well, almost every—day since then as the temporary possessor of the written record of mankind's greatest heroes and villains as well as the countless individuals who wittingly or unwittingly became a part of the dramas of history.

The following year I published my first catalog, consisting entirely of American presidents—the collection I had acquired the previous year. During the period from 1960 to 1965, my catalogs began to offer historical letters and documents in many areas of American history, beginning with the Revolution and gradually moving forward in time as I expanded my knowledge of the historical facts, the lives of the participants, and, most important, the autograph material—its rarity, the kinds of letters people wrote, the types of documents they signed, whether anyone ever signed for them, and the dozens of other details that are necessary for the accurate

Kenneth W. Rendell's first catalog, 1960

evaluation of autograph material. During the last five years of that decade, I continued to include more areas—first American literature, then English history and literature, and finally Continental history and literature.

It was also during this time that I began to appraise archival collections, a part of the business that was to become very important in the 1970s. In the following twenty years I evaluated a large percentage of the major collections donated to American institutions, including the literary archives of Random House, the archives of the

Northern Pacific Railroad (ten million pieces), the Franklin D. Roosevelt family papers, papers of Samuel L. Clemens, Johannes Brahms, Igor Stravinsky, George Gershwin, Jerome Kern, and Admiral Byrd, the archives of RKO and Paramount Pictures, and literally thousands of others. Appraisal clients included virtually every major library and museum in the country, including the Library of Congress and the National Archives as well as the National Archives of Canada, the Federal Bureau of Investigation, and the Internal Revenue Service. In the 1970s, two appraisals set the legal standards for determining the fair market value of historical letters and documents: in the first, the Otto Kerner case, I represented the Internal Revenue Service; and in the second, I represented the taxpayer, the Northern Pacific Railroad. In both cases my evaluation was upheld with no compromise. These are the only cases to date in which the Tax Court has not compromised between two conflicting values. (I write about appraisals in the past tense because in recent years my time has been devoted to working with collectors, leaving little time for institutional appraisals. However, at the time of this writing, I am actively working on an evaluation of Richard Nixon's White House papers comprising forty-four million pieces and forty-five hundred hours of tapes—a challenge worth getting involved in!)

The second half of the 1960s was also a period of developing and expanding ties with scholarly groups. I began speaking regularly at the annual meetings of the Manuscript Society, the Society of American Archivists, the American Library Association, and the Association of College and Research Libraries and writing articles for their journals. (Later, I was to become president of the Manuscript Society and the International League of Autograph and Manuscript Dealers and was unanimously nominated president of the Antiquarian Booksellers Association of America.)

The 1970s might be termed the "European Decade." In the early years I opened offices in London and Paris, and for most of the decade, I literally commuted, averaging eighteen trips a year. This was the last period when catalogs of historical letters and documents that comprehensively illustrated the history of major periods could be published by a dealer. I began with *The Ancient World* (140 pages), which was followed by *The Medieval World* (285 pages), *Renaissance Europe* (354 pages), *French Artists and Authors* (205 pages), and a three-volume series on the American frontier (729 pages). All represented the most comprehensive catalogs ever published on these subjects by a dealer. Unfortunately, none of them could be rivaled today; the material is simply not available.

In 1979, I was involved as co-editor of *Autographs and Manuscripts: A Collector's Manual* (560 pages), sponsored by the Manuscript Society and published by Charles Scribner's Sons. Selected by the American Library Association as one of the outstanding reference books of its year, it was the most comprehensive book ever published on the subject.

If the 1970s was the "European Decade," the 1980s seemed to be the decade of "going public." In 1983, I was hired by *Newsweek* as their special consultant on the

Hitler diaries. Many weeks were spent trying to determine how these outrageous forgeries had become such an international news story, and all of the publicity had a tremendous effect in making the world of historical letters and documents much better known to the general public.

Two years later, historical letters and documents were back on front pages of newspapers as Mark Hofmann, the Mormon forger, killed two people in an attempt to cover up his forgeries. This extremely complex case remained in the news for the next two years.

In 1987, the New York department store that had pioneered the idea of offering framed historical letters and documents to the general public, B. Altman & Co., was sold, and the new owners closed the departments that did not conform to their retailing concepts; this included the autograph department. As Altman's largest supplier in this area, I knew the great success they had had in offering material to the general public, and I therefore opened my own gallery in New York. Originally, it was across from Carnegie Hall on 57th Street; shortly afterward, I moved it to the Places des Antiquaires on East 57th Street, and in 1993, to our present location at 989 Madison Avenue between 76th and 77th streets.

The Kenneth W. Rendell Gallery in New York

An interior view of the New York gallery

By the late 1980s, the entire business of historical letters and documents had very significantly shifted its focus from institutional to private collectors. This was a result both of decreased institutional budgets, particularly as the availability of major collections declined, and my own personal preference for wanting to share more directly in the enthusiasm and fun of building private collections.

The first few years of the 1990s have seen a continuation of efforts to introduce more people to the idea that historical letters and documents can be collected for relatively modest sums. In 1990, we were invited to exhibit at New York's Winter Antiques Show, the most prestigious antiques show in the United States. During the next two years, we began exhibiting at several other shows. This has given us the pleasure of meeting many new collectors who never knew of the availability of historical letters and documents.

Also in 1990, we converted a bank building in the historic town of South Natick, Massachusetts, where John Eliot preached to the Indians in the seventeenth century, to an office building where we do all of our research, cataloging, conservation, and administration. Our reference library is unrivaled, and we also have the most sophisticated conservation and questioned documents laboratory in the field.

In the fall of 1992, shortly after opening the gallery on Madison Avenue in New York City, we opened a second gallery at 309 North Beverly Drive (at Dayton Way) in Beverly Hills. This decision reflects the fact that many of our clients live in the Beverly Hills area.

Administrative offices of Kenneth W. Rendell, Inc. in South Natick, Massachusetts

Kenneth Rendell at the entrance of the autograph vault in South Natick

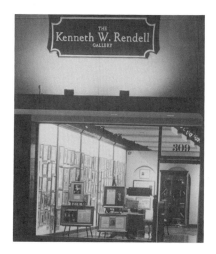

The Rendell gallery in Beverly Hills

An interior view of the Beverly Hills gallery

What about the future? The trend in the past few years has certainly been one of new people discovering the field and being astonished at what they can acquire relatively inexpensively compared to other collecting fields. Several new dealers who have been well established in the coin or stamp field have entered the field of historical letters and documents, putting a great emphasis on investment. I have never offered autograph material as an investment—although it has clearly been a very good one—because the material is so difficult to find that I do not wish simply to sell it to someone for his or her "portfolio." My pleasure is in building collections and friendships with collectors, not in developing their investment portfolios.

Kenneth W Rendell

THE WORLD OF
HISTORICAL
LETTERS & DOCUMENTS

1

WHY PEOPLE COLLECT

The world of historical letters and documents is a virtual time machine that takes us into the lives of those persons in culture and history whose genius has touched us, whose lives and accomplishments have inspired us, whose efforts have created our heritage and influenced our present. History and the people who made it are the keys to who we are today and who we may be tomorrow.

Letters and documents are the most direct link we can have to the heroes and heroines, villains, and ordinary people of the past. They show these men and women as human beings, dealing with matters on a scale that all of us can relate to. We begin to appreciate that their lives may not be all that different from our own—that people of the past confronted the same feelings and fears that we all do, that they persevered to achieve the goals—both great and small—of their lives.

Perhaps the greatest emotion elicited by historical letters and documents is inspiration. While many may think of collecting as an intellectual pursuit, it is an emotional one as well. Many collectors have told me of their being overwhelmed with emotion sitting in a room at home with the "presence" of those they admire. One told me that he walked through the rooms of his home every night in awe of those whose letters and documents he had displayed on his walls. Another described how during low moments, when inspiration escaped her in her work, she sat gazing at her collection and reflecting on the highs and lows of these people's lives and how they had overcome the difficult times and persevered to attain greatness.

Historical letters and documents open doors into times, events, and lives and bring them alive, allowing us literally to touch them and to be touched by them. For many, Winston Churchill's life is the greatest inspiration. No person facing late middle age could fail to be inspired by a man whose political career seemed to be finished during the First World War, who for the decade of the thirties was considered a crackpot by everyone, including his closest friends, and who then, at the age of sixty-five years took over the helm of the English government at a time when it ought to have been conquered by Germany, and, in a very real sense, who through the power of his personality alone inspired his nation to heroic feats unparalleled in modern history.

The greatest autograph and rare book dealer of all time, Dr. A. S. W. Rosenbach, who in the earlier part of the twentieth century brought some of the great collections of Europe to America, thereby helping to create the Huntington and many other great libraries, wrote in his autobiography,

Every true collector is strongly moved when he sees the autograph of a great personage. . . . And, after all, the printed word must have a certain coldness and formality. Indeed, it is perhaps a part of its beauty. But words written down by the actor himself as he helps to complete the drama are personal things which unfailingly appeal to the imagination. . . . There is also some impalpable quality in a great man's handwriting which draws one to it; people who have never dreamed of collecting, who never heard of the collecting mania, will suddenly react to old letters and documents. They are mad to own them. Some human attraction exists in the written word . . . quite different from the appeal made by printing. This appeal is primarily emotional. . . . Especially this is true of autograph letters. They naturally hold a more personal message, in that they interpret the spirit and reflect the period of the writer, who in informal letters is off his guard, quite unlike the mood that an author brings to his work when he knows it may be published. I have known people to weep with delight at the sight of one of those charmingly familiar letters written by Bobbie Burns. Indeed, I once became rather dizzy with joy myself, when I bought the . . . famous letter of Charles Dickens about the inception of *Pickwick*.

Malcolm Forbes, in his book on his collections and his life, *More Than I Have Dreamed,* wrote, "Unquestionably my favorite among the collections are the autograph . . . documents. . . . Such documents give us in many ways a better conception of a person than it is possible to get from a formal portrait or, in later years, from a photograph. They remind us that these are more than historical figures—they were people pouring their hopes, sadnesses, reactions and directions onto paper. Their letters and documents are what makes flesh and blood of key figures in our country's history."

WHAT YOU CAN COLLECT

People whose names have a place in history were generally able to write their own names by the time of the Renaissance in Europe, about 1500. During medieval times writing was still mostly done by professional scribes, and those of prominence "signed" their names, if at all, with a mark that was then embellished and witnessed by a scribe [1].

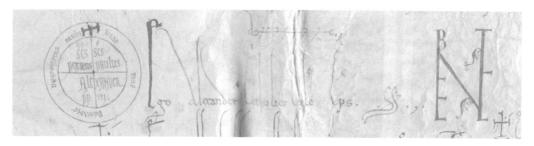

1   A papal signature of Alexander III, the form of which was developed by Pope Leo IX about 1048 for use on privilege grants. It consists of certain elements written by the pope and certain elements written by a notary. The double S's (an abbreviation for the word *subscripsi*, meaning "I have signed") were written by the pope, as was a portion of the rota (a cross placed inside two concentric circles) and the *E* in *Ego*. The upper quadrants of the rota bear the names of Saint Peter and Saint Paul and the lower quadrants bear the name of the pope himself, *Alexander PP* ["Papa" or "Pope"] *III*. The monogram *Benevalete* means "fare well."

By the year 1500, writing had changed significantly, and manuscripts bearing the signatures of most of the well-known people since that time have survived. A number of factors determine whether a person's handwriting is obtainable. A major factor affecting rarity is whether the person was in a position to create letters and documents. Most prominent government positions require a person to sign many letters and documents, and, depending on other factors, many of these would likely have been preserved in family archives. Autograph material of a person who did not have a career requiring the writing of letters and documents is generally much scarcer than the material of those who did. Nathaniel Hawthorne, for example, is far more available in documents signed as the American consul in Liverpool, England, than he is in his capacity as a writer.

A person's life span also affects availability. Autograph material of Frédéric Chopin, who died at a very young age, is very rare, despite his great popularity during his lifetime. Whether a person was well known or not during his lifetime is an important factor. Oliver Wendell Holmes, the writer, was very well known; Herman Melville, author of *Moby Dick,* was scarcely known at all. Today the autograph material of Holmes is fairly common and that of Melville very rare. The notoriety of a person after death has a similar effect. A bundle of letters by a forgotten author whose writings had not as yet been discovered by a future generation would probably be discarded, but a group of Charles Dickens's letters would be preserved.

Perhaps the most important factor affecting current rarity of the papers of prominent figures is whether they have been actively collected by institutional libraries and museums in the past (or whether the person in question gave his or her own papers to an institution). Many major figures wrote numerous letters and documents, and virtually all of them are now in permanent institutional collections. Autograph materials of Mozart and Beethoven are good examples; their letters and manuscripts have been pursued by libraries and museums virtually since their lifetimes (but are still not impossible to obtain).

Generally, people new to the field of historical letters and documents are very surprised at what they can acquire. While autographs of Christopher Columbus are unobtainable, those of his patron, Queen Isabella of Spain, can be found. Autographs of Shakespeare are also unobtainable, but those of some of his contemporaries, particularly in other fields, can be found. The autographs of Galileo are virtually impossible to find (two have been offered on the market in the last twenty years), but those of Isaac Newton, though rare, occasionally turn up. In the various chapters in this book I discuss in detail the important personalities in the various areas of western culture and the type of autograph material that the collector can expect, or hope, to find.

Many collectors of historical letters and documents have formed collections based on specific themes, such as music, literature (usually of a particular country), and historical events, such as the American Civil War. Others form eclectic collections, based solely on persons and events that interest them. Some have concentrated on one individual and then broadened their collection to include the people in that individual's circle—that is, those who influenced that person or were involved in that person's career and accomplishments. In this context, a collection of the letters of Claude Monet could be expanded to include those of the earlier artists who influenced his style as well as his contemporaries who influenced his work.

One of the most popular types of collection is that based on a fixed number of individuals who have one accomplishment in common, the most popular collection of this kind being a set of autographs of all the presidents of the United States. Other sets that are popular with collectors are the signers of the Declaration of Independence and the signers of the U.S. Constitution, as well as the monarchs of different countries, particularly of England, France, and Spain. In most collections, there is a mélange of different types of autograph material: handwritten letters or dictated letters signed, documents, signatures, signed photographs, and so on.

Depending on the individual of interest and the field, various forms of autograph material can be found, and some collections are based solely on a particular form of signed document. Signed bank checks, for example, have been a popular type of collection, and in recent years collections of signed photographs have become very popular. Books from the libraries of prominent persons, preferably signed in ownership inscriptions or otherwise bearing evidence of ownership, are the specialty of a number of collectors. Collections of books signed by their authors and prints and photographs of artwork signed by their creators are other areas, as are signed stock certificates. A form unique to a specific field may be appealing, such as vignettes of the White House signed by each president who issued them, or White House cards signed by the presidents. The availability of these types of signed pieces is discussed in the chapters that follow.

A collector should not be bound by any rules of collecting except those created by his or her own interests and ideas. Many of the greatest collections have been formed by collectors pioneering new areas at a time when their interest or specialty was not appreciated by others. Signed photographs, now very popular as a collecting specialty, were deemed of little interest about twenty-five years ago. One collector's search for them as representing how signers wanted others to see them led him to form the greatest collection of signed photographs, write a popular book about them, and inspire many others in this interesting area of specialization.

3

WHO COLLECTS

Scholars and serious collectors were the principal, indeed almost the only, collectors of historical letters and documents as recently as twenty to thirty years ago. Prices were low, large numbers of letters and documents were available, and most university and public libraries as well as historical societies had special collections divisions that were very active in locating and purchasing historical letters.

During the past decade and a half, the situation has changed dramatically. From the mid-1950s through about 1980, university and public libraries and historical societies sought out the papers of nearly every prominent person in most fields, with the result that many major archives are now in permanent research collections. Any group of papers that could be called a collection found an immediate buyer among the hundreds of university libraries that were funded with federal and state money intended to support research institutions. Graduate schools needed original material for students to use in research projects, and many employed full-time field agents not only to seek out an author's or family's papers but also to contact persons whom the subject of the collection would have written to and obtain those letters as well. Many individual letters and correspondences escaped the grasp of the institutions, but an overwhelming number of historical letters and documents were acquired by institutions during this time.

Today, relatively few archival collections or major correspondences are offered for sale because so little remains in private hands. Funds for research libraries have been cut drastically in recent years, but so much material has already been bought by institutions that these cuts have had less effect than would otherwise be the case.

Changes have also taken place with private collectors. Thirty years ago collectors of the American Revolution might have hundreds of letters and documents in their collections, but as these collectors have since disposed of their collections, individual letters and documents have been sold to a number of other collectors. With prices rising and many new private collectors entering the field, the material has been spread out among a much greater number of collectors. A collection of five hundred pieces might have been sold to fifty different collectors, and each of these collections will in turn be sold to more than one collector.

In my experience, today's collector is typically a fairly well-read person, frequently an entrepreneur, a decision maker, who has a strong interest in the people and events that have made our culture and world what it is today. Many collect in areas that relate to their professions, such as legal, financial, or medical history, but the majority collect in the areas in which they read. There have been and are a large number of very well known and accomplished people collecting historical letters and documents (Pierpont Morgan's first collection was letters and documents). We never divulge information about clients—and few collectors seek such publicity—but a few, such as the late Malcolm Forbes and Armand Hammer as well as Ross Perot, have been very public about their collecting of historical letters and documents. It seems natural that popular singers collect musical manuscripts, that a leading director and producer of movies collects pieces relating to the history of film, that a number of modern composers collect letters and manuscripts of composers of the past, and that writers collect letters of the people about whom they have written. America's best-known science writer collects early scientists. Many of our clients are as fascinating and well known as the people whose letters they are collecting. What they all have in common is a respect for and interest in the genius and accomplishments of others.

While public museums and libraries are for the most part no longer the major competitors for historical letters, manuscripts, and documents, a small number of private libraries and museums have been formed which are very active and important in the field. The Forbes Magazine Collection, for example, housed in the magazine's headquarters building in New York City, offers changing exhibits taken from their very extensive collections of historical letters and documents.

4

WHERE MANUSCRIPTS ARE FOUND

My principal sources of historical letters and documents are the descendants of those who were the original recipients and private collectors who have decided to sell their collections. A family that possesses correspondence written to ancestors or a series of presidential appointments or land grants issued to family members will frequently keep them in the family until they become aware that the financial value of the family papers exceeds their "sentimental value." Having been a dealer in letters and documents for more than thirty years, I have sold many millions of dollars worth of autograph material to private collectors; and as collectors change their interests, or their personal situations change, many collections that I have developed for my clients are offered back to me.

The proverbial "find in the attic" is the most commonly overrated source of historical letters and documents. While discoveries are made like this, they represent a very small portion of what appears on the market. With all of the publicity given to substantial discoveries in recent years, there are very few owners of family papers or collectors who have not explored their value. Owners almost always know the relative value of what they have; the question is primarily whether they have a sentimental value that is greater or lesser than the market value.

Prior to 1934, when the National Archives was established, official U.S. government papers, in many cases, were eventually discarded. Since the founding of the national repository, that is no longer the case, and the only official documents now coming into the market are those issued to individuals, mostly appointments to various government positions.

Library deaccessions have become an important source of historical letters and documents in recent years. Many libraries were given collections years ago for which they now have no use. As budget problems have plagued libraries, it has made sense to convert unwanted collections into funds needed for other activities. Many important institutional collections have been sold, including sets of presidents and signers of the Declaration of Independence as well as the holdings of one entire library, the Doheny.

For the collector, dealers specializing in historical letters and documents are the most reliable source of material. Specialist dealers offer knowledge based on years of experience, both in terms of availability and rarity and authenticity. Experienced dealers keep rarity in perspective. They know how many pieces they have seen or have handled over the decades and are not basing their judgment on a few years of experience, which usually results in an exaggerated statement of rarity. Dealers handling many fields cannot keep informed about what is being offered and have a very limited perspective on rarity.

The best specialist dealers also offer unconditional guarantees of authenticity, guarantees that should be without a time limit. A collector usually does not decide to sell his collection for many years, and if a piece proves not to be genuine, the guarantee should be in effect. The dealers either are confident in the authenticity of the material or they are not. If they are, then the guarantees should be lifetime guarantees. If they restrict the guarantees with a time limit, they are putting an unreasonable burden on the collector to determine the genuineness of the piece within that period—a responsibility that was the dealers' in the first place. Collectors should ask specialist dealers about their experience, their number of years in business, and the areas they specialize in and form an idea of the basis for the dealers' opinions. There are a relatively large number of part-time dealers, some with an excellent perspective on the field but many with virtually none.

Auctions are another source for historical letters and documents, but collectors must be extremely cautious in this market. Many auction houses offer autograph material as one of the numerous categories they handle, but only very few have any real professional, developed expertise in the field. As a result, rarities can be undercataloged and undervalued. That is rarely the case, however, because most auction house catalogers have no perspective in the field and can often overvalue what they offer. There is also the very significant problem of authenticity, and collectors should determine for themselves the quality of the opinion they are relying on and very carefully understand the terms of sale. Only a very few auction houses offer any form of guarantee of authenticity.

Some auction houses base their estimates on what owners want for their pieces, not on what the auction houses actually think they are worth. This practice is very misleading. It is not uncommon for the auction houses to have "bidding wars" among themselves, offering consignors higher estimates and reserves (the minimum bid acceptable) in order to get the consignment. Some auction houses are forced to "try out" pieces at high estimates, and if inexperienced collectors are willing to accept the estimates and pay the prices, they end up purchasing overvalued items. If the pieces are not sold at the auction, they are simply returned to the consignors and the only loss is the space in the catalog.

The specialist dealer, in contrast, almost always has invested his own money in what he is offering, and if his prices are too high and not in keeping with the market, his reputation will suffer among knowledgeable and experienced collectors who have a good sense of market value. His reputation is on the line when he sets prices. The specialist dealer, unlike the auction house, has a financial investment that can only be realized with the sale of the piece: he has not only his reputation but his capital at stake.

Many times, the high estimates and reserves of auction houses are significantly exceeded because inexperienced collectors assume that they are bidding against knowledgeable collectors and that if they overpay at auction, it is only by their last and winning bid. What they do not realize is that the underbidder frequently is acting under the same misapprehension and, in fact, serious and knowledgeable collectors have either dropped out or were never bidding. It is an enticing idea that at auction a bidder needs to bid only one bid beyond what informed, veteran collectors are willing to pay, but this theory is applied by so many people that items in many fields frequently sell for well above normal market value.

New collectors should be wary of the "country" auction. Many items offered in these sales, which offer no guarantees of any sort (everything is sold "as is"), are pieces that were previously offered for sale to specialist dealers or larger, established auction houses but were rejected for various reasons. Many clearly forged pieces and facsimiles make their way into these sales, as do pieces in poor condition. It has been my experience that prices for items in poor condition are usually much higher in such locations than similar quality material offered by specialist dealers and the larger auction houses.

A few years ago, a Boston television station covered the auction of a George Washington letter on Cape Cod. My wife was the news anchor and showed me the script of the story. When I saw the producer after the broadcast, I mentioned that the letter was very routine and sold for far more than better letters in my stock. I remarked that I had really historically interesting letters for the same price as the one sold at the auction, and if they were sufficiently interested to send a camera crew to Cape Cod, they should do a story on what I had. I was told that my offering of George Washington letters was not a news story—there was no romance to it—whereas a George Washington letter being discovered and sold in a country auction was.

The following week, I was talking to an enterprising Boston collector who mentioned the story. I commented on the high price, whereupon he told me that it had been his letter. He had consigned it to the country auction on Cape Cod hoping that it would receive far more attention than its content or rarity would warrant in regular collecting circles. When I congratulated him on his entrepreneurial skills, he reminded me that he had bought the letter from me six months earlier for about a third of the price it had brought at the auction! It was an important lesson in how the market setting can drastically affect prices.

Flea markets are the major source of letters and documents that are either not genuine or were not signed by the person represented. The documents may be signed by *a* genuine "John Hancock" but not *the* John Hancock who signed the Declaration of Independence. In Boston, during the Revolution, there were also many people with the name "Sam Adams." Genuine bargains do come from flea markets, but so much misrepresented material is brought to us from such sources that it is apparent they are the places in the market chain where the most mistakes and misidentities are found. The people who bring these pieces to us have no recourse: there are no guarantees or rights of return in markets.

The collector should always keep in mind that if a historical letter or document is offered at a price that seems too good to be true, there is a good chance that it probably is not!

5

THE DETECTION OF FORGERIES

Virtually since the beginning of writing, people have been trying to affect our knowledge of current events, our history, and our literature by forging the principal means by which such information is conveyed to us—letters, manuscripts, documents, and diaries. The written word, even in this modern era of video, telephone, and satellite communication, is the basis of much of today's news, and hence tomorrow's history. The forging of manuscript material has more commonly been done to change history than to achieve financial gain.

The most famous modern forgery cases, notably, the Hitler diaries and the Mormon forgeries, have contained elements of both: efforts to change history and swindle people out of money. This chapter is principally about the forging of documents for financial gain. These have generally been the far more sophisticated forgeries, in which the forger has combined research of the texts of the manuscripts with the use of scientific knowledge and extraordinary skill in their physical creation. The forgeries created mainly to change history have been the more sophisticated hoaxes involving elaborate provenance and situations wherein the victims of the forgeries end up playing as important a role as the proponents of the forgeries and frauds.

The authentication of autograph material is a painstaking and meticulous procedure for the expert, requiring a thorough knowledge of the characteristics of forged and genuine writing; technical data concerning paper, ink, and writing instruments; effective methods of comparing handwritings; common habits of forgers; and the necessary equipment for reaching a definitive conclusion. Many of the factors considered in examining handwriting are not conclusive proof of authenticity by themselves and must be evaluated in relation to other evidence. Obvious points, such as paper manufactured after the purported date of the document, instantly indicate a forgery. However, it can be an error to conclude from an examination of only a few factors that the writing is genuine or forged.

Various factors other than forgery can cause a change in a person's handwriting. The two principal ones are age and illness. Handwriting from different periods of a person's life may differ markedly. Unusual circumstances in the way in which a letter or document was written or signed may also give the appearance of forgery. Most people, for example, write a much clearer signature when affixing it to an important legal document than to a routine check; it is an important event, and the signature is usually written with more care. People *sign* their names, in most cases, quite differently from the way in which they would *write* their names (for example, in the text of a letter). And an individual's signature may vary according to the space available. If a signature

Mount Vernon May 16th 1785:

Dear Sir,

In for a penny, in for a
pound is an old adage. — I am so hackney ed
to the touches of the Painters pencil, that I
am now altogether at their back, and set
like patience on a monument whilst they
are delineating the lines of my face. —

It is a proof among many others,
of what habit & custom can effect. — at first
I was as impatient at the request, and
as restive under the operation, as a
Colt is of the Saddle — The next time, I
submitted very reluctantly, but with less
flouncing. — Now, no dray moves more
readily to the Thill, than I do to the Pain
ters Chair. — It may easily be conceived
therefore that I yielded a ready obedience
to your request, and to the views of Mr
Pine.

Letters from England, recommen
datory of this Gentleman, came to my hand
previous to his arrival in America —
not only as an Artist of acknowledged
eminence, but as one who had discover
ed a friendly disposition towards this Coun
try for which, it seems, he had been marked.

It gave me pleasure to hear from
you — I shall always feel an interest in
your happiness — and with Mrs Washing
tons compliments, & best wishes joined
to my own, for Mrs Hopkinson & yourself.

I am — Dr Sir,
Yr most Obedt & affecte
Hble Servant

G Washington

Frans Hopkinson Esqr

2 Forged letter of George Washington written with characteristic shaky and drawn strokes

12

hazarding sentiments upon a super
ficial view of things, when it will
appear, ultimately, that he has had
important objects in view, and has
accomplished them. —

I take the liberty of address
sing the inclosed letter to your care
& to assure you of the respect and
esteem with which I have the honor
to be,

Sir,

Y.r most obed.t &c

G.º Washington

.D. m. A.

is altered to fit a small space, the letter formations are likely to be more characteristic of his writing in the body of a letter.

Collectors are frequently advised to buy only from "reliable and reputable" dealers, but how is a new collector to make such a determination? First of all, buy only from those who give an unconditional guarantee of authenticity. Ask dealers about their experience—not just in terms of years but also how much similar material they have handled. Ask about articles published in scholarly journals, papers delivered before archival and library groups, recognition by their peers. But, most important, ask dealers how they authenticated the pieces in question.

It is true that an initial element that many call "intuition" does play an important part in any examination of questioned documents. But what is frequently called intuition is a simultaneous observation of combinations of facts reflected against the mental images stored during decades of experience, giving an initial indication of whether the document in question meets the general criteria of genuine documents of the period and circumstances.

General Characteristics of Forged Writing

I will demonstrate that authentication of historical letters and documents is based neither on "intuition" nor on "gut feelings." Authentication of historical letters and documents uses an analytic approach that can be illustrated and proven. Dealers who cannot explain their methods of authentication to your satisfaction are ones you should avoid.

The most immediately apparent characteristics of forged writing are its drawn or labored appearance and slow hesitating strokes intermingled with shaky strokes, frequently exhibiting far too much attention to detail and too much care in the formation of individual letters. The forged George Washington autograph letter [2] is reasonably well done, but when compared with a genuine autograph letter of Washington [3], the shaky strokes and excessive care taken in the writing become

4–6
Forged signatures of Civil War generals
George B. McClellan and William Tecumseh
Sherman and of the playwright and critic
George Bernard Shaw, written with hesitating
starts and stops; the Shaw, in addition, shows
retouching in the writing

immediately apparent. These characteristics are all a result of attempting to imitate someone else's writing patterns rather than instinctively following one's own. Normal writing is written with speed, flow, and smoothness, without interruption and with a lack of attention to detail and individual letter formations. (There are, of course, exceptions, particularly in the case of illness or advanced age.)

The two Civil War signatures and the signature of George Bernard Shaw [4–6] also show the shaky lines and telltale "drawn" appearance of forgeries. Additionally, they illustrate the fact that not all forgeries are created for financial or literary reasons. These examples, of relatively little value, were probably forged while the purported authors were living and collectors competed with each other to obtain their autographs.

The care taken in executing forgeries will often produce signatures that are much more legible than genuine examples. This is demonstrated in the genuine and fake signatures of Charles Dickens [7, 8].

7 Genuine signature of Charles Dickens   8 Forged Dickens signature

Normal genuine writing begins and ends with what can be called flying starts and endings; the initial stroke commences as a very fine line, broadening as it approaches the initial formation of the character. The writer terminates the writing by removing the pen rapidly from the surface of the paper, resulting in a final stroke that decreases in width until it disappears [9]. While this is not necessarily true of all writers, few people begin writing by boldly putting the pen onto the paper directly and then beginning the stroke. Nor do they hesitate after finishing the final stroke and then lift the pen directly off the paper [10]. This method of writing is, however, very common among forgers, who, of course, are not writing in a normal manner.

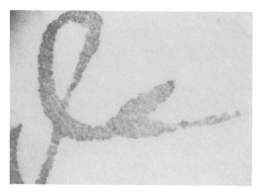 

9 Genuine writing showing the effect of rapidly removing the pen from the surface of the paper

10 Forged writing showing a heavy concentration of ink at the end of the stroke

15

Lifting the pen when writing individual letters has been the habit of some less accomplished forgers, and unless it is known that the author of the writing in question had this habit, such pen lifts can suggest the probability of forgery. The more skillful forger can align the continuing stroke after a pen lift, but in many cases the ink from the continuing stroke will flow back onto the first stroke, creating a double thickness of ink. (Ballpoint pens, particularly the early models, and pencils create writing in which pen lifts are virtually impossible to detect.)

Rewriting or retouching is unusual in genuine writing and is done only to improve legibility. Great care is not normally taken by the writer. If a pen runs out of ink, or otherwise fails, a writer will begin again where the quality of the writing was affected. Rewriting or retouching that shows an intention of continuing a smooth form, in the absence of ink depletion, should always be a signal of a possible forgery. The *h* in George Washington's signature has clearly been retouched after the pen was lifted off the writing surface [11, 12].

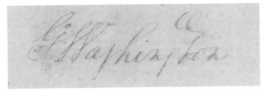

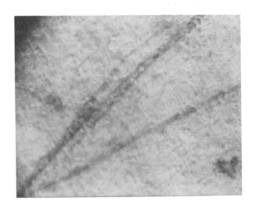

11 Forged signature of George Washington revealing evidence of retouching

12 Enlargement of the letter *h* in Washington's signature showing some retouching of the loop

A significant number of writers do not use the same form of capital letters in their writing as they do in their signatures. Their signatures have more stylized, more individual capitals, and many forgers have used the signature form of a capital in the body of the text. This was one of the glaring errors of Konrad Kujau, the forger of the Hitler diaries. With little of Hitler's genuine handwriting to study, Kujau wrote all of the capital *H*'s in the text with the highly stylized *H* from Hitler's signature, when in fact Hitler always employed a very plain *H* in the body of his writing [13, 14].

13 Hitler generally wrote the letter *H* in a straight-forward manner

14 The forger Kujau used the stylized form of the letter

Tracings are not often encountered in the field of historical documents, but they do occur. Those made by placing paper over a genuine signature and using transmitted light to project the image are rarely seen, since they require that both the genuine example and the forgery be written on translucent paper, which would be suspect in itself. A more common but relatively crude method is to place a facsimile or photocopy of a genuine signature over the paper to be forged and with a sharp instrument trace the genuine facsimile. The resulting indented line on the blank paper is then filled in with ink, but traces of it are nearly impossible to erase. Equally inept are traced signatures initially done with pencil and then with ink; the pencil markings are later erased. Microscopic examination will show signs of both the indented line and the pencil tracing. The poor line quality of such tracings, however, rarely necessitates such a detailed examination.

A characteristic that I have found surprisingly common is the forger's habit of using the same form of writing when forging sections supposedly written by different persons. Dockets and endorsements or other notations that would have been written by the recipient will sometimes contain identical word formations as the document.

A recent forgery illustrating this error is the letter purportedly written by Clyde Barrow and signed by him and Bonnie Parker. Having varied the two capital letters, the forger has written "Parker" in Bonnie Parker's signature in the same style as the body of the letter, which was supposedly written by Clyde Barrow [15].

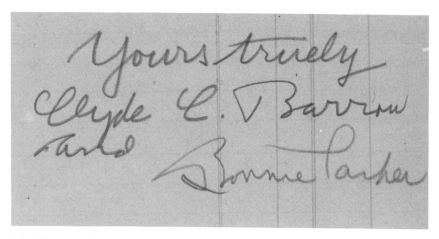

15 Closing and signatures of Clyde C. Barrow and Bonnie Parker from a forged letter

Sections of forged writing added to genuine documents are usually detected (if the forgery was added sometime later, as is usually the case) by the feathering effect of writing on old, porous paper (this is discussed in detail under the heading "Ink"). Another factor to consider is if the person would have signed such a document [16]. For example, there is no apparent reason for Samuel L. Clemens to have signed the shipping document shown here. One must also be alert to the possibility that the genuineness of the document does not necessarily authenticate the writing that makes it valuable. The Button Gwinnett signature added to a genuine eighteenth-century account book is forged [18], as is the stylized signature of Frederic Remington and the sketch of a bucking horse added to a page that does bear genuine writing of the American western artist [17].

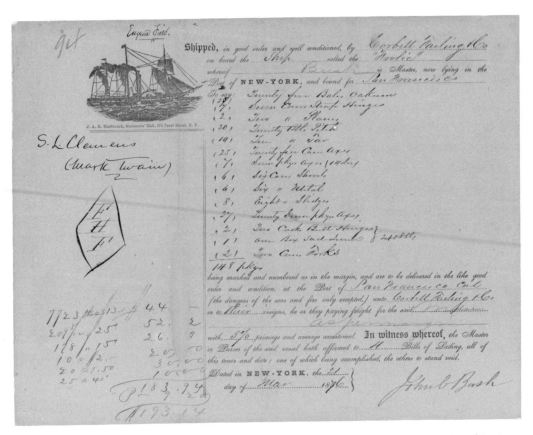

16 Forged signature of Samuel Langhorne Clemens added sometime later to a genuine shipping document dated March 21, 1876

17 Forged drawing of a bucking horse and signature of Frederic Remington added to a page bearing genuine writing by the artist

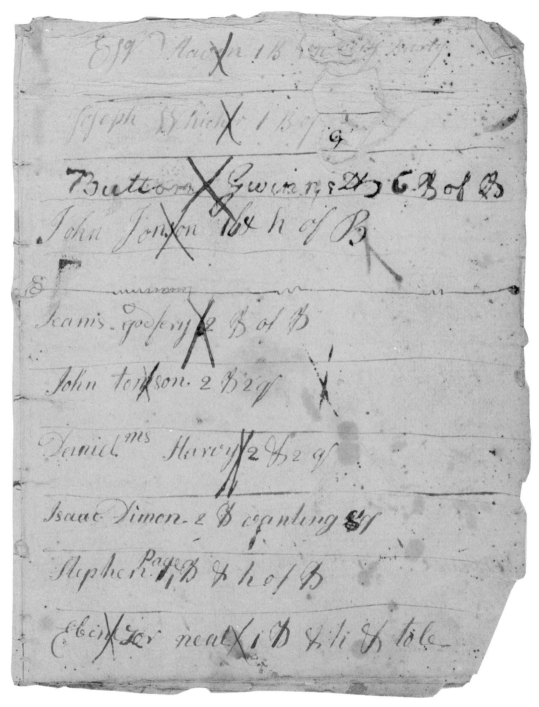

18 Forged signature of Button Gwinnett added to a genuine eighteenth-century account book

Another consideration in examining the writing alone is consistency of style and form with national characteristics of writing systems of the time. The system of forming letters, linking the characters, and spacing varies widely between countries and periods of time. A system of writing that was common in the United States during the early nineteenth century would be most suspect if it were employed in a letter supposedly written by a native German living in his own country at that time.

Terminology, forms of address, salutations, closings, and the general layout and folding of letters have all changed significantly through the years, and a detailed knowledge of these factors is very important in examining historical documents and letters. The three examples of Charles Dickens, Lord Tennyson, and George Washington, all indicate that the forgers had no idea of the genuine terminology of the time [19–21]. The forger of the Washington letter might as well have written the closing, "Have a Nice Day, George."

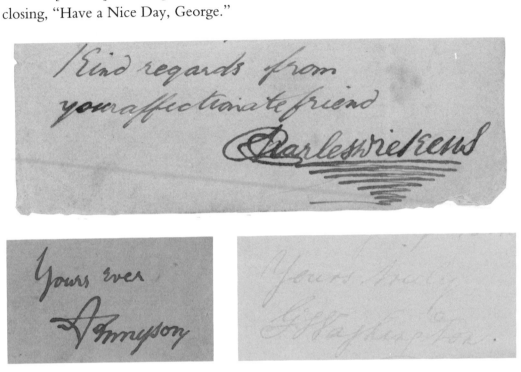

19–21 Forged examples of Charles Dickens, Lord Tennyson, and George Washington, showing the use of anachronistic terminology in their closings

The text or content of the letter or document is of great importance in uncovering forgeries. In many cases it is the content that immediately unmasks them. Forgers have actually dated letters and documents after the death of the supposed author. An important exception to this are presidential documents that were signed in blank and then filled in and dated later. It is therefore possible to have a presidential document dated after the death of the president or after his administration ended. Another exception exists in situations where checks were postdated and the writers died before the date that appears on the checks. An example of this occurred when Charles Dickens wrote a check dated June 10, 1870, in payment of his estranged wife's quarterly allowance but died the day before the date of the check, June 9. Facts, in addition to the date, should be verified: was it likely the writer was in the stated city at that time?— are the facts in the text accurate?—is it likely the person would have written a letter with this specific content at this time in his life? (George Washington writing in 1797 praising the wisdom of the Louisiana Purchase of 1804 would be a clear sign of forgery!)

The content of the letter or document is also one of the two principal areas of examination for determining if the real person wrote the item in question (the other is handwriting comparison). There were, for example, many people in Boston at the end of the eighteenth century named Samuel Adams and John Adams, but it is unlikely that they would have written letters or signed documents similar to those the patriots did, excluding, of course, routine personal notes. (In these cases, exacting comparisons of handwriting are necessary.)

In the case of the Hitler diaries, the greatest failings cannot be attributed to the journalists but to the historians they had hired and on whom they had relied. These historians had access to the content of the diaries long before publication but failed to discover, as other historians did later, that there were no facts in the diaries that were not contained in either a privately printed book by Max Domarus entitled *Hitler: Speeches and Proclamations, 1932–1945,* or *Volkischer Beobachter,* the Nazi party's daily newspaper. The diaries even repeated a typographical error in addition to copying factual errors from the Domarus book.

The Materials: Paper, Ink, and Writing Instruments

PAPER

Examination of the paper or parchment can readily unmask many forgeries. A substantial number of forgers have neglected the importance of the paper in dating letters and manuscripts and have used types of paper that were not yet or no longer in use at the time of the purported document. Prior to 1300, parchment or vellum, made from animal skin, was used almost exclusively (papyri and other ancient materials predate the scope of the present work). Documents written on paper and dated before the fourteenth century are very unlikely to be genuine; certainly great care would need to be taken in accepting them as authentic. Paper made from linen rags and on a wire frame (resulting in a grid pattern that can be seen when the paper is held up to the light), which is called "laid" paper, was used concurrently with vellum after 1400, the paper being used almost exclusively for letters and routine matters such as bookkeeping and the vellum, for documents. The use of vellum for important (usually legal) documents continued well into the nineteenth century, and a modern version is still encountered in some unusual cases today. Laid paper has also continued in use until the present time, especially for fine quality writing paper. Wove paper without the grid pattern came into general use in America beginning about 1800 and in Europe, about 1765. In 1867, wood pulp paper was commercially introduced; the acidity of this paper varies, but it is almost always far less stable than paper made from cloth rags.

An examination of the kind of paper used provides a range of possible dates. Some papers are watermarked with a decorative design or the name of the maker and sometimes also with the date of the manufacture of the paper mold on which the paper was made. While it may seem unlikely that a forger would fail to notice a dated watermark, it does happen. A well-written forgery of John F. Kennedy's famous quotation from his inaugural address, "Ask not what your country can do for you, ask what you can do for your country," was written on genuine White House stationery watermarked 1981, eighteen years after the president's assassination. The skill of the forger did not extend to common sense enough to hold the blank piece of White House stationery up to the light.

The skillful forger, however, can usually obtain the correct paper of the period without too much difficulty. Contemporary journals and account books with blank pages and the unused leaves of contemporary letters provide the sophisticated forger with his basic materials. The forger of the Mormon documents, Mark Hofmann, for example, obtained the right paper by buying single-page letters with integral address leaves and separated the letters, leaving blank pages for his forgeries. In other cases he removed blank end leaves from contemporary books in libraries, the common resort of nineteenth-century European forgers.

Particular sizes of paper were used at different periods, as were different colors, and size and color can provide the initial clue to a forgery. Oblong folio vellum was the most popular size for documents prior to 1600, as was legal folio paper (about 8-1/2 by 14 inches) for letters. In the late seventeenth century, quarto (approximately 8-1/2 by 11 inches) became the most popular size for letters, with legal documents frequently being written on larger sheets or membranes of vellum. Octavo sizes (about 8 by 6 inches) for letters became common in the early part of the nineteenth century. A glance at the George Washington forgery of a receipt dated June 10, 1767, indicates that the forger was unaware that Washington would not have written a document of this type on vellum; nor would such a small and damaged piece have been used.

One of the curious aspects of forgery is the false aging of the paper or vellum. While the skillful forger obtains paper contemporary with the period, the amateur attempts to duplicate aged paper by soaking it in tea, burning it, tearing small holes in it, rubbing dirt into the fibers, or other cosmetic means. When he writes on the paper, the amateur forger invariably avoids the holes and particles of dirt. A slightly less amateurish forger obtains paper that actually is old and follows some of the same "aging" processes to avoid having the paper look too new. These forgers are unaware that most historical letters and documents are in fine condition (especially when written on laid paper) and that persons normally wrote letters and documents on paper that was in excellent condition, without holes or other defects. A significant exception to this general statement are the holes that can naturally appear in parchment or vellum documents. These holes are caused by natural defects in the animal skin and are not the result of damage or deterioration. Parchment with these holes already present was used by scribes; they naturally avoided the holes when writing the text, and legal and business documents with these natural characteristics are sometimes encountered.

Chemical tests are very useful when examining paper made during the past thirty years, a period in which many new chemical combinations have been used in papermaking. Like the chemical analysis of ink, this is a very complex area, and is best undertaken by specialists in paper analysis. Determining whether paper contains an optical brightener can be readily done with a good high-intensity ultraviolet light. The optical brightener fluoresces a brilliant white and is unmistakable evidence that the paper was produced after 1950. Many manufacturers have varied their watermarks and other patterns over time, so that the precise year of manufacture can be determined. Some makers of account books, for example, have varied very slightly the width of the columns so that backdated ledgers can be detected.

Anyone examining forgeries of historical documents must be aware of the existence of large numbers of unused genuine printed forms that have been, and are, available to forgers. During the final days of World War II, as Allied soldiers raced through Germany, large quantities of unused printed forms and stationery were taken as souvenirs. Unused stationery of Adolf Hitler, embossed in gold with his name and the Nazi eagle, is occasionally sold in the ephemera markets. The genuineness of the paper and printing is, therefore, only one factor in determining authenticity.

INK

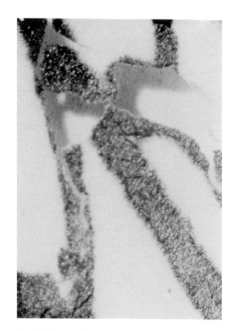

An examination of ink is important for determining the earliest date that a letter or document could have been written. As with paper, there are relatively few types of ink to be concerned with until very recent times, when the subject becomes much more complex and it becomes necessary to analyze inks chemically to differentiate the many different types of compounds and their dates of use.

The earliest ink was made from finely ground carbon; extremely stable, it did not attack the vellum or paper on which it was used. Iron gall ink, the type most often encountered in collecting, was invented in the Middle Ages; it was likely to be acidic in content and to attack the paper. Iron gall also changes color with time, and the reddish tones acquired by many inks of this type are very distinctive and almost impossible to imitate. Equally difficult to imitate is the effect of the high acidity of this type of ink

22 Writing from a genuine Robert Morris signature on a document, illustrating the corrosion of paper caused by highly acidic iron gall ink, an effect that is difficult for forgers to duplicate

on paper, as is evidenced in the signature on a genuine Robert Morris document written just after the American Revolution. The ink has literally eaten through the paper, leaving only an outline of where some of the writing was [22].

Coloring matter was found in iron gall ink as early as the American Revolution, although its presence so early is quite unusual. Colored inks did become increasingly popular, particularly in Europe, after 1835. Indigo, with its characteristic bluish tint, was more commonly added to iron gall ink after 1836 but can be encountered before this date. Iron nut gall ink, invented in 1836, differs from other inks, particularly iron gall, in that a considerable part of the coloring matter is held in suspension and as a result penetrates the fibers of the paper instead of drying on the surface.

The year 1856 was significant from the collector's standpoint since that is when aniline inks were invented. The chief characteristic of this ink is its solubility in water, with the result that the ink will run on contact with water; its primary advantage is that it does not attack the paper as iron gall ink does.

India ink has a uniformity of shading that is comparable to printer's ink. It is frequently confused with printing and sometimes mistaken for a facsimile. The sheen of India ink is one means of differentiating between this ink and the dull finish of printer's ink; another is the fact that India ink is water based, whereas printer's ink is oil based, a difference that is easy to spot under analysis.

Modern inks can only be dated through chemical testing. Modern ink manufacturers, like papermakers, have added compounds to their products at one time or another, with the result that their dates of manufacture can often be established. A procedure

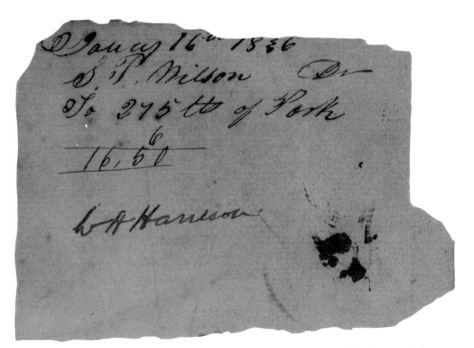

23 Forgery of William H. Harrison's signature on a genuine early-nineteenth-century document showing the absorbency of the paper, which causes the ink to feather out

has also been developed for establishing the length of time an ink has been on the paper based on the migration of ions into the paper. This test is effective only with inks containing iron.

As paper ages, it becomes more absorbent. Ink applied to old paper will in most cases be rapidly absorbed, spreading out in a feathery pattern and creating an outline to the main strokes. The William Henry Harrison signature was forged on a genuine document of the early nineteenth century [23]. The unusual flow of the ink is apparent in this enlargement [24]. (In unusual circumstances, this can occur in genuine writing, but it is generally an immediate indication of forgery.)

The forger of the Mormon documents prevented this "feathering" from occurring with

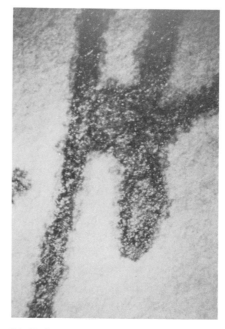

24 Enlargement of the letter *H* in the Harrison signature

great skill, by covering the paper with ammonia hydrochloride or hydrogen peroxide. Two tests did, however, indicate this fake aging. Examination under high-powered ultraviolet light showed a blue fluorescence from the ammonia hydrochloride, immediately giving evidence of chemical treatment. The second effect—tiny cracks that made each stroke appear like a reptile's skin—could only be seen under high magnification and its importance understood only when one realizes that all the letters and documents that fluoresced blue also showed a cracking of the ink. The ammonia hydrochloride had prevented the feathering pattern of new ink on old paper by raising the pH factor, which caused the ink to coagulate, harden, and crack (pH 7 is the neutral value between acidity or alkalinity; when it is raised, an increase in alkalinity is indicated). A third element was immediately visible to the naked eye in many of Hofmann's forgeries: the chemical used to prevent feathering had caused this ink to run slightly, giving the overall writing a slightly blurred appearance.

WRITING INSTRUMENTS

The traditional quill pen is the oldest writing instrument normally encountered in autograph collecting. The steel pen began to be used in the latter part of the eighteenth century, a fact frequently overlooked by some forgers who, mistakenly believing that quill pens were employed until recent times, have used them on letters written in the earlier part of the twentieth century. The writing of a quill pen differs notably from that of a steel pen, particularly in downstrokes and lateral strokes, which are broadly

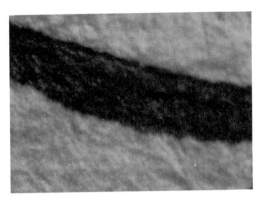

25 Enlargement of a letter written with a quill pen. The quill pen makes no furrows and the writing appears as a smooth stroke.

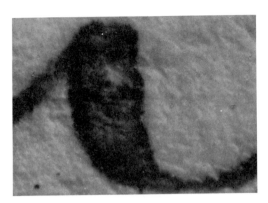

26 Enlargement of a letter written with a steel nib pen showing readily visible nib marks

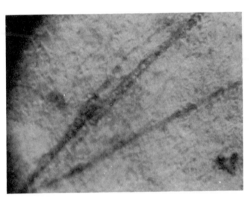

27 Enlargement of the letter *h* from a forged George Washington letter written with a steel nib pen

shaded because of the flexibility of the quill [25]. In addition, under microscopic examination, the nib marks of steel pens (which create two "furrows" with ink in between them) are clearly visible [26]. Many writers did continue to use the earlier instrument well into the nineteenth century, but the dealer or collector should be aware of its decreasing popularity and consequent comparative rarity during the middle and later part of the century.

The presence of nib marks rather than the absence of shaded lateral and downward strokes will instantly unmask many forgeries in which a steel pen was used to write what purports to be a pre-1780 letter or document. Frequently these marks are so strong as to be clearly visible to the naked eye. The forger of the George Washington receipt [27] failed to keep enough ink on his pen to cover even superficially his use of a steel pen in a letter where it would have been most unlikely to find a steel pen used.

The ballpoint pen began to be used widely at the end of the Second World War in America and somewhat earlier in Europe. The early examples created very blunt and heavy initial strokes and were prone to skip over the paper fibers without depositing ink. These defects coupled with the poor line quality can give the appearance of being forgeries. In contrast, the fiber or felt-tip pen introduced in 1964 creates a ribbonlike smooth flow of ink.

The use of a defective pen, such as one with a broken nib that spattered or distributed the ink unevenly, usually indicates that the document is genuine. Forgers generally take great care to use perfect materials and to avoid any variation from the normal so as not to attract attention.

Pencils came into general use about 1785 but were rarely used for letters or documents. Forged pencil writing can be difficult to detect because it can easily be retouched without any indication, and it is not always possible to determine in which direction the stroke was written (the side of the paper fibers on which the carbon is deposited can indicate the direction of writing). The propensity for pencil to smudge may indicate that a pocket diary in clear pencil without smudges is suspect, or that a clear and sharp pencil entry among other entries that are slightly smudged was done at a later date. (The pencil writing in the Hitler diaries was clear and fresh, with no smudging. The width of the stroke never varied, indicating it was written with a mechanical pencil, introduced in 1822, which would not have become dull with use.)

POSTAL MARKINGS

Few forgers have given proper consideration to the importance of postal markings, and well-accomplished forgeries can appear to be amateurish attempts when viewed philatelically. The first postal hand stamps came into use in England in 1661; they consisted of the month and day printed in a small circle; in 1695, a straight-line postmark bearing the name of the post town was introduced. Germany adopted this practice of incorporating the name of the town in 1720. Italy followed in 1740 and the United States, in 1756. Adhesive postage stamps were first used in England in May 1840 and in the United States seven years later (although private mailing companies employed their own adhesive stamps commencing in 1842, and the postmasters in New York, Providence, and St. Louis issued their own adhesive postage stamps in 1845). A comprehensive postal history guide will approximately date both the postal markings and postage stamps independent of the purported date on the letter.

The Mormon forger, Hofmann, had a knowledge of philately and consequently forged some letters by obtaining an unimportant letter of the correct period written on one page with the integral address and postmarked leaf attached. The leaf with the letter was detached and discarded and the forgery written on the verso of the correctly postmarked address leaf (this did, however, leave the problem of the address panel being written in a different hand from the purported letter on the other side).

Before 1845, letters were normally folded to use the center of the final leaf as the address panel, and the folded letter was then sealed with wax for transmittal. Envelopes are rarely encountered prior to this date, although they became quite popular once they were introduced and rapidly replaced the older method. Before the introduction of the envelope, a separate piece of paper was sometimes, though infrequently, folded around the letter to cover it for mailing.

FACSIMILES

The overwhelming majority of facsimiles (which are in fact engraved, lithographed, or printed reproductions of handwriting) are readily apparent under low magnification (10X, the maximum size of an easily used magnifying glass). The most noticeable characteristics are the flat, even appearance of the ink, with no variation in flow and areas within the pen stroke that are not inked. (The same effect can indicate a genuine piece if the paper fibers are depressed in a spot and the pen skips over the area, leaving it untouched; in most facsimiles these uninked spots occur throughout the writing, not just in one isolated area.) Some facsimiles are, especially if lithographed, very deceptive. Among the most difficult to detect and the most frequently offered as genuine are military documents bearing Adolf Hitler's lithographed signature and letters thanking his unnamed correspondent for birthday or Christmas greetings [29, 31].

28 Genuine signature of Hitler   **29** Lithographed signature of Hitler

 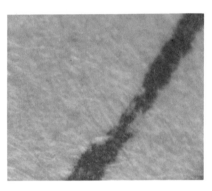

30 Enlargement of a letter from a geniune Hitler signature

31 Enlargement of a letter from a lithographed Hitler signature

 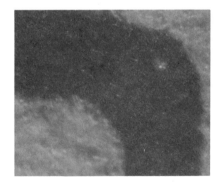

32 Enlargement from a genuine letter of George V showing a smooth flow of ink

33 Enlargement from a facsimile letter of George V showing an ink void

Many facsimiles are also of a nature that should make an examiner suspicious. Supposedly handwritten letters without a specific salutation sending thanks for birthday or Christmas greetings, or written just after an important event, such as an election or award (when the writer would receive a large number of letters), automatically should be suspect. It should seem unlikely to all but the most gullible that George V could have sent a personal message to every soldier who served in the First World War [32, 33], or that Churchill could have personally written to all those who commiserated with him over the loss of the election in 1945 or those who wrote each year congratulating him on his birthday.

"Authorized" Forgeries

SECRETARIAL SIGNATURES

Many people in prominent positions, who are required to sign innumerable letters and documents, have at one time or another authorized others to sign their names for them. In most instances there was no intention to deceive the recipient by attempting to imitate the signature, the not uncommon practice being for the proxy signer to place his own initials after the secretarial signature. While one does need to be aware of such secretarial or proxy signatures, these are not what we are concerned with in collecting historical letters and documents.

"Authorized" forgeries in which a signature is imitated in an attempt to deceive the recipient into believing it was signed by the person named generally began about the turn of the twentieth century. There were, of course, earlier exceptions, but it was not until about 1900 that it became somewhat commonplace to be deceptive about secretarial signatures.

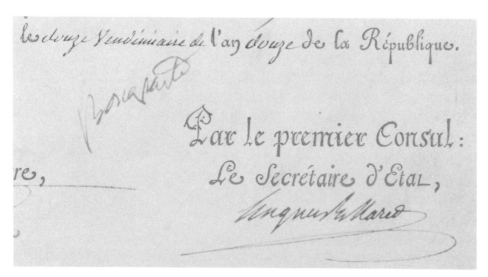

34 Secretarial signature of Bonaparte by his secretary of state, Hughes Maret, when Bonaparte was First Consul

Trésozier général

de nôtre Maison et finance Sr De Marc antoine
françois Marie Randon de la Tour, à vous Voulons
et vous mandons que de Sr deniers de vôtre dest fau fonct
par l'état arrêté pour l'entretenement et nourriture
de plusieurs de nos officiers pendant la presente année
Vous payez comptant au Sr Jean Baptiste Henry
frotteur de nôtre appartement La somme de Deux cent
Livres que nous lui avons accordée pour ses salaires,
tant pour lui que pour ceux qu'il a employé de frotter
et de nétoyer les parquets de nôtre dit appartement
pendant le quartier de Janvier, février et mars de cette
et rapportant par vous La présente avec Quittance
sur ce suffisant La ditte Somme de deux cent
livres sera passée et allouée en la dépense de
vos Comptes par nos Chers et bien aimés Les
Gens des Comptes du Roy nôtre très honoré
Seigneur et Epoux à Paris. Lesquels prions
et néantmoins mandons ainsi le faire sans
difficulté. Car tel est nôtre plaisir. Donné à Versailles Le premier avril
mil sept cent quatre vingt six.

Marie antoinette

payez
Marie antoinette

Beaugeard

In eighteenth-century France, kings rarely signed routine official documents and their relatively simple signatures were imitated by *secrétaires de main*. In many instances an arrow was drawn from the royal "signature" to that of the secretary below. This custom cannot, however, always be relied on because many secretaries omitted the line or arrow. Unless the royal signature is very distinctly genuine, which is relatively unusual, all such signatures are suspect. These documents signed by secretaries must have been treated with less authority than intended as the kings and queens, especially Marie Antoinette, took to adding notes and a second, genuine, royal signature [35].

More deceptive are the "Bonaparte" signatures signed on documents by his secretary of state, Hughes Maret, when Bonaparte was first consul [34]. Other than documents of this type, Napoleon did not authorize others to sign for him.

In America, little or no effort was made to imitate the presidents' signatures after secretaries were authorized to sign presidential land grants partway through Andrew Jackson's administration. Despite the very clear statement on this type of document indicating a secretarial signature, they continue to be the most common type of secretarially signed documents offered for sale as genuine.

Some wives, for instance, so commonly wrote and signed their husbands' correspondence that letters penned by them are frequently mistaken for those of their illustrious husbands. One of the most deceptive was Varina Davis, who imitated Jefferson Davis's handwriting so well that only the period she placed after her versions is an immediate sign that she, not her husband, wrote them [36, 37].

36
Genuine signature of Jefferson Davis

37
Signature of the Confederate president by his wife, Varina, who added a period after the signature as a subtle mark of her authorship

While several American presidents from the early part of the nineteenth century authorized secretaries to sign routine nonofficial documents for them, it was not until Andrew Johnson's time, in 1865, that really deceptive official documents appear. Two months after becoming president, Johnson began the practice of having military and naval appointments bear a stamped signature that can be very misleading to the uninformed.

Theodore Roosevelt frequently employed a rubber stamp before becoming president, but even an untrained eye cannot mistake it for a genuine signature. Likewise, the secretary who signed for William Howard Taft could not deceive anyone who has

35
Document of Marie Antoinette signed with a second and genuine royal signature
—the bold signature with the word *payez* above it (opposite page)

a genuine signature with which to compare it, nor should anyone be fooled by Woodrow Wilson's rubber-stamped signature when he was governor of New Jersey from 1911 to 1913 [38, 39].

George B. Christian, Warren G. Harding's secretary, was a different matter. He signed so many of Harding's letters that for many years it was not understood which were the genuinely signed examples [40, 41]. This practice was discontinued when Harding entered the White House. Calvin Coolidge's secretary, when Coolidge was governor of Massachusetts, made a serious attempt at imitating the characteristics of his master's writing. Like his predecessors, though, Coolidge personally signed all White House letters [42, 43]. Later in the decade, Herbert Hoover, as secretary of commerce, employed one A. G. Shankey who became very proficient at imitating her boss's signature, to the extent that she boasted of it in a letter to Christian Herter [44, 45].

38 Genuine signature of
Woodrow Wilson

39 Rubber stamp signature of Wilson

40 Genuine signature of Warren G. Harding

41 Secretarial signature of Harding by
George B. Christian

42 Genuine signature of
Calvin Coolidge

43 Signature of Coolidge by
his secretary when he was
governor of Massachusetts

44 Genuine signature of Herbert Hoover

45 Signature of Hoover by his
secretary, A. G. Shankey

Franklin D. Roosevelt, before becoming president, employed a number of persons to sign his name, commencing with his first position, assistant secretary of the navy. The illustrations below right show the work of some of these secretaries [47]. Three genuine signatures appear below left [46]. Except for a few brief periods, Harry Truman always wrote his own signature, and when, as president, he did authorize a secretarial version on White House cards, a period was added after his middle initial, S.

Assistant Secretary of the Navy.

46
Genuine signatures of Franklin D. Roosevelt signed (from top to bottom) when he was assistant secretary of the Navy, president, and in failing health

Very sincerely yours,

47 Secretarial signatures of FDR

Dwight D. Eisenhower was the last president who did not allow secretaries and machines to sign his name extensively. Even during the Second World War, Eisenhower signed all of the letters that were written in his name. In a letter to his wife, he wrote that it was simply impossible for him to keep up with the volume of correspondence and that while his letters had to be composed by secretaries, he personally signed every one. While he was president of Columbia University and during the first presidential campaign, in the fall of 1952, it was necessary for Eisenhower to authorize a secretary to sign his name as well as to use a machine to write his signature. It was not until the last years of his life that he again authorized a secretary to sign his name but this time with the middle initial omitted.

John F. Kennedy has been credited with bringing a new atmosphere to Washington; he also brought the practice of rarely signing one's name personally. Beginning with his first years in Washington and continuing through his presidency, he authorized more than a dozen secretaries to sign his name and also extensively used signing machines, called "autopens," with many different writing patterns. This same policy has been carried on, in varying degrees, by all of Kennedy's successors.

The practice is now so common and well established that even though Ronald Reagan frequently drafted letters in his own handwriting, the drafts were then typed and a machine signature added. In 1986, a group of these drafts was uncovered. The drafts showed Reagan's habit when he was governor of California of taking the time personally to write long, detailed, and very articulate responses to letters. His secretary would then type them on official stationery and apply the signature appropriate to the manner in which he signed the draft. Reagan's missives are no more likely to be genuine when written from his movie star days.

The deceptive use of machines that, based on a matrix of a genuine signature, sign a person's name with a pen duplicating the unevenness of genuine writing has revolutionized the collecting of modern presidential letters. Unless there is strong evidence to the contrary, it should be assumed that any letter from a president since 1960 does not bear a genuine signature (although the letter may be genuine). President Kennedy and his successors had many different signature patterns in use, and a collector could have half a dozen letters all bearing different signatures which could still have been signed by machines. Presidents Ford and Carter, prior to their presidency, had refused the use of such machines, but the pressure of the tremendous volume of mail was sufficient to change their minds once they assumed office. A number of books and monographs have reproduced the known machine signature patterns of modern presidents and must be consulted when examining presidential material after 1960 (see the bibliography).

AUTOPEN SIGNATURES

It should always be assumed that any contemporary letter, signed photograph, or other piece not of a truly personal or important business nature could have been signed by a machine if it is from a well-known person who would have received many routine letters requiring an answer. The astronauts, for example, found it necessary to resort to machine signatures on the souvenirs sent out from NASA headquarters. And, in the field of entertainment, it is not realistic to believe that actors and actresses have the time to sign hundreds of photographs each day.

The original autopen machine has been superseded in recent years by a more sophisticated machine that can write handwritten messages of any length. The only certain way of determining whether a piece is signed by machine is to obtain another identical signature or handwriting pattern and to place one on top of the other to confirm their common machine origin.

A much more in-depth discussion of forgery detection is found in
Forging History: The Detection of Fake Letters and Documents
by Kenneth W. Rendell

◆

This 185-page work contains over four hundred illustrations. In addition to a more detailed discussion of the factors considered here, the book concerns famous forgeries and their unmasking, including chapters on the Hitler diaries and Mormon forgeries, as well as comparisons of handwriting and typewriting and the equipment used in detecting forgeries.

6

HOW VALUES ARE DETERMINED

It is frequently stated that the fair market value in a collecting field is what someone is willing to pay or another is daring to ask for the material. That statement is only half true in the field of historical letters and documents. Fair market value is also in part determined by the price that must be offered to the owner to convince him to part with the material.

This was dramatically illustrated in the mid-1970s when the most important collection of letters and documents formed in this century—that of Philip D. Sang—was sold at auction. Before the Sang sale, major rarities were almost never seen on the public market; many had gone into private or institutional collections decades earlier. Sang had acquired his incredible collection mainly through private purchases from dealers. Historical letters did not then sell for very high prices, and collectors and families who owned them, as well as institutions, did not have significant financial incentive to part with them. The Sang sale offered over a period of a few days the rarest and most interesting letters and documents that many collectors had seen in their lifetimes. Many thought that collectors and dealers would be overwhelmed with so much important material (the first lot alone consisted of ten letters by John Adams to Benjamin Rush, all with incredibly important content). Just the opposite happened. The availability of so many important, rare, and interesting letters and documents attracted many new collectors and revived or expanded the interest of many who were already collectors but who had never been offered such great pieces. Among this group was Malcolm Forbes, who had been an active but average collector. The opportunity to acquire great letters was not one Forbes wanted to miss, and he was one of the biggest buyers. Record prices were set, but the quality of the letters and documents warranted them. The most lasting and important effect of the Sang sale was, however, to cause many older collectors, families, and institutions to consider parting with material no longer relevant to their interests when they realized the high prices that could be obtained.

An excellent example of higher prices attracting material to the market is illustrated in the autographs of Button Gwinnett, the rarest autograph of any of those who signed the Declaration of Independence. The year before the Sang sale, I had acquired a document signed by Gwinnett. I found it very difficult to arrive at a price because it was the first one offered in decades; I sold it for $45,000. At the Sang sale, a comparable example fetched three times that amount, which caused a number of owners to sell their documents, and for a period of a few years Gwinnett was quite readily available in the $100,000 to $150,000 price range.

This balance between the price that will interest a seller and what a collector is willing to pay is at the heart of evaluating rare and important pieces. More common pieces— and occasionally, rare and important pieces—do come onto the market to be sold at whatever a buyer will pay. These circumstances usually involve estates or collectors needing to sell for financial reasons or flagging interest, in which case the determination of value is based solely on the perceptions of the buyer.

Establishing the fair market value is an equation that takes into account a number of factors, each to a greater or lesser degree, resulting in a value factor that is then altered by an unusual demand on the part of a particular collector or a lack of availability (which requires a value that will entice an owner to part with a piece). The first of these factors is the importance of the individual in history and in his field. In most cases, the creator of a major idea is of more importance than the developer of that idea. The composer is almost always more important than the performer, the inventor more important than the developer. Generally, the value of letters and documents most reflects the historical importance of the individual, tempered, however, sometimes significantly, by other factors.

Demand by collectors is nearly as important. Mozart is as important as a person can be to collectors, and there is a tremendous demand from collectors in the United States, Europe, and Japan for anything in his hand. There is no national or language barrier to interest in music. In contrast, there are many important historical figures (for example, most British prime ministers) who have not particularly interested collectors, and the value of their letters is not in keeping with their roles in history.

Value is also affected by the importance to collectors of the individual's area of prominence. The manuscripts of an important person in the field of science tend to be much more valuable in monetary terms than the most important person in the field of theater history. General collector interest in a field elevates the value of nearly everyone in the field.

Content is the variable that causes the greatest fluctuation of prices for letters of the same person. The content of a letter will also affect people differently, and not everyone will agree on the interest and the degree of importance of a particular letter. Among the most important functions of a dealer is placing the content of a letter in perspective for a collector. A witty and amusing letter of George Bernard Shaw is common, a similar letter of T. E. Lawrence quite unusual.

The subject matter of a letter is also important in another way. Generally, the most valuable content relates directly to what the writer is best known for. Arthur Conan Doyle is a popular figure whose autograph material is widely collected. His most interesting letters are about spiritualism, the subject that most interested him in the later decades of his life. However, all of these letters, revealing a great deal about Doyle's interests and beliefs, sell for less than any letter mentioning Sherlock Holmes, no matter how insignificant. Letters of composers writing about their most famous works command higher prices than more significant letters about less famous works.

Rarity is, of course, a major factor, but only one of many. Generally, rarity is determined by the following factors: the length of a person's life; involvement in activities that either did or did not result in the individual writing many letters and signing documents; whether the individual was well known during and after his or her lifetime (causing people to save the writings), or became well known decades after death (by which time much material would have been discarded). Active collecting may have made letters and documents rare which were once common. Many institutions and some private collectors have collected so aggressively that they have virtually everything a particular person has written.

The recipient of a letter can also affect value. A letter written to an important collaborator or fellow author may give greater importance to the content than may be immediately apparent.

Condition is important when other similar letters or documents can be found without any defects. A military appointment signed by Abraham Lincoln that has a hole in it is less appealing than another that is intact. To find a collector for the damaged document, the price must be made appropriately attractive. However, if a letter is important in terms of its content, condition is much less of a factor. If a rare letter or document has some foxing (brown spots) caused by mildew, wear in the folds, or a tear that has not affected the text, the value is unaffected because that letter or document cannot be found in better condition. (Any flaws that could possibly deteriorate further must be arrested with proper preservation techniques.)

The effect of the publication of letters and manuscripts on value is a much debated subject. Scholars often request that collectors give them copies of letters, diaries, manuscripts, and so forth, so that they can publish them. They usually suggest that publication will enhance the value of the material because it will give it a stature it did not have previously. In this regard, there are a number of important factors for the collector to consider.

First, the collector does not own publication rights to letters and manuscripts that he acquires; he or she acquires only the physical object itself—the letter, for example— but not the rights to publish its contents. Except with modern, usually living, personalities, this is almost never a problem, but in some contemporary situations no one except the legal owner of the copyright can publish the letters or manuscripts. A collector cannot usually publish a collection of letters of a modern figure without permission. A few years ago, J. D. Salinger blocked publication of a book that was based on the content of letters he had sent to various people.

Scholars frequently ask collectors for copies of letters for publication. They do so because no copies are available other than the original material in the collectors' possession. Literary publication rights must be secured from the estate of the writer unless the material is legally in the public domain.

Generally, publication of historical (as distinguished from literary) letters does not decrease their value to a considerable extent. In the case of a substantial, connected correspondence, a manuscript, or, most importantly, a diary, allowing publication may adversely affect value to a considerable extent. Many years ago I sold to the Library of Congress the complete correspondence of Oliver Wendell Holmes (the jurist) to Lady Castletown (described in the chapter on American legal history). I had obtained these letters from Lady Castletown's descendants in Ireland; to the best of everyone's knowledge, they had never been published. The sale was rescinded, however, when it was discovered that a scholar visiting the family in the 1930s had made handwritten copies of the letters and deposited them in the Harvard Law Library. The Library of Congress's policy was not to purchase material if copies are available elsewhere. Fortunately, in that case, the individual value of the letters was much greater than the price I had placed on the correspondence in its entirety.

With historical material, it is important to consult a very knowledgeable dealer if you are concerned about the effect of publication on value. Many collectors have no great concern about future value because they do not intend to part with their collections and receive great satisfaction in seeing material from their collections published. This is both an individual and a financial decision.

In the case of literary material, the situation is quite different. Unpublished correspondences of authors are usually significantly more valuable than published ones. The reason is that many libraries have budgets to acquire literary material unavailable elsewhere. They want to acquire material for their library that is unique. The collector usually need not be concerned with individual letters, but if a collection is formed, it may definitely have a greater financial value if it remains unpublished.

All of these factors are evaluated by the specialist dealer in considering the fair market value. Several of these are quite subjective, and all are affected by the dealer's knowledge and experience in the field. In discussing values, it is worthwhile to consider Malcolm Forbes's comments about his collection of historical letters and documents as quoted by John Marion, chairman and chief auctioneer at Sotheby's, in his book, *The Best of Everything*: "This area remains a potential gold mine for collectors. . . . A letter can be so revealing, full of color and anecdotes—it can tell you so much more about a person than any artist's rendering. Compared to other areas, autograph material is vastly underpriced."

7

HOW TO KEEP AND PRESERVE
YOUR COLLECTION

When a framed historical letter or document is acquired from a responsible dealer, he or she will have examined the original before framing it to determine if there is any inherent potential preservation problem, perhaps a high acidity in the paper, the presence of pressure-sensitive tape that will later cause irreversible stains, or discoloration indicating the beginnings of mold. Deacidifying paper and arresting mold growth are relatively simple procedures and should always be undertaken if there is any question of a potential future problem. The removal of transparent pressure-sensitive tape is much more complex but if not done, will result in permanent stains.

The collector should also be assured that the framing is done with acid-free materials, that is, the original letter or document is not placed in contact with any material containing acid, which can migrate into the original letter or document. Neither normal glass nor nonreflective glass blocks out one of the most harmful elements, ultraviolet rays. Plexiglas UF-3 should be used as it does block out harmful ultraviolet rays while having the same appearance as glass. Framed historical letters and documents should not be hung in direct sunlight. Nor should they be hung over a source of heat such as a radiator or a fireplace, as excessive heat is the second most damaging element to paper. An average temperature of seventy degrees Fahrenheit is acceptable. Humidity is the third most important factor to consider. Humidity in excess of 55 percent encourages the growth of mold, especially at higher room temperatures. Some molds are colorless and may later react with properties in the paper, causing the brown spots commonly called foxing. An unusual softness in a section of a letter may indicate an invisible mold already at work (most are visible under high-intensity ultraviolet examination).

Material that is not framed may be kept in sleeves made of polyester (also called Mylar), polypropylene, or polyethylene, then kept in individual file folders, boxes, or albums. One of the simplest methods is to keep items in acid-free folders in a fireproof filing cabinet. A more attractive method is to have cloth or leather folders made for each letter or document. The original can be displayed on the right side, with a description or portrait on the facing left side. Folders with several mylar sleeves can also be made to accommodate multiple-page originals. The lettering on the spine and front cover can be done on a leather label to give as complete a description as desired. Books can also be boxed in cloth or leather with the title on the spine, making it much more convenient to handle, display, and preserve.

The use of custom-made albums can prevent potential damage from the metal rings commonly used in ring binders. If the original material moves toward the gutter of the ring binder, it can easily rub against the rings and be damaged. This is a very common problem, and regularly available commercial albums should not be used for this reason. In my business, we work with a fine binder in creating individual folders, boxes, and albums for different collectors' needs, and we have designed various bindings to meet specific demands.

However they are kept, original letters and documents should never be placed in contact with materials, particularly newspaper clippings that are not acid-free. Most newspaper clippings, since they are made of highly acidic wood pulp paper, will transfer their acidic properties to the original. Another problem is offsetting: I have seen many albums assembled in the last century in which an engraved portrait was put with the original letter or document and the ink used for the image of the portrait has offset onto the original piece. Early forms of photostats or any other chemically treated paper can also destroy the original item if left in contact with it.

The nonprofessional should never attempt to repair or conserve letters and documents without exact knowledge of what is required. I have had material brought to me with tears repaired with everything from masking tape to adhesive tape. All of these are expensive and difficult to remove and can do real damage over a fairly short period. Responsible dealers are happy to recommend professional conservators to collectors. Collectors need not be overly concerned about conservation if they acquire material from such a responsible dealer. If they acquire an old album of letters from an antique dealer or buy a piece framed many years ago by an unknown dealer, they should seek expert advice on what, if anything, needs to be done to protect it permanently.

The normal conditions—temperature, sunlight, and humidity—that most collectors live in are usually (though not always) the same conditions that will be proper for housing their collections.

AREAS OF COLLECTING

◆

AMERICANA

HISTORY

ARTS & LETTERS

OTHER AREAS

AMERICANA

◆

Colonial America

The American Revolution

Signers of the Declaration of Independence

The American Civil War

Presidents of the United States

The American West

American Legal History

General Americana

DEFINING RARITY

Defining the rarity of historical letters and documents that are not readily available on the market is difficult when it is necessary for the definitions to be valid for sometime. Many otherwise fine books on collecting have been misleading because they based descriptions of availability on information from past years without considering the overall trends in each area, and accounting for the fact that much material is acquired permanently by libraries and museums and is very unlikely to ever be available again.

In the past few years the availability of historical letters and documents has changed relatively quickly. More people than ever before are collecting in this field, and material of many people that was usually available on the market is now seen very infrequently. Fine material is being offered for sale by collectors and families, and occasionally by libraries, but this material is sold much more readily than in the past. Today's collectors must take advantage of opportunities to acquire pieces that are difficult to find or they may have to wait years for another opportunity.

In discussing the subject areas of collecting, I have used three terms as consistently as possible, and the following definitions represent my opinion of the situation for the next few years:

Extremely rare: an item that is possible to find, but it may be offered once in a ten- to fifteen-year period.

Very rare: an item that is likely to be available every five years.

Rare: an item that is not readily available but can be found perhaps in a year or two.

8

COLONIAL AMERICA

It is nearly impossible to obtain autograph material of the well-known personalities of seventeenth-century America. Collectors generally have to content themselves with a document of this period, usually from the Massachusetts Bay Colony, as a relic from the early years of America's founding.

Autographs of most early colonial leaders such as **Myles Standish** are unobtainable; a few, such as those of **John Alden**, have appeared on the market in the past and may appear in the future, but such occurrences would be extremely rare. The same is true for autograph material of early government officials, for example, anything signed by either of the two **John Winthrop**s of the Massachusetts Bay Colony. A very colorful seventeenth-century personality whose autograph is also extremely rare is the Dutch governor of New Amsterdam, **Peter Stuyvesant**. Forced to surrender the Dutch colony to the English in 1664, he returned to New York, after an inquiry in Holland, to retire.

The earliest major figure in the colonization of America whose autograph material a collector can reasonably expect to obtain is **William Penn**. He signed many land grants during his colonization of Pennsylvania, and there is a steady interest among collectors in these. Those signed while Penn was in Philadelphia are rarer. One of the more important governors of this time was **Edmund Andros** who was at various times governor of New York, New Jersey, and New England during a period when the boundaries of the colonies were being defined. Although his autographs are extremely rare, there is less demand for them, so the collector can have a hope of finding a piece signed by him.

Myles Standish

John Alden

John Winthrop

John Winthrop, the Younger

Peter Stuyvesant

William Penn

Edmund Andros

Sam Sewall

Samuel Sewall

Cotton Mather

Cotton Mather

W Shirley

William Shirley

Jeff Amherst

Jeffrey Amherst

Montcalm

Marquis de Montcalm

Jam: Wolfe

James Wolfe

Wm Pepperell

William Pepperell

Thos Hutchinson

Thomas Hutchinson

An interesting person representing the period of the Salem witch trials is **Samuel Sewall**, one of several special commissioners who condemned fourteen women and five men to death by hanging. Sewall was the only judge who ever publicly admitted that he had erred in this judgment. Documents signed by this colonial jurist are rare, but there is a likelihood of locating one. It is also possible to find documents of the important colonial preacher **Cotton Mather**, though they are becoming increasingly rare.

It is more feasible to collect autograph material of the well-known figures of eighteenth-century America. One of the most important is **William Shirley**, the governor of Massachusetts just before the French and Indian War. Shirley, who became commander in chief of the British forces in America during the war, signed many documents as governor, and they are relatively common. The autograph of another major military figure of this time, **Jeffrey Amherst**, can also usually be acquired. The two opposing commanders of the French and Indian War, the French **Marquis de Montcalm** and the British commander **James Wolfe**, clashed at Quebec, where both were killed. Letters and documents of the victorious Wolfe are very rarely seen, and those of Montcalm are equally rare. An American general who led troops in the attack on Louisbourg and who was also a noted colonial merchant was **William Pepperell**. His commercial documents are much more commonly encountered than material of the other participants.

Thomas Hutchinson, the judge who upheld the legality of the Stamp Act (and had his house burned to the ground as a result), was appointed royal governor of Massachusetts shortly after that decision and upheld many of the British actions that led to the outbreak of the American Revolution. His documents are scarce, but pieces can usually be obtained.

Documents of many colonial governors are collectable over time. Autograph material of everyone from eighteenth-century America is actually quite scarce or rare, and if only one or two collectors were to focus on this period, the small amount of material that becomes available would disappear rapidly.

9

THE AMERICAN REVOLUTION

Opportunities for collecting autograph material of the people who played important roles in the American Revolution have diminished very significantly in the past thirty years. The Revolution, along with the Civil War and the presidency, has been one of the most popular areas of collecting, and revolutionary war material, even more so than that of the Civil War, has gone into institutional collections. Letters and documents of most of the prominent people written during the Revolution are rare, though collectors can generally expect to find pieces written before or after the Revolution.

Autograph material of **Thomas Paine**, the author of *Common Sense,* has always been scarce, and Paine's popularity among collectors has placed his material in the very rare category. Material of **Samuel Adams**, one of the original firebrands of the early revolutionary movement, is much more available, mainly in the form of documents signed as governor of Massachusetts. His letters are much rarer. Another of the early revolutionary leaders and orators whose autograph material can be collected is **James Otis**. While his documents are not common, they have not been as popularly collected and are relatively inexpensive. Documents of **Patrick Henry**, the articulate leader who set the tone of the Revolution with his speech "Give me liberty, or give me death" can also be obtained. His documents signed as governor of Virginia have become more scarce, and his letters are quite rare. Autograph material of the patriot and silversmith whose name has become synonymous with the outbreak of the Revolution, **Paul Revere**, is very difficult to find. (His son, and namesake, had very similar handwriting, and documents or letters written when the two were working at the same time must be very carefully examined.)

Thomas Paine

Samuel Adams

James Otis

Patrick Henry

Paul Revere

Edmund Burke

Edmund Burke

John Hancock

John Hancock

B Franklin

Benjamin Franklin

Adams

John Adams

Th Jefferson

Thomas Jefferson

One of the most ardent supporters of the American Revolution was the British statesman **Edmund Burke**, who made pro-American speeches in England and wrote pamphlets attacking taxation in the colonies and promoting conciliation with them. Burke's autograph material has been very heavily collected, but documents and brief letters are encountered.

The early days of the new government, led by the the Founding Fathers, produced many leaders. Among the most famous was **John Hancock**, president of the Continental Congress, who in July 1776 was the first to sign the Declaration of Independence. Hancock material has always been extremely popular, as he was seen as representing the founding of the country. Fortunately, Hancock's merchant career, his terms in Congress, and his service as governor of Massachusetts led to his signing many documents that were usually preserved because they bore such a well-known and legible signature. The value of his documents represents his popularity more than the rarity of his autograph material, and documents can usually be found.

Autograph material of **Benjamin Franklin**, one of the most important Americans of the eighteenth century, is now much rarer. His letters have been very aggressively collected by institutions, and his documents, principally as governor of Pennsylvania, have been very much in demand. Franklin material is seen less and less often.

Autograph material of **John Adams** has also been in demand among collectors, both for his role in the Revolution and as president. His presidential documents have always been scarce, and now his earlier legal documents have also become scarce. Of the Founding Fathers, Adams was one of the best letter writers, and there is great interest when his letters are offered.

Thomas Jefferson, the principal author of the Declaration of Independence, is not rare in documents, but he is one of the most popular revolutionary leaders and presidents, and the value of his material reflects this. Fine letters by him have been collected by several institutions and are rarely offered for sale.

Another revolutionary war leader whose autograph material is collected for several reasons is the Philadelphia physician **Benjamin Rush**, who is as well known as a physician as he is as a signer of the Declaration of Independence. While examples of Rush turn up over time, they are not readily available. Autograph material of Rush's fellow Pennsylvanian and signer, **Robert Morris**, is also collected by those interested in financial history. Morris's numerous financial and business dealings led to the creation of many letters and documents, and his material is among the most available of the leaders of the Revolution.

Several presidents of the Continental Congress who were not in the Congress in July 1776 played leading roles in the Revolution. **John Jay**, president from 1778 to 1779, was later minister to Spain, then negotiated the Treaty of Paris to end the Revolution. He became the first secretary of foreign affairs, the first chief justice of the U.S. Supreme Court, and governor of New York. Documents signed by Jay as governor of New York are the most commonly found, but occasionally a letter written to his wife, Sally, is available. Generally, material of John Jay is scarcer than his long career would indicate, because it has been collected for many years by Columbia University. Jay's predecessor as president of the Continental Congress, **Henry Laurens**, was sent by the Congress to negotiate a treaty with the Dutch but was captured at sea and later exchanged for Lord Cornwallis. Letters of Laurens have been collected by a South Carolina institution and are rarely seen; documents signed by him, particularly those as president of the Continental Congress, are rare.

Many of the more interesting documents relating to the Continental Congress during the Revolution are signed by its secretary, **Charles Thomson**. He signed extracts from the proceedings that are generally scarce, and those with interesting content are rare but possible to obtain.

Benjamin Rush

Robert Morris

John Jay

Henry Laurens

Charles Thomson

53

George Clinton

George Washington

Many governors played important roles during the Revolution, particularly **George Clinton**, who was governor of New York from 1777 to 1795. Much of the war took place in his state, and his autograph material is included in many collections. Clinton's long gubernatorial term led to his signing of many documents, and his material is regularly offered.

George Washington is synonymous with the Revolution, and his autograph material is the most popularly collected in this very popular field. Fortunately, Washington signed many official and personal documents and wrote many letters that later generations preserved. Many major collectors have specialized in Washington letters as well as the Revolution, and nearly all of their collections have been acquired by institutions. Most Washington letters are now permanently housed in libraries, though examples are occasionally available. Documents, however, are still available. The most attractive type relating to the Revolution is a membership certificate of the Society of the Cincinnati [48], an organization of officers who served in the Revolution. These ornately engraved documents signed by Washington are usually in faded condition because they were framed and hung in the homes of the members and their descendants for more

48
Membership certificate of the Society of the Cincinnati signed by Washington

54

Ethan Allen

Ethan Allen

Benedict Arnold

Benedict Arnold

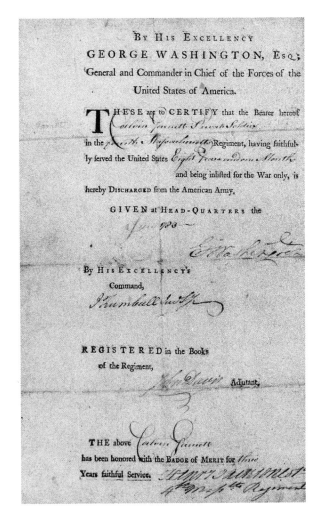

49 Discharge from the revolutionary army
signed by Washington

George Rogers Clark

George Rogers Clark

Horatio Gates

Horatio Gates

than a century. The other type of revolutionary war document Washington signed are discharges from the revolutionary army [49]. These are also usually found in only fair condition; they were folded and unfolded many times by the discharged soldiers and are virtually never found in fine condition. Other types of nonrevolutionary war documents can also be collected, and these are discussed more fully in the chapter on presidents of the United States.

Ethan Allen, the leader of the Green Mountain Boys who seized Fort Ticonderoga in 1775, was later captured by the British and exchanged. Documents and letters signed by him are very rarely seen. Autographs of **Benedict Arnold** are not readily available, but commercial documents can sometimes be acquired. **George Rogers Clark**, like Ethan Allen, made his career in a frontier environment, and material signed by him is only slightly less rare. Clark organized and led his fellow frontiersmen against Indians in raids at the beginning of the Revolution, then went on to capture many key points in the Northwest Territories (present-day Illinois and Kentucky) and held them for the colonies. Letters are extremely rare; the few documents that are offered concern land transactions.

Horatio Gates, the general who defeated Burgoyne at Saratoga, the turning point of the Revolution, can

Nathanael Greene

William Heath

John Paul Jones

John Barry

Henry Knox

Lafayette

Charles Lee

"Light-Horse Harry" Lee

Benjamin Lincoln

occasionally be found in postrevolutionary war letters, though they are not readily available. Letters of **Nathanael Greene**, the general put in command of the Army of the South in 1780, have been collected by an institutional library, and while he wrote many letters, especially as quartermaster of the army, they are infrequently seen today. **William Heath**, also a general, signed various legal documents after the Revolution, and these are more readily found. Material signed by America's naval hero, **John Paul Jones**, whose ship the *Bonhomme Richard* sank the British ship *Serapis,* is extremely rare. Autographs of **John Barry**, a less well known but very important figure in the revolutionary war, are also rare but in less demand, so they are more frequently seen.

One of the revolutionary war personalities whose letters are more readily obtained is **Henry Knox**, a general and close adviser to Washington. Knox later served as Washington's secretary of war and in this capacity signed many documents and official letters that occasionally are offered. Another revolutionary war leader whose autograph material is more commonly encountered is **Marquis de Lafayette**, who was long-lived and led a very active social, political, and business life after his return to France. Letters by this interesting figure are usually available.

Charles Lee, the second highest ranking general in the Revolution and the subject of great historical controversy, was captured by the British and later exchanged. His retreat at the Battle of Monmouth was, according to many historians, prearranged with the British. He was subsequently relieved of his command and became a bitter foe of Washington. His letters are rarely seen on the market. Material signed by the cavalry commander **"Light-Horse Harry" Lee** would also be rare were it not for his service as governor of Virginia. Land grants signed by him are frequently found. Another general whose documents are more common is **Benjamin Lincoln**, who was captured with his army in the South and later was present at Yorktown to receive Cornwallis's sword in surrender.

Lincoln held various minor positions in Massachusetts before the war, and documents as collector of the port of Boston are quite common. The opposite is true of "the Swamp Fox," **Francis Marion**, who led a military group in South Carolina. His letters are very rare. Almost equally rare is anything signed by **Israel Putnam**, the general at the battle of Bunker Hill who was incapacitated by a stroke in 1779.

Francis Marion

Israel Putnam

Philip Schuyler

John Stark

Baron von Steuben

Joseph Warren

Anthony Wayne

Autograph material of **Philip Schuyler**, the principal general in command of the northern department, is obtainable though not of war date. Business letters written after the war appear for sale fairly frequently. Autograph material of **John Stark** of New Hampshire, the general who fought at Bunker Hill and later won the battle of Bennington, is very rare. **Baron von Steuben**, the Prussian military officer who came to America to aid the colonial effort, is most known for his training and organization of troops during the bitter Valley Forge winter of 1777. His letters are rare, but financial documents signed by him, though not common, can be acquired. **Joseph Warren**, reputed to have ordered at the battle of Bunker Hill, "Don't shoot until you can see the whites of their eyes," was himself killed there. His autographs are extremely rare. The type of document collectors are most likely to encounter is an official one signed when Warren was president pro tempore of the provincial Congress. "Mad" **Anthony Wayne** was engaged in many revolutionary battles, particularly at Germantown, and continued a very active military career after the war. Documents or letters of Wayne are infrequently seen, though in time they can be obtained.

One of the revolutionary war personalities whose autograph material is most readily available is King

George III

Sir William Howe

Richard Howe

Henry Clinton

John Burgoyne

John André

Jeffrey Amherst

George III. The monarch who tried to tax and keep the American colonies as part of his empire signed many documents during his long reign, and though many are not in good condition, fine examples are available. His letters are less frequently seen. After the war, George III had bouts of madness and became blind; his later signatures, written before his son took over as regent, clearly show this deterioration.

Sir William Howe was Britain's commander in chief in America and, according to some military historians' views, led the British forces with a notable lack of commitment to defeating the Americans. Howe was in command at Bunker Hill, but in later engagements he failed to follow up on his victories and allowed American forces to retreat when he had an opportunity to defeat them. His letters and documents are not common, but collectors have not been as interested in the British side of the Revolution, and they are consequently available with some frequency. Autograph material of his brother, **Richard Howe**, an admiral in the British navy who saw considerable revolutionary war service, is usually available and not expensive. **Sir Henry Clinton**, Howe's successor as commander in chief in America, pursued the war much more vigorously than did Howe. Clinton's material, like that of Howe, is not common but, with a little patience, can usually be found.

Letters and documents of **John Burgoyne**, who was defeated at the battle of Saratoga and captured, are much rarer and in greater demand. Another personality on the British side whose autographs are very rare is **John André**, who had been appointed to negotiate with Benedict Arnold the betrayal of West Point to the British but was captured while returning to New York and hanged as a spy. Autograph material of **Jeffrey Amherst**, the overall commander in chief of the British army, though most noted for his service in the French and Indian War, is included in many revolutionary war collections. Military letters or documents of his can usually be found. **Guy**

Carleton, the commander of British forces in Canada, repelled various American attacks on Quebec; his autograph material is generally available as well. Letters of **Lord Cornwallis**, whose defeat at Yorktown effectively ended the military operations of the Revolution, can also usually be acquired in examples written in his later military capacities.

Letters and diaries of the ordinary soldiers in the Revolution are much rarer than those of the Civil War. Even fairly routine military documents signed by lesser officers have been heavily collected, and almost any material dated during the war is in demand.

Guy Carleton

Lord Cornwallis

10

SIGNERS

OF THE

DECLARATION OF INDEPENDENCE

In 1970, I wrote an article for the quarterly publication of the Manuscript Society comparing the rarity, at that time, of autograph material of the signers of the Declaration of Independence with a listing prepared in 1930 by Thomas F. Madigan, the leading dealer of his day. It was interesting to compare the two lists in terms of how rarity had changed over those forty years; but in examining the 1970 article today, it is evident that even more changes have taken place in these twenty-four years than in the preceding forty-year period. In 1970, I had written that it was nearly impossible to complete a set of all fifty-six signers but that it was relatively easy to collect material of forty to forty-five of them, though it was very difficult to find pieces of the others. In 1970, examples of forty to forty-five of the signers were usually available from dealers, in the form of legal documents and also, though more rarely, in the form of letters. Examples of five of the rarer signers would probably be offered within a year and documents of three or four more, within two or three years. The last two, Thomas Lynch, Jr. and Button Gwinnett, might not appear on the market for many years.

In the article I commented, "With only a few exceptions, a person forming a collection of any one of the more common signers would significantly affect rarity. Material of Charles Carroll of Carrollton, the last surviving signer, is a good example. . . . Traditionally Carroll's material had been quite low on everyone's list of rarities, but there are simply not *that* many of his letters and documents outside of institutions. Several years ago, a private collector purchased all of the Robert Morris material available at one time. This required a relatively small expenditure, but it did create a scarcity which was readily apparent."

Today, the situation is dramatically different. Few collectors have made an attempt to complete sets of the signers of the Declaration of Independence. Most have collected material of the various signers that they can locate without regard to how far they might get toward a complete collection. This has been a major change in the attitude of collectors, and it has removed from the market many of the signed documents that were once readily available. Thirty years ago, most collectors would not have embarked on a collection in this area if they could not obtain material of nearly all the personalities, but today a representative selection is the goal of the modern collector.

This has resulted in much greater demand for the more common pieces, and consequently, very few documents of the signers are readily available for acquisition.

In 1970, I had listed the signers in three groups according to rarity. In 1994, it seems more accurate to group the signers into five categories of rarity. The differences within each group are relatively slight, and the signers are listed alphabetically, not in an ascending or descending order of rarity. The autograph material considered within these groups of relative rarity pertain to legal or official documents of the signers, not letters, and only in the case of Thomas Lynch, Jr., does it pertain to signatures.

EXTREMELY RARE: In 1930, autograph material of Thomas Lynch, Jr., was listed by Madigan as the rarest; in 1970, I reversed this order, putting Gwinnett material as the rarest and that of Lynch, the second rarest. I wrote then, "There are approximately four times as many letters and documents by Gwinnett as there are by Lynch; but if cut signatures are added, then the total number of letters, documents and signatures of Lynch exceeds those of Gwinnett by approximately ten. Gwinnett obviously has enjoyed much greater public attention than Lynch, in part because of his name, and in part because a document signed by him was sold in 1927 for $51,000 (the *Encyclopedia Britannica* gives scant biographical information and states that he is most noted for the value of his autograph). Today, a signature of Lynch is still more likely to be obtained than something bearing Gwinnett's signature."

VERY RARE: Material signed by the following is offered very infrequently, and there may be no opportunity to acquire a document of these individuals for a period of years: Lyman Hall, Joseph Hewes, William Hooper, Francis Lightfoot Lee, Francis Lewis, Arthur Middleton, Thomas Nelson, Jr., John Penn, Richard Stockton, Thomas Stone, George Taylor, and John Witherspoon.

RARE: Documents signed by this group are likely to be found during the course of a year: John Adams, Carter Braxton, Samuel Chase, Abraham Clark, William Floyd, Elbridge Gerry, Stephen Hopkins, Richard Henry Lee, Philip Livingston, Lewis Morris, William Paca, Benjamin Rush, Matthew Thornton, William Whipple, and George Wythe.

SCARCE: Documents of the signers in this category should be frequently available, but some patience may be necessary: Samuel Adams, Josiah Bartlett, Benjamin Franklin, John Hancock, Thomas Heyward, Jr., Francis Hopkinson, Thomas Jefferson, John Morton, George Read, Caesar Rodney, Edward Rutledge, Roger Sherman, James Smith, and James Wilson.

USUALLY AVAILABLE: Documents of the following are regularly offered for sale: Charles Carroll of Carrollton, George Clymer, William Ellery, Benjamin Harrison, John Hart, Samuel Huntington, Thomas McKean, Robert Morris, Robert Treat Paine, George Ross, George Walton, William Williams, and Oliver Wolcott.

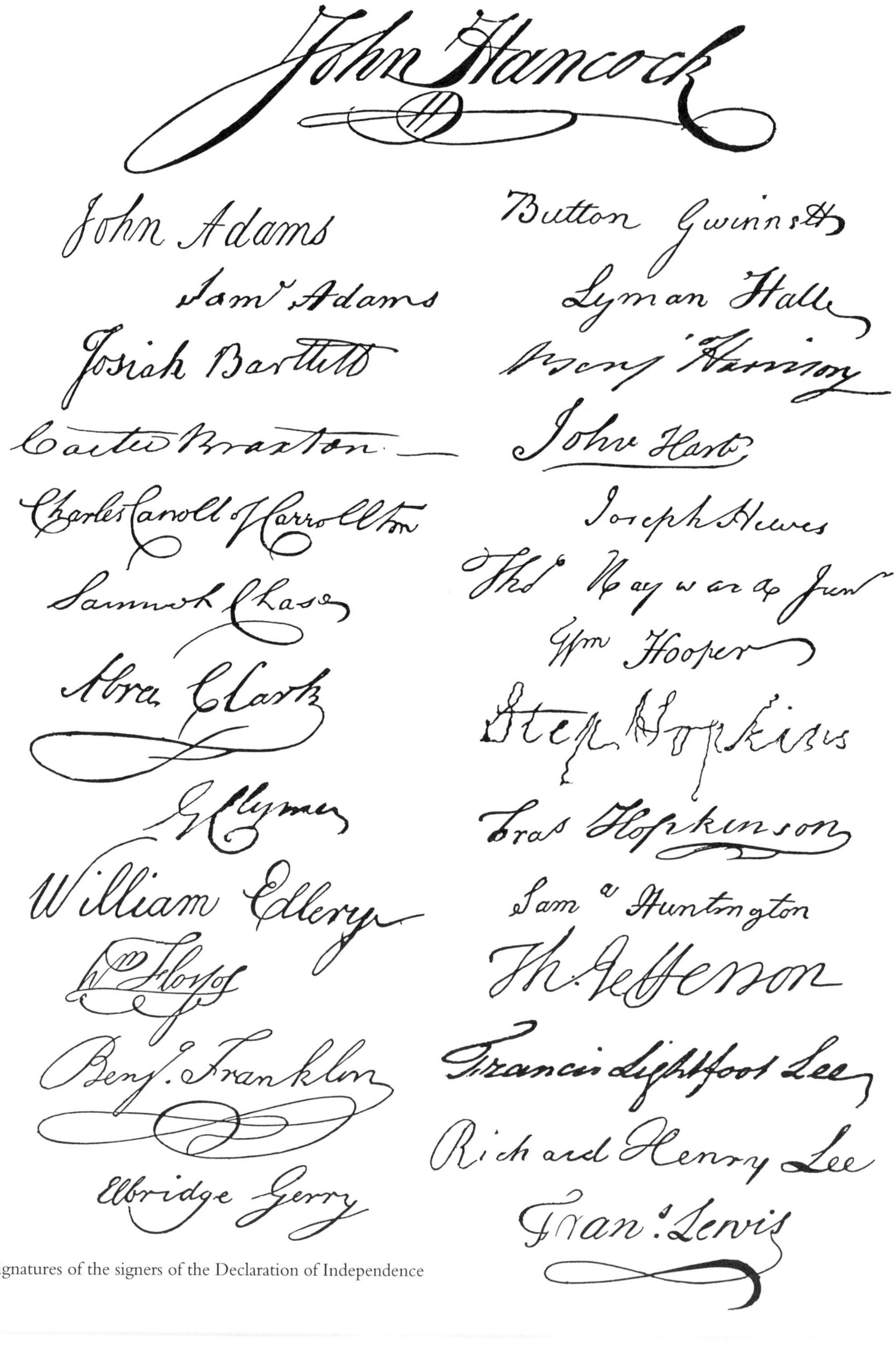

John Hancock

John Adams

Sam¹ Adams

Josiah Bartlett

Carter Braxton

Charles Carroll of Carrollton

Samuel Chase

Abra Clark

G. Clymer

William Ellery

W. Floyd

Benj. Franklin

Elbridge Gerry

Button Gwinnett

Lyman Hall

Benj Harrison

John Hart

Joseph Hewes

Tho⁵ Hayward jun

Wm Hooper

Step Hopkins

Fras Hopkinson

Sam⁴ Huntington

Th. Jefferson

Francis Lightfoot Lee

Richard Henry Lee

Fran⁵ Lewis

Signatures of the signers of the Declaration of Independence

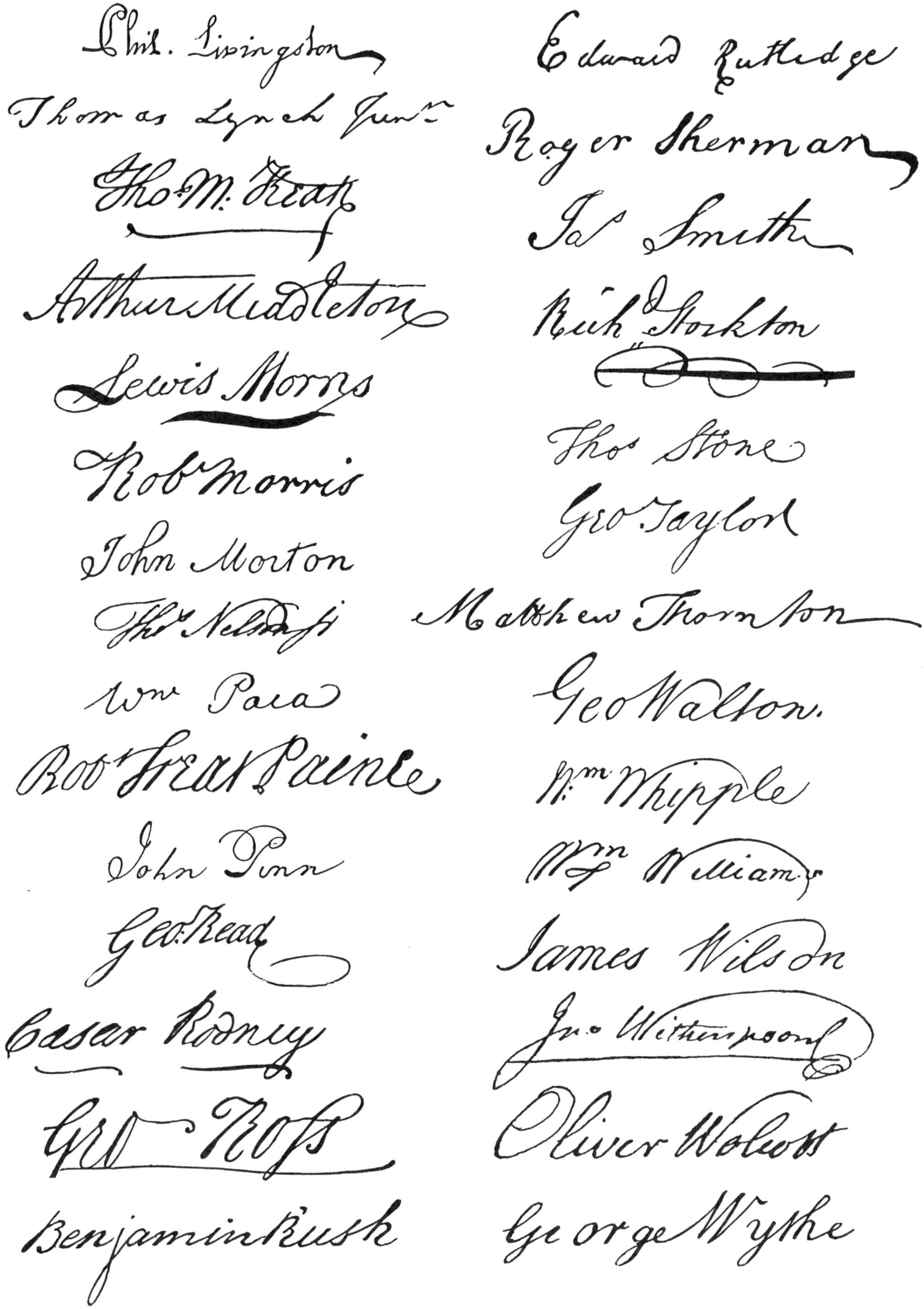

Phil. Livingston

Thomas Lynch Junr.

Thos M: Kean

Arthur Middleton

Lewis Morris

Robt Morris

John Morton

Thos Nelson ji

Wm Paca

Robt Treat Paine

John Penn

Geo. Read

Casar Rodney

Geo Ross

Benjamin Rush

Edward Rutledge

Roger Sherman

Jas Smith

Richd Stockton

Thos Stone

Geo. Taylor

Matthew Thornton

Geo Walton.

Wm Whipple

Wm Williams

James Wilson

Jno Witherspoon

Oliver Wolcott

George Wythe

11

THE AMERICAN CIVIL WAR

Popular interest in the American Civil War has always been very strong. It has been demonstrated by the steady flow of visitors to battlefields, the making of popular films about the Civil War, and the thousands of books that have been published on the subject. In this generation, there have been numerous television programs about the war. This interest has also been expressed in the collecting of Civil War letters and documents. For many years, pieces signed by the Civil War generals who had long life spans were available in relatively large numbers. The administrative needs of the war required officers to sign many documents, and there was an abundant supply of these available. All of this has changed during the last decade, and generally, autograph material of nearly everyone of Civil War date is scarce.

Many of the leading generals in the war also had important roles in the Mexican War, and their signed material is more available in military documents and letters of this period. Other generals, like Jeb Stuart, had active military careers during the 1850s, and documents from this period are more likely to be found. Others who became well known for their careers in the Civil War led long lives afterward in very public positions and wrote many letters and documents. Being well known, their letters were usually saved. Despite all of these circumstances, signed material by many of the personalities has become quite scarce. It is, however, still possible to acquire letters and documents by many, if not most, of the leading figures of the Civil War, though not always of war date, and this field continues to be one of the most popular areas of collecting. The Civil War is a much more collectable subject than the American Revolution.

As a general rule, material of the Confederates is scarcer than that of Union leaders. This is true for pieces signed by generals as well as for letters written by ordinary soldiers. Diaries of Confederate soldiers are much scarcer than Union ones, and both are now rarely offered for sale.

Civil War collections often begin before 1861. During 1851 and 1852, **Harriet Beecher Stowe** first published *Uncle Tom's Cabin, or Life Among the Lowly* as a serial in an antislavery paper. Her influence was tremendous and gave great support to the abolition movement. Stowe signed many cards, quotations, and letters, and her autograph material is very popular and can almost always be found in the form of signed cards. In October 1859, the abolitionist **John Brown** seized Harper's Ferry and the government arsenal there with the intention of causing an uprising of slaves, thereby setting the tone of violence in the name of righteousness that was to follow. John Brown was executed later that year, and his autographs are rare, though there is always a chance of coming across a letter.

Abraham Lincoln's presidency was primarily concerned with the war, and examples of endorsements on letters directed to various military officers giving wartime directives are generally available. Also frequently encountered are military commissions for wartime appointments (see the chapter on presidents for illustrations of these). Letters concerning the war are very rare. Letters of **Mary Lincoln** are also very rare; many are quite sad, written after Lincoln's assassination, pleading financial hardship and showing signs of mental instability. Letters of the actor and assassin **John Wilkes Booth** have become very rare; they were always scarce but have in recent years been very heavily collected.

Within Lincoln's administration, several cabinet officers held important wartime positions. **Edwin M. Stanton**, the secretary of war whose power soared after the assassination, is commonly found in wartime letters and documents. The same is true of the secretary of the navy, **Gideon Welles**; the first secretary of

Harriet Beecher Stowe

John Brown

Abraham Lincoln

Mary Lincoln

John Wilkes Booth

Edwin Stanton

Gideon Welles

Simon Cameron

Simon Cameron

W. P. Fessenden

William P. Fessenden

Salmon P. Chase

Salmon P. Chase

James Speed

James Speed

Hannibal Hamlin

Hannibal Hamlin

Andrew Johnson

Andrew Johnson

Jefferson Davis

Jefferson Davis

Jefferson Davis.

Davis's signature by his wife, Varina,
who added a period after her version

Alexander H. Stephens

Alexander H. Stephens

Judah P. Benjamin

Judah P. Benjamin

Robert E. Lee

Robert E. Lee

war, **Simon Cameron**; and the secretaries of the treasury, **William P. Fessenden** and **Salmon P. Chase**. Several other cabinet members are very rarely seen in autograph material, particularly **James Speed**, the attorney general. Letters of Lincoln's first vice president, **Hannibal Hamlin**, are also available, but his second vice president and successor, **Andrew Johnson**, is usually encountered in signed documents (see the chapter on presidents).

In the Confederate government, **Jefferson Davis** is most commonly available in letters and documents signed as secretary of war under Franklin Pierce and in postwar letters written after he returned from exile. Wartime pieces are rare. Relatively available is autograph material of the Confederate first lady, Varina Davis, who wrote a great many of the letters bearing the signature _Jefferson Davis_. Her handwriting imitated her husband's almost exactly, but she added a period after her version of his signature, and the collector who is aware of this habit need not be concerned about the authenticity of Jefferson Davis material. Autograph material of Davis's vice president, **Alexander H. Stephens**, is scarce but not in great demand and is relatively inexpensive.

Letters and documents of most of the members of the Confederate cabinet are much scarcer than those of their Union counterparts, and there has been much more collector interest in them, particularly in the material of **Judah P. Benjamin**, who served as the Confederate secretary of state. The outstanding general of the Confederacy, **Robert E. Lee**, is extremely popular with collectors. Autograph material of war date is very difficult to obtain, but military letters written before the war and postwar letters written as president of Washington and Lee University, while very scarce, are more frequently seen. It is also possible to obtain signed _carte-de-visite_ photographs of Lee (approximately 3-7/8 by 2-3/8 inches) though these are becoming increasingly rare.

The Confederate general in command at the shelling of Fort Sumter, the event that signaled the start of the

P. G. T. Beauregard

war, was **P. G. T. Beauregard**. He had resigned from the superintendency of West Point on the eve of the war, was commander of the Army of Mississippi, and fought throughout the war. His autograph material can be found in postwar examples. One of the most popular personalities of the Confederate army was one of its most brilliant military leaders, **Jeb Stuart**, who was killed in 1864 at Spotsylvania Courthouse. His letters are rare from any period, but most frequently seen are those from his frontier service in the late 1850s. The most popular Confederate leader among collectors, after Robert E. Lee, is **T. J. Stonewall Jackson**. The early death of this brilliant military commander in 1863 (he was accidentally shot by his own troops at Chancellorsville) has contributed to both the rarity of his autograph material and his popularity. Another famous Confederate leader whose autographs are rare is **George Pickett**, who led the famous charge at Gettysburg.

Letters and documents of **Jubal A. Early**, who led the raid down the Shenandoah Valley toward Washington and was defeated by Sheridan, are less rare. The same is true of **Braxton Bragg**, who won the Battle of Chickamauga, though pieces signed by either Early or Bragg are not readily available. Signed material of both **James Longstreet**, the Confederate commander at the Second Battle of Bull Run, and **Joseph E. Johnston**, who lost Vicksburg to Grant, is only slightly less scarce. **Ambrose P. Hill** and **Albert Sidney Johnston** were both killed in battles, and the rarity of their autographs reflects this. The cavalry general **Joseph Wheeler** had an active law practice after the war, which has made his letters much more frequently seen. Letters and documents of another cavalry commander, **Nathan B. Forrest**, are much

Jeb Stuart

Stonewall Jackson

George A. Pickett

Jubal A. Early

Braxton Bragg

James Longstreet

Joseph E. Johnston

Ambrose P. Hill

Albert Sidney Johnston

Joseph Wheeler

Nathan B. Forrest

John H. Morgan

John S. Mosby

E. Kirby Smith

Winfield Scott

Robert Anderson

Nathaniel Lyon

Ulysses S. Grant

Henry W. Halleck

George B. McClellan

George G. Meade

rarer, and he is found virtually only in signed bonds. Anything signed by **John H. Morgan**, the raider killed in 1864, is very rare. Fortunately for collectors, **John S. Mosby**, "the Grey Ghost," the most famous Confederate raider, had a long life and wrote many postwar letters, although these are now less and less frequently seen. Autograph material of the last Confederate commander to surrender, **E. Kirby Smith**, is very scarce though occasionally encountered.

At the outbreak of the war, the Union army was still commanded by the Mexican War hero **Winfield Scott**, who retired in 1861. His letters from all periods, except the Mexican War, are relatively common. The Union commander of Fort Sumter at the start of the war, **Robert Anderson**, was very popular in his day, and he signed many autographs. **Nathaniel Lyon**, one of the first noted Union generals to be killed in the war (1861), wrote many letters during his service in the Mexican War and the years before 1861, and it is possible to obtain his military letters.

The North's most important general rode to the presidency on his wartime successes. **Ulysses S. Grant** signed great numbers of wartime documents, but they have become increasingly difficult to find; wartime letters are even scarcer. Material from after the war is much more readily available, and occasionally documents from the Mexican War are found (see the chapter on presidents).

Autograph material of **Henry W. Halleck**, the Union general in chief from 1862 to 1864, is not particularly rare though not always immediately available. Letters and documents of **George B. McClellan**, the commander of the Army of the Potomac and leader of the Peninsular Campaign, are more commonly seen. Equally available is signed material of **George G. Meade**, who also commanded the Army of the Potomac from 1863 to 1865. One of the most important and most popular Union generals, **William Tecumseh Sherman**, is scarce in wartime documents; wartime letters are rare, but postwar letters can still be found fairly readily. The interest in Sherman is very strong and likely to make all of his material rare before long.

William Tecumseh Sherman

Lew Wallace

Philip Kearney

Oliver Otis Howard

The Union general **Lew Wallace** is far better known for his literary efforts. After the war, he wrote *Ben Hur,* among other works, and his letters, while having been strongly collected from a literary standpoint, can occasionally be found. Much rarer is material of **Philip Kearny**, the general killed in 1862. Letters and documents of **Nathaniel P. Banks**, the general commanding the department of the Gulf from 1862 to 1865, are relatively common. Banks has never inspired the imagination of collectors, and the value of his letters and documents reflects this. The prices for postwar letters of **Oliver Otis Howard**, who commanded the Army of Tennessee in Sherman's March to the Sea, are also relatively inexpensive but are actually not common.

Nathaniel P. Banks

Ambrose E. Burnside

The commander of the Army of the Potomac, Union general **Ambrose E. Burnside,**so noted for his whiskers that he inspired the term "sideburns," is usually available in postwar letters. The same is true of **Benjamin F. Butler**, who commanded the land forces in the capture of New Orleans. One of the more important northern generals, **Philip H. Sheridan**, who fought in numerous successful battles and blocked Lee's retreat at Appomattox, can usually be found in postwar letters, but they are becoming much scarcer. The same is true of **"Fighting" Joe Hooker**, another commander of the Army of the Potomac.

Benjamin F. Butler

Philip H. Sheridan

"Fighting" Joe Hooker

[signature]

David G. Farragut

[signature]

David D. Porter

[signature]

James B. McPherson

Even more scarce is material of **James B. McPherson**, who was killed in 1864.

On the naval side of the war, Admiral **David G. Farragut**'s autograph material is scarce, based in part on the strong interest he inspires among collectors. Much more commonly seen are letters of Admiral **David D. Porter**.

12

PRESIDENTS
OF THE
UNITED STATES

The presidents of the United States are one of the most popularly collected areas of historical letters and documents in America. The importance of the presidency itself—the power and prestige—is certainly a major reason. The men who have held the office interest collectors simply because they were presidents but more frequently because of their accomplishments as president, their careers before the presidency (notably those of Washington, John Adams, Jefferson, Madison, Taylor, Grant, and Eisenhower), or the particular character they brought to the White House. Harry Truman's unexpected rise to the demands of the presidency and Andrew Jackson's western style have attracted collectors, as have the robust personality of Theodore Roosevelt and the statesmanship and leadership of Franklin D. Roosevelt.

In 1962, Arthur M. Schlesinger wrote an article in the *New York Times Magazine* reporting on the results of a poll of historians on the historical importance of individual American presidents. The seventy-five historians considered only presidential careers and excluded William Henry Harrison and James A. Garfield because of the brevity of their terms in office and presidents after Eisenhower. Schlesinger's article rated the presidents as follows:

GREAT: Lincoln, Washington, F. D. Roosevelt, Wilson, and Jefferson

NEAR GREAT: Jackson, T. Roosevelt, Polk, Truman, John Adams, and Cleveland

AVERAGE: Madison, J. Q. Adams, Hayes, McKinley, Taft, Van Buren, Monroe, Hoover, Benjamin Harrison, Arthur, Eisenhower, and Andrew Johnson

BELOW AVERAGE: Taylor, Tyler, Fillmore, Coolidge, Pierce, and Buchanan

FAILURES: Grant and Harding

The interest of collectors frequently does not follow the historians' ratings of thirty years ago. Military leaders of three of the major wars—Zachary Taylor, Ulysses S. Grant, and Dwight D. Eisenhower—are avidly collected because of their military careers, not their presidencies. Eisenhower's administration has been very favorably reconsidered by modern historians. James Madison, one of the authors of the Constitution, is of much greater interest to collectors than the other presidents with whom he shared a place in the "average" group. Grover Cleveland, in contrast, while rated a "near great," is of little interest to collectors. Interest among collectors and Schlesinger's rating of historical importance, are, however, more closely correlated with many of the other presidents.

The earliest presidents tended to be by far the best letter writers. The eloquence of George Washington (reflected in his handwriting), the lengthy, detailed, and philosophical letters of John Adams, and the thoughtful and articulate writings of Thomas Jefferson were indicative of great men, times in which great decisions had to be made, and also, perhaps, a period during which the volume of the business of the presidency was not such that thoughtful letter writing was an impossibility.

The quality of the content of presidential letters has certainly not been dependent on education. Andrew Johnson's bad grammar and poor spelling did not prevent him from expressing his thoughts and feelings eloquently, nor did a military background hinder Andrew Jackson from writing very forceful and well-focused letters dealing with the issues of his presidency. Abraham Lincoln reflects his times as well as his personality in his carefully worded and succinct letters.

Those new to the field of collecting historical letters and documents are usually quite surprised to find that autograph material of the most important and popular presidents is not the rarest. Autographs of Abraham Lincoln and George Washington, two of the most popular, are relatively common in terms of the number of letters and documents that survived them, but not by any means the least expensive. Both had pre-presidential careers—Washington in the Revolution and Lincoln as an attorney—in which they signed many letters and documents. There have been few Americans who did not instantly recognize both their names, and this is an important factor in understanding rarity. When a person's fame dies with him, caches of letters and documents discovered a generation or so later have frequently been discarded by the finders, who are not familiar with that person's fame during their lifetime. Fifty years after his presidency, few Americans knew the name of James K. Polk, and his correspondence could easily have been discarded. That certainly was never the case with Washington or Lincoln.

These are two of the principal factors in the equation determining rarity—whether the president held previous positions requiring the writing of many letters and documents, and whether his fame succeeded him so that future generations saved his papers. Institutional and private collecting are other factors. Autograph material of both Washington and Lincoln, for example, has been very actively collected by libraries and private collectors; while many letters and documents were created, few appear on the market. It is also important to distinguish between rarity in collections and rarity on the market. There are many presidents whose autograph material is much rarer than that of Washington or Lincoln, but since they have not been collected by institutions or private collectors, except for an example in a presidential set, many more of their documents and letters are available.

Autographs of three presidents do stand out as rarities simply because they signed very few pieces while president. William Henry Harrison is the president with the briefest term in office; he caught a cold during his inauguration and died a month later. His autograph material signed as president is, not surprisingly, the rarest. Presidential autograph material of James Garfield, who was shot by Charles Guiteau on July 2, 1881, and died on September 19, is the next in rarity; and signed material of Zachary Taylor, who also died in office after a term of a year and four months, follows in terms of rarity.

Many collectors approaching the field of American presidents inquire about the type of autograph material to collect. This is a decision that should be worked out with a knowledgeable dealer based on the collectors' personal interests, finances, goals, and, most important of all, what appeals to them. A collector desiring, for example, to collect only signed handwritten letters, will have less difficulty with the first century of presidents, as letters written by secretaries and signed by the presidents are actually much scarcer than letters written by the presidents themselves. This situation changes dramatically at the turn of the twentieth century with the increased use of the type-writer. Handwritten letters of modern presidents are usually rather rare.

In the latter part of this chapter, I comment on each president (and, where appropriate, First Lady) as to the quality of their letters, rarity, and demand and also provide information concerning the collecting of bank checks, signed photographs, and signed books. Signed photographs are, of course, impossible to obtain for the earlier presidents because they predate the invention of photography, while twentieth-century presidents are relatively common in this form, though one has to make sure that they are actually signed by the president himself. Bank checks can be quite common, as in the case of Calvin Coolidge, whose checks were dispersed in quantity many years ago, or extremely rare, as in the case of more than a dozen presidents. Signed copies of books are generally available for the presidents who were authors. Some personal presidential libraries have been broken up and sold—notably, those of George Washington and Franklin D. Roosevelt—making volumes from their libraries much more common than those of presidents who had few personal books, all of which may have been acquired by an institution decades ago.

Many different types of documents were signed by presidents, and I have illustrated several of those commonly collected. Presidential appointments and commissions come in various sizes and typographical layouts depending on the position to which the individual is appointed [50, 52]. Military commissions are among the most visually attractive of presidential documents. They are partly printed, on parchment, with ornate military vignettes at the top and bottom. The earlier version [51] has a vignette at the top that is different from the later one, which is more commonly encountered [53]. Naval commissions have an even more attractive engraved naval vignette and are scarcer than commissions for the army [54].

Land grants are relatively common from the term of Thomas Jefferson through the end of the first term of Andrew Jackson. There are three types [55, 56, and 57], the most common being the one in illustration 55. At the beginning of his second term, Jackson found the task of signing these documents too burdensome, and from that time onward, secretaries signed land grants for all the presidents (there are very rare exceptions).

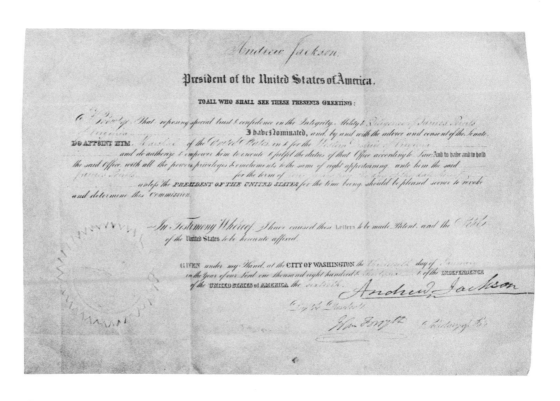

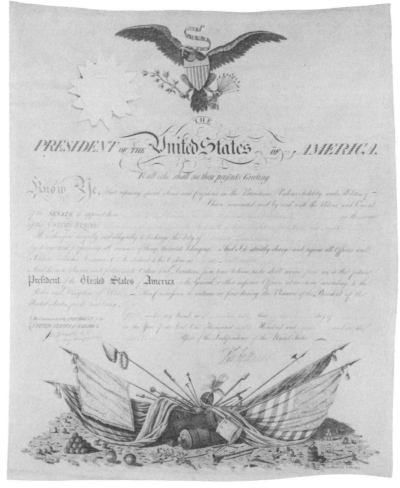

50
Presidential appointment signed by Andrew Jackson (above)

51
Military commission signed by Thomas Jefferson (left)

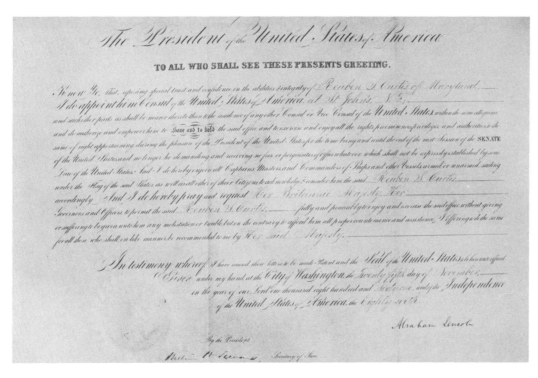

52

Presidential appointment signed by Abraham Lincoln as president and by William H. Seward as secretary of state (above)

53

Military commission signed by Lincoln as president and by Edwin M. Stanton as secretary of state (right)

54
Naval commission signed by
Abraham Lincoln as president and
by Gideon Welles as secretary of
the navy (left)

55
Land grant signed by John Quincy
Adams (below)

56
Land grant signed by John
Adams as president and by
John Marshall as secretary
of state (right)

57
Land grant signed by James
Monroe (below)

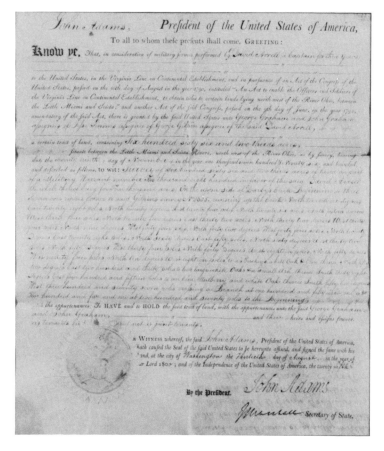

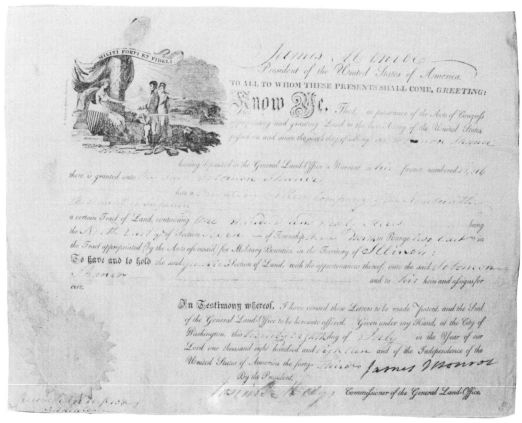

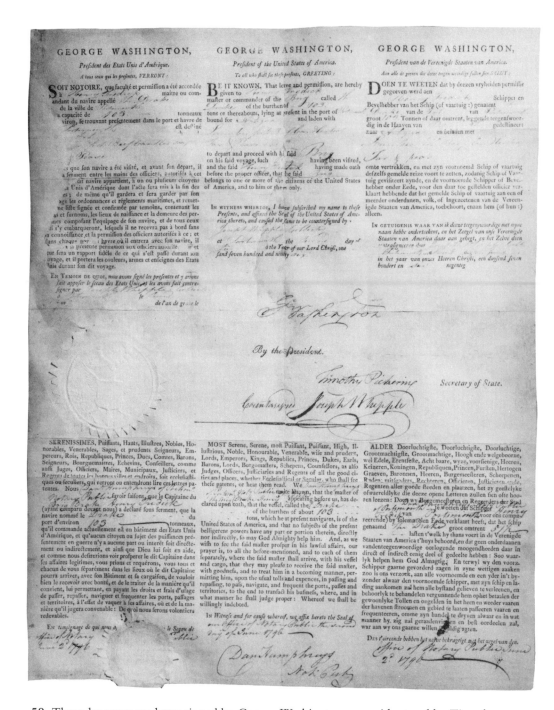

58 Three-language sea letter signed by George Washington as president and by Timothy Pickering as secretary of state

Sea letters in four languages—English, French, Spanish, and Dutch—were printed on paper; their purpose was to obtain safe passage for the ship and its crew. These documents were used in foreign voyages, except to the Mediterranean, and were signed by the president and secretary of state. (The earliest versions are in three languages [58].) These documents are frequently worn because of constant folding and unfolding.

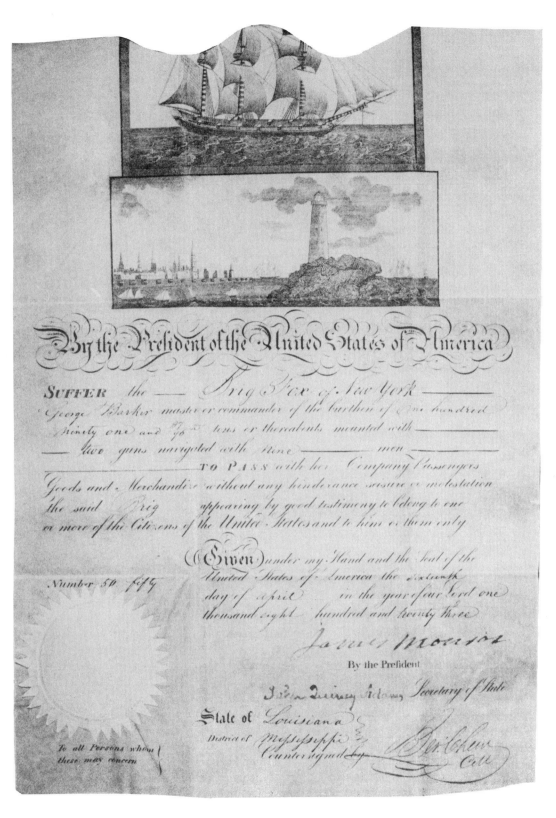

59 Ship's passport signed by James Monroe as president and by John Quincy Adams as secretary of state

Ships' passports for the Mediterranean are considered by many collectors to be the most attractive presidential documents. The upper portion contains an engraved naval scene and has a scalloped top edge. Printed on parchment, this type of document was the result of an agreement with Algiers in 1795 to allow the unmolested passage of American ships in return for tribute paid to the Barbary pirates. The Algerian ships would match the scalloped top of the ship's passport with their model to verify its authenticity, following the example of indentures [59].

Executive Mansion cards bear the imprint *Executive Mansion/Washington* in the upper right-hand corner. While the use of these cards was initiated by Grant, examples signed by him are extremely rare. It was during the administration of Rutherford B. Hayes that they began to be used extensively for both notes and autographs. They measure approximately 2-3/4 by 4-1/4 inches [60]. Theodore Roosevelt, apparently disliking the pretentiousness of the title *Executive Mansion,* changed the imprint to read *White House* at the beginning of his administration. Executive Mansion or White House vignette cards measure 3-5/8 by 4-3/4 inches; they bear an engraved view of the front or back of the White House [61].

Documents in which the president authorizes and directs the secretary of state to affix the seal of the United States to a particular official document or letter are, for some presidents, the type of documents most frequently found [62].

Presidential documents conferring patents are relatively rare. These attractive documents, which give details of the invention, are frequently accompanied by drawings and additional details [63].

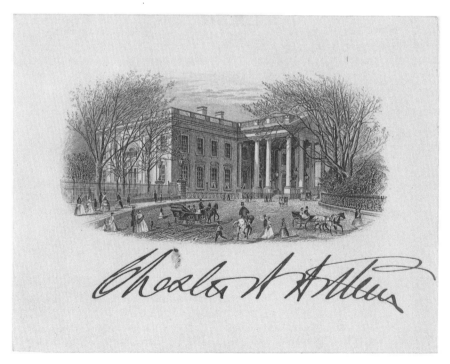

61 Executive mansion vignette signed by Chester A. Arthur

60
White House card signed
by Herbert Hoover
(right)

62
Authorization for the
secretary of state to affix
the seal of the United
States signed by Ulysses S.
Grant (below)

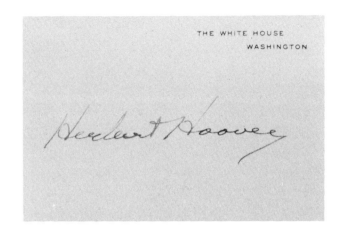

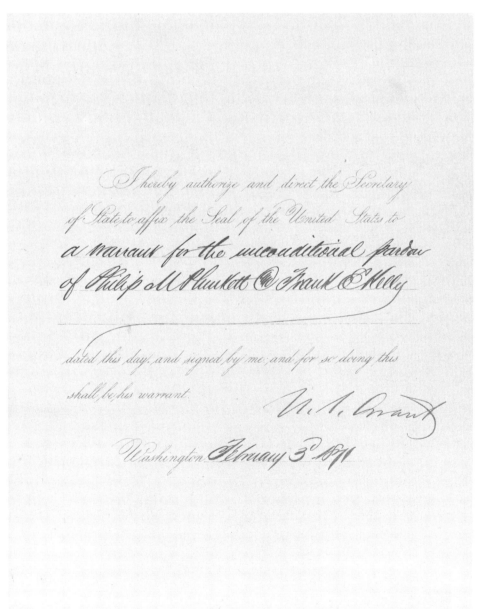

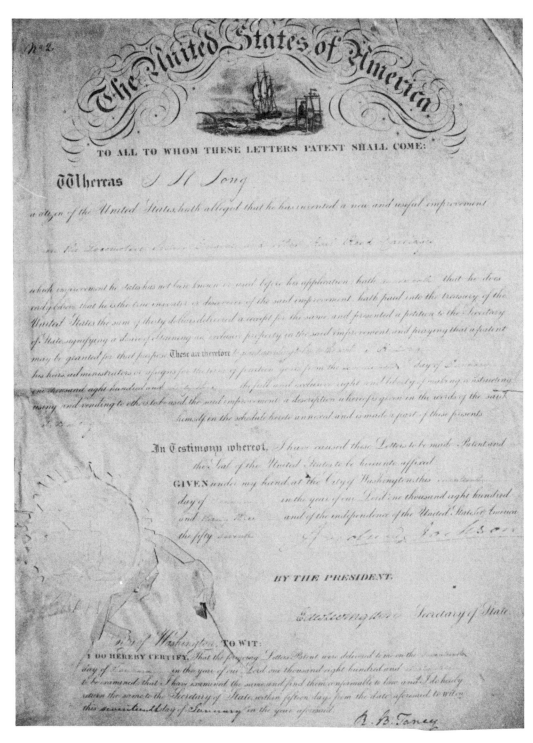

63 Patent signed by Andrew Jackson as president and by Roger B. Taney as attorney general

THE
PRESIDENTS
&
FIRST LADIES

GEORGE WASHINGTON
1732–1799
April 30, 1789–March 3, 1797

The leadership, intelligence, style, and power of the personality of the first president are reflected in his letters, which he wrote in magnificent calligraphy. His letters are thoughtfully and carefully worded, presenting his ideas in a very logical way. Washington chose his words so carefully that it is sometimes necessary to read his letters several times to be certain of the exact meaning he intended.

In his early adult life, Washington was a surveyor; his land surveys, which are now quite rare, have been very popular with collectors when available. During the revolutionary war most of his letters were dictated to secretaries and signed by him, while most of his presidential and postpresidential letters were completely written in his own hand. His later letters generally concern the affairs of Mount Vernon.

At the end of the Revolution, Washington personally signed soldiers' discharges. Because these documents were frequently folded and unfolded, those that survive are usually badly worn in the folds and in relatively poor condition [49, p. 55]. Washington also signed very ornate certificates of membership in the Society of the Cincinnati for those who served as officers in the war. These important family heirlooms were frequently framed and hung for many decades, resulting in a fading of the ink in the text and signatures. They are sometimes encountered with writing so faint as to be almost illegible, particularly Washington's signature [48, p. 54]. Sea letters issued during his presidency are also usually badly worn in the folds [58, p. 78]; other presidential appointments are more likely to be in better condition. Lottery tickets signed by Washington are infrequently found; general legal documents signed by Washington during various periods of his life are more common.

Books from Washington's library of 884 volumes generally bear his armorial bookplate and signature at the top of the title page. Many of these were acquired by the Boston Atheneum in the last century, and although many others have appeared on the market in past decades, they are now rare. Checks signed by the first president are also rare. (Washington checks were very commonly forged by Robert Spring, a master forger of Washington, and any example must be carefully examined.)

As one of the most popular and valuable presidents, Washington's autograph material has been extensively forged by most of the major forgers, especially Spring and Joseph Cosey. Revolutionary war passes, in addition to checks, are particularly suspect, and several forgers did not hesitate to forge complete handwritten letters (see the chapter on the detection of forgeries for a complete discussion).

M. Washington

MARTHA CUSTIS WASHINGTON
1731–1802

Letters of Martha Washington have appeared on the market, and for many years the Mount Vernon Ladies Association has acquired virtually all of those offered. Consequently, her letters are very difficult to obtain.

John Adams

JOHN ADAMS
1735–1826
March 4, 1797–March 3, 1801

The second president was probably the finest letter writer among all the presidents. Throughout his career he wrote letters that revealed his thoughts and feelings on the issues of the day. After his presidency he would, on occasion, write long, philosophical letters. Those to his lifelong friend, Benjamin Rush, are particularly outstanding. Adams's letters of presidential date are considerably rarer than those of other periods, and it is interesting that his handwriting became larger when he rose to the presidency. His presidential signature was frequently three times the height of his pre-presidential signature. Toward the end of his life, in the 1820s, many of his letters were dictated to a secretary; they bear his shaky signature. Presidential documents are very scarce, as are the early legal documents that are sometimes found. Books signed by Adams are very rare and checks signed by him extremely rare.

John Adams is sometimes confused with other contemporary Bostonians bearing the same name, so one must be careful that the letter or document being collected is in fact by the John Adams who was president.

The demand for material of John Adams is very strong; collectors are interested in him as an individual, as a signer of the Declaration of Independence, and as president. His letters with interesting content command very significant prices when offered.

A Adams

ABIGAIL SMITH ADAMS
1744–1818

Although a fair number of letters of Abigail Adams have come onto the market during the past thirty years, her autograph is certainly rare. Her autograph material has always been met with very substantial interest among collectors and has quickly disappeared into collections. Unfortunately, letters revealing her very strong character, particularly in advice to her husband, never appear for sale.

THOMAS JEFFERSON
1743–1826
March 4, 1801–March 3, 1809

While a large number of Jefferson's letters are of a routine nature, he was capable of writing very fine letters of great philosophical interest. Unfortunately, these are extremely rare, and even letters discussing the domestic affairs of Monticello are now much less frequently encountered. Jefferson was the first president to begin the practice of writing third-person letters (*Th: Jefferson presents his compliments . . .*). Ships' passports and sea letters from his presidency are scarcer than land grants and general appointments. Books from his library as well as checks signed by him are very rarely seen on the market.

The interest of collectors in Jefferson has always been very strong because of his role as an early statesman, as a drafter and signer of the Declaration of Independence, and as president. The University of Virginia has collected his letters for many years, and in recent years even those with routine content have become rare.

MARTHA SKELTON JEFFERSON
1748–1782

Autograph material of Jefferson's wife, who died at the age of thirty-four, is extremely rare.

JAMES MADISON
1751–1836
March 4, 1809–March 3, 1817

The overwhelming majority of James Madison's letters concern government and personal affairs of a routine nature, especially when compared to his three predecessors in the presidency. Letters with interesting content are very rarely found. As with Jefferson, James Madison's land grants are by far the most common presidential documents, although he did sign many ships' papers, sea letters, and appointments. While books signed by Madison are extremely rare, checks signed by him are in the scarce category and can occasionally be obtained.

The interest of collectors in Madison, whose influence largely shaped the final draft of the Constitution, is much stronger than for the majority of the presidents but not nearly as great as the interest in his three predecessors.

DOROTHEA (DOLLEY) TODD MADISON
1768–1849

Dolley Madison is one of the best-known First Ladies, largely because she set a new tone in the White House with her lively personality and great personal popularity. Her letters have been saved, and they are occasionally obtainable. Poems in her handwriting, usually unsigned, are more frequently found. Many of James Madison's letters written later in life were dictated to her, written in her hand, then signed by the former president with a feeble and shaky signature.

JAMES MONROE
1758–1831
March 4, 1817–March 3, 1825

The decline in the general quality of the content of letters continues with the fifth president. While he occasionally wrote good and, under unusual circumstances, very fine letters, this was not generally the case. Most of James Monroe's letters discuss personal business. Documents as governor of Virginia are occasionally offered but are not particularly sought after by collectors. Ships' passports and appointments as president are frequently encountered, and land grants signed by Monroe are relatively common. Books signed by him are extremely rare and his signed checks are very rare.

The interest of collectors in James Monroe as an individual is far outweighed by the interest in obtaining a letter or document for a presidential collection.

ELIZABETH KORTRIGHT MONROE
1763?–1830

As with Martha Jefferson, autograph material of Elizabeth Monroe is extremely rare.

John Quincy Adams

JOHN QUINCY ADAMS
1767–1848
March 4, 1825–March 3, 1829

The overwhelming majority of John Quincy Adams's letters discuss his affairs as a congressman, and only rarely does one encounter a letter with important content; he certainly was not his father's son in his propensity to write important and interesting letters. Adams occasionally wrote poems, and in some instances they are quite interesting. His early letters are more likely to be interesting and charming. As with James Monroe, his land grants are by far the most common form of presidential documents encountered. Adams is the first president whose signed images can be obtained, although these signed steel engravings are very rare. Books signed by him are less rare and would be in the scarce category, while signed checks are very rare.

The interest among collectors in John Quincy Adams is mostly limited to completing sets of presidents, though some have collected his autograph material because of a personal interest.

Louisa Catherine Adams

LOUISA C. JOHNSON ADAMS
1775–1852

As with her mother-in-law, Louisa Adams's letters do appear occasionally on the market.

Andrew Jackson

ANDREW JACKSON
1767–1845
March 4, 1829–March 2, 1837

Andrew Jackson was the first westerner to occupy the White House, and his fiery and dynamic personality was occasionally expressed forcefully in his letters. His writing style was different from his predecessors, but his letters reflect his feelings as well as any of them. Most of his letters are concerned with military or personal matters, but on very rare occasions, wonderful letters of Jackson can be found. The most commonly encountered Jackson documents are his presidential land grants. At the beginning of his second term in office, Andrew Jackson stopped signing land grants, and from this time onward, they are signed by secretaries. (All future presidents followed his policy, and except for Indian land grants, all were signed by secretaries.) Military and other appointments are less common, and patents signed by him are the rarest. As might be expected, books signed by Jackson are extremely rare and checks signed by him very scarce.

The interest among collectors in Andrew Jackson is very strong. His career as Indian fighter, as Hero of New Orleans, and as president have made Jackson, as an individual, one of the most collected presidents.

RACHEL ROBARDS JACKSON
1767–1828

Letters of Rachel Jackson are extremely rare. Some letters previously thought to have been written by her are apparently written from her dictation and are neither in her hand nor signed by her.

MARTIN VAN BUREN
1782–1862
March 4, 1837–March 3, 1841

The quality of Martin Van Buren's letters matches his importance as a president. Occasionally, political letters are encountered, but he had none of the letterwriting abilities of his predecessors, nor did he have great events to write about. Routine letters overwhelmingly dominate what is found. Early legal documents bearing the signature *Martin Van Buren* appear with some frequency on the market, but it is evident that many of these were signed for Van Buren during his early legal career in New York. Presidential documents are considerably scarcer than those of Monroe, John Quincy Adams, and Andrew Jackson, primarily because he is the first president not to have signed land grants. Books signed by him are extremely rare and checks signed by him very rare.

The interest in Van Buren among collectors is mostly to complete presidential sets.

HANNAH HOES VAN BUREN
1783–1819

Autograph material of Hannah Van Buren is virtually unobtainable.

W. H. Harrison [signature]

WILLIAM HENRY HARRISON
1773–1841
March 4, 1841–April 4, 1841

Letters written by this western Indian fighter are much scarcer than those written by his predecessors. Extremely few have interesting content. Autograph material of Harrison would be the rarest of all the presidents up to his time were it not for a large group of documents signed as aide-de-camp to General Anthony Wayne while fighting Indians in the Northwest Territories. These came onto the market many decades ago, and although all were dispersed into collections, their reappearance makes it possible for collectors to obtain a good example of his signature at a relatively reasonable cost. These documents usually concern orders for military supplies. Documents signed as governor of the Northwest Territories are much scarcer and more attractive. Checks signed by Harrison are scarce, while books signed by him, like those of his fellow westerner, Andrew Jackson, are extremely rare.

William Henry Harrison caught a cold at his own inauguration and died one month later. As a result, material signed as president is, by far, the rarest of any president. Three signed autograph letters, two or three signed letters, and somewhere between fifteen and twenty-five documents signed as president are known to exist.

Collectors interested in the history of the Northwest Territories and the Indian wars have collected Harrison's letters written during his western career. Otherwise, he is collected principally to complete sets of presidents.

Anna. Harrison [signature]

ANNA SYMMES HARRISON
1775–1864

Some years ago, approximately two dozen letters of Anna Harrison appeared on the market and were quickly absorbed into collections. They have reappeared infrequently, and her autograph material is now rare.

[signature: J. Tyler]

JOHN TYLER
1790–1862
April 6, 1841–March 3, 1845

John Tyler very rarely wrote about important subjects. His presidential documents are usually available, the most common being authorizations to the secretary of state to affix the seal of the United States. Books signed by Tyler, as well as signed checks, are extremely rare.

Collector interest in Tyler is almost exclusively to complete sets of presidents.

LETITIA CHRISTIAN TYLER
1790–1842

[signature: Julia G Tyler]

JULIA GARDINER TYLER
1820–1889

Autograph material by Tyler's first wife is extremely rare; that of his second wife is very rare.

JAMES K. POLK
1795–1849
March 4, 1845–March 3, 1849

Though not comparable to the quality of the letters of the Founding Fathers, James K. Polk was the first president since Jackson who could write a good political letter. All of his letters are relatively rare, much scarcer than those of his precedessors, Tyler or Van Buren. Letters discussing or mentioning the Mexican War are extremely rare. Presidential documents are scarcer than those of most of the presidents of the period. Books from his library are rarely offered, but it is possible over time to find an example. Checks written by him are virtually unobtainable.

There is some demand among collectors for material by Polk because of his involvement with the Mexican War; however, most is based on the need to complete presidential collections.

SARAH CHILDRESS POLK
1803–1891

Autograph material by Sarah Polk is rarely offered for sale.

ZACHARY TAYLOR
1784–1850
March 5, 1849–July 9, 1850

Letters and documents of Zachary Taylor during his early career as an Indian fighter in Florida and in the Northwest can be quite interesting. He spent many years chasing and fighting the Indians, and his frustrations were expressed at times in his correspondence. Most of his military letters and documents concern appointments and supplies. Checks and books signed by him are virtually unobtainable.

Taylor served as president for only fifteen months, and during this time most of his letters were dictated to secretaries and signed by him. His letters written during his presidency are therefore rare, although they are not nearly as rare as those of William Henry Harrison. Documents from his presidency are also rare. One of the reasons for the scarcity of letters with important content is that a member of the Beinecke family actively collected Taylor's letters for many years and donated them to Yale University.

Collector interest in Taylor is quite strong, as an Indian fighter and victorious Mexican War general and to complete sets of presidents.

MARGARET SMITH TAYLOR
1788–1852

Autograph material of Margaret Taylor is extremely rare.

MILLARD FILLMORE
1800–1874
July 10, 1850–March 3, 1853

The quality of Millard Fillmore's letters certainly represents him accurately as one of the forgotten presidents (ironically, he has become somewhat known to the public precisely because of his obscurity). Interesting letters by Fillmore are very rare. Presidential documents are fairly common, particularly appointments and authorizations to the secretary of state. Signed books from his library have been more common than those of any previous president, although few of these have survived in good condition. Checks signed by him are extremely rare, as are signed engravings or photographs.

The interest in Fillmore among collectors is mostly to complete sets of presidents.

ABIGAIL POWERS FILLMORE
1798–1853

CAROLINE MCINTOSH FILLMORE
1813–1881

Autograph material of Abigail Fillmore is extremely rare. Examples in the hand of Caroline Fillmore, who married Fillmore after his presidential term, are very rare.

Franklin Pierce [signature]

FRANKLIN PIERCE
1804–1869
March 4, 1853–March 3, 1857

Franklin Pierce rarely wrote an interesting letter. Almost all his letters, while they may be lengthy, merely express general thoughts and deal with ordinary matters. Presidential documents are usually available and in the same category with his contemporaries. Books signed by him are very rare, while signed checks or portraits are extremely rare.

The only interest in Pierce is to complete presidential sets.

Jane A. Pierce [signature]

JANE APPLETON PIERCE
1806–1863

Previously extremely rare, a small group of letters by Jane Pierce appeared on the market in the last decade and have been slowly absorbed into collections. Their infrequent reappearance for sale has made them more collectable.

James Buchanan [signature]

JAMES BUCHANAN
1791–1868
March 4, 1857–March 3, 1861

James Buchanan wrote many fine political letters during his early political career in Pennsylvania. His later letters are usually very routine. Presidential documents are fairly common; books from his library are very rare; and signed checks or portraits are extremely rare.

The interest in Buchanan among collectors is mostly to complete sets.

ABRAHAM LINCOLN
1809–1865
March 4, 1861–April 15, 1865

In 1861, there is a return to greatness among presidents with the election of Abraham Lincoln, a superb letter writer who for decades has attracted institutional collectors, and today a Lincoln letter dealing with more important military or domestic issues is extremely rare. Any Lincoln letter is now uncommon.

Lincoln's early legal briefs are usually written in his hand and signed by him with the name of the law firm, *Lincoln & Herndon, Lincoln & Logan,* or *Stuart & Lincoln.* These have always been very popular with lawyers and are now much less frequently encountered than in the past. During his presidency, Lincoln endorsed and signed letters sent to him, and these endorsements provided many of the examples in collections. Military appointments, because of the tremendous wartime need for officers, are generally available. Books signed by Lincoln frequently bear the stamp of his law firm, *Lincoln & Herndon,* and, while his signed photographs and checks are not nearly as rare as many of his predecessors, they are, along with his books, very desirable and eagerly sought after by many collectors.

As might be expected, Abraham Lincoln has been the most forged president. Half a dozen major forgers have specialized in imitating his handwriting. All have failed to replicate its force and its very idiosyncratic nature. None realized that Lincoln never wrote his last name, *Lincoln,* on a consistent baseline and that the letter *c* is consistently below this baseline, while the *ln* is always above it. A few have even made the mistake of signing *Abe Lincoln,* a signature he never used. (For a more complete discussion, see the chapter on forgeries.)

The interest in Abraham Lincoln is tremendous. He is perhaps more popular than Washington, and this popularity extends beyond presidential and Americana collectors (one of the best Lincoln collections formed in recent years is in a Japanese university).

MARY TODD LINCOLN
1818–1882

There is a great demand for letters of Mary Lincoln, which are not as rare as many earlier First Ladies but are more expensive. Mary Lincoln's letters written after the assassination of her husband show the tremendous mental and financial strain she was suffering.

ANDREW JOHNSON
1808–1875
April 15, 1865–March 3, 1869

The humble background of the president who succeeded Lincoln is reflected in his letters, which frequently contain misspellings. The former tailor could write very strongly worded and quite interesting letters expressing his views, but these are now extremely rare on the market. Handwritten letters as president are virtually unobtainable, although signed letters are occasionally offered. During his presidency, Andrew Johnson injured his right hand, and he is the first president to use a stamp to sign most of his military appointments. Other documents that are offered, principally directions to the secretary of state to affix the seal of the United States, bear his genuine signature. Books signed by Johnson are extremely rare. Portraits and checks signed by him are very rare.

There is an interest among collectors in Andrew Johnson because of his role in the Civil War and subsequent impeachment. Interest in him as president is to complete sets.

ELIZA MCCARDLE JOHNSON
1810–1876

Autograph material of Eliza Johnson is virtually unobtainable.

ULYSSES S. GRANT
1822–1885
March 4, 1869–March 3, 1877

Like many other presidents, Ulysses Grant wrote letters that reflect his career. His Civil War letters are forceful and decisive, with logical views and arguments; his presidential letters are considerably less interesting and indicative of the general malaise that affected his administration. Grant's letters after the presidency are almost always social. Endorsements from the Civil War are scarce, but documents from his presidency are not rare. Grant introduced the Executive Mansion card for short notes, but examples signed by him are extremely rare. Signed checks by Grant are scarce, while books signed by him are very rare. Signed engraved portraits are relatively scarce but frequently available; signed photographs are rarer and less frequently seen.

There is very strong interest among collectors in Grant as a Civil War general—far more than there is in him as president, where he is only sought after to complete sets. His letters written during the Civil War, once commonly available, are now seen less and less frequently.

JULIA DENT GRANT
1826–1902

Autograph material of Julia Grant, while somewhat scarce, is usually obtainable.

RUTHERFORD B. HAYES
1822–1893
March 5, 1877–March 3, 1881

Most of Rutherford B. Hayes's correspondence deals with ordinary and routine matters. The Rutherford B. Hayes Library in Ohio has over a period of many years collected nearly all of the letters with important content that have been offered for sale, and this has made such letters very rare. Documents signed as president are readily available. Signed portraits, checks, and books are all in the rare category.

Interest in Hayes among collectors is only to complete sets of presidents.

LUCY WEBB HAYES
1831–1889

Autograph material of Lucy Hayes is rare.

JAMES A. GARFIELD
1831–1881
March 4, 1881–September 19, 1881

Before his election to the presidency, James A. Garfield served for many years as a representative from Ohio. Letters during this period are relatively common and concern the daily affairs of a congressman; letters with good content are very rare. Presidential letters of Garfield, who was shot on July 2, 1881, and died on September 19, are extremely rare, as are documents signed during this period. He is second only to William Henry Harrison in rarity during his presidency. Checks signed by Garfield are scarce unless one includes drafts addressed to the sergeant-at-arms of the House of Representatives. Portraits signed by him are scarce, and books signed by him are very rare.

The demand among collectors is almost exclusively to complete sets of presidents.

LUCRETIA RUDOLPH GARFIELD
1832–1918

Autograph material of Lucretia Garfield, who lived for many years after her husband was assassinated, is relatively common.

CHESTER A. ARTHUR
1830–1886
September 19, 1881–March 3, 1885

Letters of Chester Arthur are of uniformly poor content; interesting letters are never found. He is quite rare in handwritten letters signed as president, and letters signed by him as president are scarce. Signed presidential documents are less common than those of his contemporaries. Arthur is the first president to make extensive use of the Executive Mansion card, and he introduced a second type of card as well, bearing an engraved scene of the Executive Mansion. Checks signed by Arthur are scarce; books from his library and signed portraits are very rare.

The interest among collectors is only to complete sets of presidents.

ELLEN HERNDON ARTHUR
1837–1880

Autograph material of Ellen Arthur is virtually unobtainable.

GROVER CLEVELAND
1837–1908
March 4, 1885–March 3, 1889
March 4, 1893–March 3, 1897

Grover Cleveland's letters can frequently be very interesting, and he wrote a relatively large number of letters on many subjects that have good content—in marked contrast to many of his predecessors and successors in the presidency. Presidential documents are very common. Books signed by Cleveland do occasionally turn up but could be termed scarce; checks signed by him are very rare, while signed portraits are much more readily available.

Despite the relatively high quality of the content of Cleveland's letters, few collectors have sought his letters because of a personal interest in him.

FRANCES FOLSOM CLEVELAND
1864–1947

Autograph material of Frances Cleveland is very common.

[signature: Benj Harrison]

BENJAMIN HARRISON
1833–1901
March 4, 1889–March 3, 1893

While a better letter writer than Chester Arthur, Benjamin Harrison was not nearly as interesting as his predecessor or successor, Grover Cleveland. An occasional good letter is encountered, but the overwhelming majority concern business or social matters. As with letters of Hayes, those of Harrison have been collected extensively by an institution in his home state, and this may account for the rarity of interesting letters. Presidential documents are fairly common. Checks signed by Harrison are scarce, while signed portraits are rare, and books signed by him are extremely rare.

Interest in Harrison is almost exclusively to complete sets of presidents.

[signature: Carrie S. Harrison]

CAROLINE SCOTT HARRISON
1832–1892

[signature: Mary Lord Harrison]

MARY DIMMOCK HARRISON
1858–1948

Autograph material of Caroline Harrison is rare. She died before Harrison's election to the presidency. Autograph material of Mary Harrison, who married Harrison after his presidential term, is very common.

WILLIAM MCKINLEY
1843–1901
March 4, 1897–September 14, 1901

William McKinley's letters, both before and during the presidency, rarely discuss important issues. His early legal documents are popular with legal history collectors, but his material as governor of Ohio is of little interest to collectors. Presidential documents are slightly scarce. Portraits signed by McKinley are relatively common, while checks and books signed by him are both scarce.

The interest in McKinley among collectors is to complete sets of presidents.

IDA SAXTON MCKINLEY
1847–1907

Autograph material signed by Ida McKinley is rare.

Theodore Roosevelt [signature]

THEODORE ROOSEVELT
1858–1919
September 14, 1901–March 3, 1909

Theodore Roosevelt is one of the best presidential letter writers. Many of his letters, expressing his very strong feelings on many subjects, reflect his feisty personality. His later letters, particularly those concerning his personal involvement in the First World War and his sons' participation are very open, honest, and warm and reflect his own pride, anguish, and pain. Letters of this quality have been very actively collected; the largest such collection is now at Boston University. Many of his typewritten letters, particularly as president, bear corrections by him or additions to the dictated text. Handwritten letters signed as president are very rare. Teddy Roosevelt's letters provide a true insight into the thoughts and feelings of the man.

Adding a common touch to his presidency, Roosevelt changed the printed name from *Executive Mansion* to *White House* on the cards commonly used to give autographs. Checks signed by Roosevelt are at this time relatively common, as are books signed by him. Signed portraits are also frequently available, although particularly fine ones are rare. While letters and documents from other times in his life are fairly available, anything concerning his activity as a Rough Rider is very rare and in great demand

At various times before the presidency, Roosevelt used a stamp for his signature, although this should not deceive anyone familiar with genuine signatures. As governor and vice-president, he also authorized a secretary to sign his name.

Roosevelt is one of the most popular presidents, and many collectors specialize in collecting letters written throughout his long career. Those with interesting content are now rare.

ALICE LEE ROOSEVELT
1861–1884

Edith K. Roosevelt [signature]

EDITH CAROW ROOSEVELT
1861–1948

Autograph material of Roosevelt's first wife, Alice Roosevelt, is unobtainable. Autograph material of Edith Roosevelt, who outlived her husband by many years, is very common.

WILLIAM HOWARD TAFT
1857–1930
March 4, 1909–March 3, 1913

The overwhelming majority of letters written by William Howard Taft concerns various business and government affairs, but occasionally letters with fine content do appear. Presidential documents are very common, as are signed photographs, while signed checks and books are only slightly less available.

There is some interest among collectors in Taft's postpresidential career as chief justice, but he is mostly collected by those interested in completing sets and by those interested in his considerable accomplishments as president.

HELEN HERRON TAFT
1861–1943

Autograph material of Helen Taft is commonly available.

WOODROW WILSON
1856–1924
March 4, 1913–March 3, 1921

On occasion, excellent letters of Woodrow Wilson surface, but they are very rare, and the overwhelming majority of his letters are about university, state, or government matters. Many of the letters offered are from his days at Princeton University or as governor of New Jersey, and his presidential letters are more likely to be interesting. Presidential documents are only slightly scarcer than those of his contemporaries. Books signed by Wilson are relatively common; signed checks are rare, while signed photographs are common.

While governor of New Jersey, Wilson used a rubber stamp to sign a large number of his letters. They are very obvious when examined.

Demand among collectors, while greater than that for letters of Taft or Coolidge, is significantly less than that for Roosevelt. Despite the fact that Woodrow Wilson played a key part in the negotiations to end World War I and founded the League of Nations, fewer collectors have specialized in his letters than might be expected.

ELLEN AXSON WILSON
1860–1914

EDITH GALT WILSON
1872–1961

Autograph material of Wilson's first wife is very rare. Wilson's second wife outlived her husband by forty years, and her letters are fairly common; unfortunately, they never deal with her role in the presidency after her husband's stroke.

WARREN G. HARDING
1865–1923
March 4, 1921–August 2, 1923

While most of Warren G. Harding's letters concern his duties in the Senate or White House, he did write a few fine letters, especially as president. The only handwritten letters encountered are from the period when he was editor of the *Marion Star* newspaper. Presidential documents are slightly scarcer than those of other presidents of the period but are still normally available. Signed photographs are fairly common, signed checks are scarce, and books signed by him are very rare.

Harding's dislike of signing letters was greater than that of any of his predecessors, and he authorized his secretary, George P. Christian, Jr., to imitate his signature from 1918 until he became president in 1921.

Interest in Harding is mostly to complete sets of presidents, but fine letters are in demand among a number of collectors specializing in him.

FLORENCE KLING HARDING
1860–1924

Letters signed by Florence Harding are common and usually discuss social or personal matters.

CALVIN COOLIDGE
1872–1933
August 3, 1923–March 3, 1929

Calvin Coolidge's letters reflect his image as Silent Cal; they say as little as he did. He rarely wrote letters with comments on the issues of the day, let alone his personal views. Presidential documents are very common, particularly appointments, as are signed photographs. His signed checks may be the most common of all the presidents. Books signed by him are also relatively common.

As governor of Massachusetts, Coolidge had his secretary imitate his signature quite well, and these signatures can be deceptive to the uninformed.

Interest in Coolidge among collectors is solely to complete sets of presidents.

GRACE GOODHUE COOLIDGE
1879–1957

Autograph material of Grace Coolidge is very common.

HERBERT HOOVER
1874–1964
March 4, 1929–March 3, 1933

Herbert Hoover rarely wrote letters containing quotable sentences; he was almost always very brief and expressed little of his philosophy. Presidential documents are scarce, as are presidential letters. Signed photographs and books are very common, while signed checks are very rare.

When secretary of commerce, Hoover authorized a secretary to sign his name on letters; she did this with considerable skill. Hoover also introduced printed form letter thank you notes in type imitating handwriting; these notes have misled many collectors.

Interest among collectors is almost exclusively to complete sets, although there has been increased interest in his autograph material in recent years.

LOU HENRY HOOVER
1874–1944

Autograph material of Lou Henry Hoover is scarce.

FRANKLIN D. ROOSEVELT
1882–1945
March 4, 1933–April 12, 1945

Franklin Roosevelt's ability to write, or at least edit, lively and interesting speeches is not reflected in his letters. His letters are friendly, sometimes warm, and as governor of New York, occasionally deal with political issues; but generally they are uninteresting. In this regard, he compares most unfavorably with his distant cousin Teddy. Roosevelt's letters to friends are occasionally signed *FDR*. Presidential documents are usually available. Books from Roosevelt's library, signed by him, have been sold by members of his family and combined with copies of his own inscribed books, have been available to collectors with some frequency. Signed portraits by him are scarce, while signed checks are rare.

Prior to the presidency, Roosevelt authorized a number of secretaries to imitate his signature, particularly when he was assistant secretary of the navy during World War I. The deterioration of Roosevelt's health is apparent in his signatures during the last year or so of his life. They have all the characteristics of forgeries, such as shaky lines, but in this case, they are indicative of his rapidly declining health and of their authenticity.

Demand for Franklin Roosevelt material is very strong, both as an individual and for presidential sets.

ANNA ELEANOR ROOSEVELT
1884–1962

Not since Dolley Madison was there a First Lady as well known and popular as Eleanor Roosevelt. She attained a stature greater than any of her predecessors or successors (so far), and her letters are very common. Unfortunately, they very rarely contain more than a hint of the role this extraordinary First Lady played, not only in influencing her husband's administration but also on the world stage.

HARRY S TRUMAN
1884–1972
April 12, 1945–January 20, 1953

Harry Truman's letters reflect his blunt, no-nonsense style; they can be very witty and to the point but are rarely philosophical. Most relate to routine government business, but overall, he is a better than average presidential letter writer. Presidential documents are scarce, probably because the families of his descendants are not yet willing to part with them. Official checks signed by him are fairly common, while personal checks are very rare. Signed books and portraits are very common. Truman was willing to sign autographs for almost anyone who asked him.

Some of his Senate correspondence was signed by secretaries, as were White House cards.

Demand for Truman material is very strong; he is collected as an interesting individual and as president.

BESS WALLACE TRUMAN
1885–1982

Autograph material of Bess Truman is very common.

(signature: Dwight D. Eisenhower)

DWIGHT D. EISENHOWER
1890–1969
January 20, 1953–January 20, 1961

Dwight Eisenhower's letters to his wife written during World War II are among the best letters written by any president at any time. All these letters to Mamie were handwritten, whereas letters written during the same period to others were always typewritten, and all except the most important ones were dictated by Eisenhower's aides (though all are genuinely signed). As president, Eisenhower occasionally wrote interesting letters but rarely a very fine one. Most of his letters concern government and social matters. Eisenhower's presidential documents, like those of his contemporaries, are rare on the market. Books signed by Eisenhower are common, as are signed photographs; checks signed by him are extremely rare. (Eisenhower once commented that all his checks had to be signed by aides because if he signed them, the recipients rarely cashed them and he could not balance his account.)

During his administration, Eisenhower sent White House cards bearing facsimile signatures to collectors requesting autographs; these cards bear a printed statement on the verso that the signature is a facsimile. While president of Columbia University, Eisenhower had many of his letters signed by machines and continued this practice while campaigning for the presidency in 1952. During the last few years of his life, he authorized a secretary to sign his letters and requests for autographs, omitting his middle initial.

Autograph material of Eisenhower is in very strong demand among collectors, particularly material from World War II. In recent years, Eisenhower's presidency has been reevaluated very favorably, and this has been reflected in the increased interest of collectors in his presidential letters.

(signature: Mamie Doud Eisenhower)

MAMIE DOUD EISENHOWER
1896–1979

Autograph material of Mamie Eisenhower is very common.

JOHN F. KENNEDY
1917–1963
January 20, 1961–November 22, 1963

The political world entered a new era in 1961 with the election of John Kennedy, and the autograph-collecting world entered the era of presidents delegating the signing of the overwhelming majority of their letters to secretaries and machines. Kennedy also had the habit of signing his name many different ways, complicating the authentication of his material even further.

Virtually all letters of this colorful, charismatic president discuss appointments and other congressional matters; important letters are very rare. Presidential documents are also very rare. Books signed by Kennedy are frequently available, checks signed by him are extremely rare, and genuine photographs signed by him are rare.

Kennedy is one of the five or six most popular presidents among collectors; he is collected in his own right as well as to complete sets of presidents.

JACQUELINE BOUVIER KENNEDY
1929–1994

Jacqueline Kennedy has been the most famous First Lady since Eleanor Roosevelt. Her fame is certainly based on criteria different from that of Eleanor Roosevelt, and her letters that have come onto the market are much scarcer.

LYNDON B. JOHNSON
1908–1973
November 22, 1963–January 20, 1969

The personality of Lyndon Johnson is not reflected in the letters that were sent out from the Senate and White House bearing his name. Many were apparently written by others for him, and most were signed by secretaries or machines. Interesting letters signed by Johnson are quite rare, and routine letters as senator or president are scarce because of his extensive use of secretaries and autopen machines. Presidential documents signed by Johnson himself, like those of all the recent presidents, are rare. Books and photographs bearing his genuine signature are scarce, while checks signed by him have not appeared on the market.

At present, with the Vietnam War still a very bad memory for Americans, there is little interest in collecting autographs of Johnson except for presidential sets.

CLAUDIA TAYLOR (LADY BIRD) JOHNSON
1912–

Material signed by Lady Bird Johnson is very common, although letters with significant content have not as yet appeared.

RICHARD M. NIXON
1913–1994
January 20, 1969–August 9. 1974

In contrast to his predecessor, Richard Nixon at times expressed strong thoughts and opinions in letters, and he tended to sign them personally. The overwhelming majority of his letters, of course, deal with the daily affairs of his office. Presidential documents are rare. Genuine signed photographs of Nixon are still relatively common, as are signed books. Signed checks of Nixon have not appeared on the market.

Like his immediate predecessors and all of his successors, Richard Nixon used autopen machines extensively to sign his letters, and he also authorized his secretaries to imitate his signatures as closely as possible.

Despite the fact that Nixon has been the only American president forced to resign, he is very popular among collectors. He will probably be remembered as much for his foreign policy as his resignation, and this seems to be reflected in the interest that collectors have taken in collecting his letters.

THELMA (PAT) RYAN NIXON
1913–1993

Autograph material of the former First Lady has routinely appeared for sale. Genuine signatures are usually signed *Pat Nixon* rather than *Patricia Nixon*.

GERALD R. FORD
1913–
August 9, 1974–January 20, 1977

Gerald Ford's letters express a warm personality, and, particularly as a congressman, he wrote forceful and lengthy letters on issues of the day. Presidential documents, like those of his contemporaries, are rare as recipients and families still keep their commissions to various posts. Signed books and photographs have been common on the market; no checks have appeared.

Demand for Ford letters has been only to complete presidential collections. As a friendly personality who seems to carry on extensive correspondences, Ford's handwritten letters may, in the future, be relatively common compared to those of his contemporaries.

ELIZABETH (BETTY) BLOOMER FORD
1918–

Betty Ford was a popular First Lady, and she was responsive to those writing to her. In time I would expect her letters to be commonly available.

JIMMY CARTER
1924–

January 20, 1977–January 20, 1981

While governor of Georgia, Jimmy Carter could occasionally be quite eloquent in expressing his opinions, particularly in handwritten letters. Too few of his presidential and postpresidential letters have come onto the market to reveal if he continued to express himself as fully in letters during these times. Signed photographs of Carter are scarce, but checks and books signed by him are common. Carter, like his contemporaries, extensively used secretaries and machines to sign his name.

The interest of collectors in Jimmy Carter autograph material has been very slight, representing only an interest in completing sets of presidents. Most of the material offered is, however, of a souvenir nature—signed statements, booklets, programs, and so on.

ROSALYN SMITH CARTER
1927–

The former First Lady's autograph material is readily available, although significant letters have not yet appeared.

RONALD REAGAN
1911–
January 20, 1981–January 20, 1989

Ronald Reagan's habits in letter writing are unique. While governor of California, Reagan would personally draft, in his own hand, many of his important as well as routine letters. These drafts were then given to a secretary who typed them and applied a machine signature, regardless of the letter's importance. According to several people who worked in the Oval Office, this practice continued into the presidency. The drafts that Reagan wrote have appeared on the market, and the contents are very well reasoned, interesting, and forceful, clearly presenting his point of view. They are among the best written by a twentieth-century president. Except for these letters, very few genuinely signed Reagan letters have appeared on the market. Virtually no presidential documents have been offered. Checks signed by Reagan, at this time, are rare. It is not presently known how scarce or common signed photographs and books will be (one suspects the former will be common).

It is very difficult to authenticate any autograph material of Ronald Reagan unless it is completely handwritten from the period after his movie career. His earliest letters, from the time of his motion picture career at Warner Brothers, were not written personally; his mother was employed by the studio to write and sign his personal correspondence. These long and personal handwritten letters very closely resemble letters in Reagan's own handwriting.

Reagan's popularity as president is reflected in the great demand for his autograph material.

NANCY DAVIS REAGAN
1923–

I have thus far been unable to discover whether or not Nancy Reagan commonly signed her own correspondence and other material.

(George Bush signature)

GEORGE BUSH
1924–
January 20, 1989–January 20, 1993

Fine letters of George Bush have at times appeared on the market. His long business and government career, before having access to signing machines, indicates that his autograph material will probably be common. A number of people who have known him for years have, literally, hundreds of handwritten thank you notes.

(Barbara Bush signature)

BARBARA PIERCE BUSH
1925–

It is too soon to know about Barbara Bush's letter-writing habits.

(Bill Clinton signature)

WILLIAM JEFFERSON "BILL" CLINTON
1946–
January 20, 1993–

(Hillary Rodham Clinton signature)

HILLARY RODHAM CLINTON
1947–

At this time, letters signed by Clinton as governor of Arkansas appear to be common; there is little demand for them. The letter-writing habits of the Clintons in the White House are not known.

13

THE AMERICAN WEST

America and indeed much of Western Europe have always had a fascination with the American frontier. This frontier, whether it was the Atlantic Coast faced by the earliest settlers, the Appalachian Mountains, the Rocky Mountains, or the Pacific Coast, was unique, distinct from the frontiers of Europe, which were essentially boundaries separating densely populated countries.

In America, the European was faced with a frontier that forced him to adapt to the ways of the wilderness and adopt many of the Indians' skills and implements. As the frontier moved farther westward and settlers began to move into the former frontier, the original European frontiersman evolved into a new personality, an American, with European origins but a lifestyle and mentality based on the challenges and living conditions in the New World.

The influence of the American frontier continues in the present day. Not only is it the subject of cinema, television, and books but frontier architecture and decorative arts are found throughout the United States. The feeling of unlimited opportunities and expansiveness that many Americans are raised with can be directly related to the heritage of free land and the prospect of a new and better life on the frontier. In a practical sense, this now exists only in Alaska, but the influence of the frontier on the American character continues.

To the eighteenth-century settlers, the American western frontier was the Appalachian Mountains, and there was no greater figure in the western history of this time than **Daniel Boone**. An illiterate backwoodsman, Boone wrote virtually no letters, and the only documents obtainable are from his career as

Daniel Boone

Simon Kenton

Isaac Shelby

Julian Dubuque

Zebulon M. Pike

Meriwether Lewis

William Clark

Manuel Lisa

Kit Carson

a land speculator after the American Revolution. These documents are rare but occasionally obtainable, although there are fewer and fewer opportunities to acquire one. Signatures of his fellow backwoodsman, **Simon Kenton**, whose adventures read like fiction, are also found only on land documents and are much rarer, though in less demand, than those of Boone. The most frequently found documents of the early western pioneers of present-day Kentucky are those signed by **Isaac Shelby**, who was very active in the Revolution and then served as Kentucky's first governor. Various types of documents, mostly signed as governor, can be acquired.

Documents signed by **Julian Dubuque**, the early explorer of present-day Iowa, are very rare but possible to obtain. Much more frequently available are documents of the western explorer for whom Pike's Peak was named, **Zebulon M. Pike**. Military documents concerning supplies, signed by Pike, provide collectors with fine examples of this pioneer explorer.

Early in his administration, Thomas Jefferson asked his private secretary, **Meriwether Lewis**, to organize an expedition to explore the newly purchased Louisiana Territory; together with **William Clark**, who had a military background, Lewis led the expedition across the northern part of present-day United States to the Pacific Ocean. Documents signed by Clark during his military career and, less frequently, those signed as governor of Missouri Territory, can be obtained. Anything signed by Lewis, who ended his own life during an attack of depression while on his way back to Washington in 1809, is very rare.

One of the most important figures in the fur trade from St. Louis was **Manuel Lisa**, whose business extended into the heart of the Rocky Mountains. Documents signed by him are very rare, but it is possible to acquire one on occasion. Very rare, and in much more demand, are pieces signed by the legend of the West, **Kit Carson**. Military documents are the only type of documents seen. Autographs of another legend of the West, **Davy Crockett**, are also very rare and in great demand.

Autograph material of **Stephen F. Austin**, the colonizer of Texas, would be in the same category were it not for the fact that he signed documents pertaining to an early Texas loan. Very popular with collectors, these relics of the founding of Texas do occasionally come onto the market. Autographs of another Texas patriot, **William B. Travis**, who died at the Alamo, are extremely rare. Documents of General **Antonio de Santa Anna**, the conqueror of the Alamo, would like those of Austin be very rare, except for mortgage bonds that he signed later in life. These very colorful bonds, discovered about 1960, have been dispersed among collectors but do get offered as collections come onto the market. Another Texan whose name is virtually synonymous with the state is **Sam Houston**. Houston's long political life caused him to write many letters, and while the demand from collectors is strong, fine examples can usually be found. (His huge signature on autograph album pages led one contemporary to remark that he had signed, "I am Houston.")

John C. Frémont carried out many well-organized military explorations of the modern West and again, because of his long military career and later business activities, signed many documents and wrote many letters.

Davy Crockett

Stephen F. Austin

William B. Travis

Antonio de Santa Anna

Sam Houston

Joseph Smith

Brigham Young

John C. Frémont

One of the most remarkable events in western history began well east of the Mississippi River as **Joseph Smith** led the Mormons to Nauvoo, Illinois. Smith is extremely rare in letters, very rare in documents, and usually only seen in currency signed as cashier of the Kirtland Safety Society Bank. After Smith's assassination in 1844, **Brigham Young** took over leadership of the Mormons and led them west to present-day Salt

John A. Sutter

Henry Wells

William Fargo

John Butterfield

Ben Holladay

Isaac C. Parker

Lake City. Young's later letters are infrequently available, but his signature, apparently frequently requested by admirers, is usually easily obtained.

In California, the Swiss-born pioneer, **John A. Sutter**, owned a sawmill where gold was discovered on January 24, 1848. Sutter was a sufficiently prominent figure in pre-gold rush California to have signed letters and documents, and although rare, the collector does have a reasonable chance of finding something signed by him. One of the most interesting pieces obtainable from the California gold rush are letter sheets that bear full-page engravings depicting scenes of the gold fields. There are several different scenes, including views of towns and various activities in the gold field, and one depicts the journey across the plains. The purpose of these illustrated letter sheets was to make it easier for the gold seeker writing home to explain his life and experiences. These letter sheets are actually quite rare, but examples can usually be located if the collector has patience.

Another very interesting pictorial piece representing the American West is a stock certificate of the American Express Company signed by **Henry Wells** and **William Fargo**, the founders of Wells, Fargo & Company and the American Express Company. A cache of these was found years ago, and while well dispersed into collections several decades ago, examples do turn up frequently. A few of these stock certificates are signed by **John Butterfield**, the founder of Butterfield, Wessen & Company. This firm merged with the companies of Wells and Fargo to form the American Express Company. His signature is much scarcer than the signatures of Wells and Fargo. **Ben Holladay**, called "the Napoleon of the Plains," founded various stagecoach companies that were sold to Wells, Fargo in 1866. Except for one type of printed document that he signed, his autographs are very rare.

Autographs of Judge **Isaac C. Parker**, the "Hanging Judge" who ruled a large part of the Western Territory from his court in

Fort Smith, Arkansas, are encountered on rare occasions in the form of Oaths of Office whereby individuals were appointed marshals within his district of jurisdiction.

The famous outlaws and gunslingers of the West are generally unobtainable. **Frank James**, co-leader with his brother Jesse of the James gang, wrote letters to his wife while awaiting trial in jail; these have been dispersed into private collections, and on rare occasions one is offered for sale. Frank James signed many of these *Ben* so that, if intercepted, they would not be published. Autographs of Jesse are virtually un-obtainable. **Pat Garrett**, the sheriff who shot Billy the Kid in a gunfight, can also be found, though not commonly, in the form of documents. **Emmett Dalton** of the Dalton gang outlived his brothers and wrote his memoirs. While his letters are rare, signed copies of his memoirs, *When the Daltons Rode,* can occasionally be obtained. Material of **Bat Masterson** and **Wyatt Earp** is extremely rare, as is that of the **Younger brothers**. Of many others, such as Wild Bill Hickok and Billy the Kid, there is nothing.

Frank James

Pat Garrett

Emmett Dalton

Bat Masterson

Wyatt Earp

Jim Younger

Bob Younger

Cole Younger

The Indian wars of the 1870s created many military documents and letters from the western forts, and autographs of some of the military leaders such as **Nelson A. Miles** and **George Crook** are fairly easily obtainable; material by the most famous of them all, **George A. Custer**, is rare, though at times available. Custer's fame has led to considerable interest in him, and the military endorsements and small notes that come onto the market are met with strong collector interest. Much rarer than autograph material of Custer are signatures of the Indian leaders

Nelson A. Miles

George Crook

George A. Custer

Sitting Bull (signature)

Sitting Bull

W. F. Cody "Buffalo Bill" 1916. (signature)

William F. "Buffalo Bill" Cody

Annie Oakley (signature)

Annie Oakley

GERONIMO (signature)

Geronimo

Geronimo and **Sitting Bull**. Both could sign their names (Geronimo by drawing the letters horizontally) and did so on cards for admirers. Today, these cards are quite rare.

The popularization of the American West was accomplished by a number of writers, but the showman most responsible for bringing the romance of the West to audiences throughout the United States and Europe was **William F. "Buffalo Bill" Cody**. As popular today as he was in his time, there is a steady interest and demand for material signed by Cody, which can usually be obtained, particularly in the form of cards and photographs signed for those attending his shows. One of Cody's star attractions developed such a strong reputation that her name became synonymous with being a sharpshooter. Autograph material of **Annie Oakley**, "Little Miss Sure Shot," is much rarer than that of Cody; it is very infrequently encountered.

14

AMERICAN LEGAL HISTORY

Collecting letters and documents by the leading personalities in the field of American legal history is very popular. **John Jay**, the first chief justice, also served in many other offices, including president of the Continental Congress, secretary of foreign affairs, one of the commissioners who negotiated the treaty to end the American Revolution, and governor of New York. All of these official positions occasioned Jay to write many letters and documents that have been saved, but they have been very aggressively collected by Columbia University and a number of private collectors. His correspondence with his wife, while away in Europe or when he was riding the court circuit, chronicle the events of the day and are occasionally available.

Autograph material of the second chief justice, **Oliver Ellsworth**, would be very rare if a group of interesting revolutionary war payment authorizations had not been found. **John Marshall**, chief justice for thirty-four years, presided over the Supreme Court at the most critical time, when the new Constitution was being interpreted. Letters and documents by Marshall are frequently available, although there is always a very strong demand for them. His letters very rarely concern anything other than legal matters.

Letters or documents of many of the associate justices of the Supreme Court during these early years are extremely rare or virtually unobtainable. Extremely few complete sets of autographs of members of the Supreme Court have ever been put together.

Letters and documents of many of the nineteenth-century associate justices are very common, such as those of **Levi Woodbury**, but most are scarce and a few are very rare. In the middle of the nineteenth

John Jay

Oliver Ellsworth

John Marshall

Levi Woodbury

Roger B. Taney

Salmon P. Chase

Oliver Wendell Holmes, Jr.

century, collectors began to ask the justices to sign their names on pages as a group, and occasionally these pages are offered. Headed by the chief justice and followed by the signatures of the entire Court, these pages, especially the earlier ones, are rare and eagerly sought after. Later in the nineteenth century, group photographs began to be taken of the entire Court, and very rarely one of these, signed by all the members on the mount below the photograph, is found.

The autographs of **Roger B. Taney**, Marshall's successor as chief justice for nearly as long a period, are as popular among collectors as those of his predecessors. Most noted for the Dred Scott decision, Taney generally upheld federal rights over state's rights in his opinions. Many legal documents and letters written in various official capacities, such as secretary of the treasury, survive, and it is not difficult to obtain examples of these. **Salmon P. Chase**, Lincoln's secretary of the treasury, resigned from Lincoln's cabinet and was appointed chief justice. His letters as secretary of the treasury are relatively common, especially the numerous official letters and documents he was required to sign. Most of the justices and chief justices of the latter half of the nineteenth century can be found in letters and documents, although any dealing with important legal issues are rare.

In 1902, one of the most important and influential justices ever to serve on the Court was appointed. The son of a famous American author, **Oliver Wendell Holmes, Jr.**, made a reputation for himself in legal history that far exceeded his father's reputation in literature. Letters of Holmes are usually available, and there is considerable demand for them. Occasionally, a letter written by Holmes to Lady Castletown is offered. Many articles have been written about this correspondence and the nature of Holmes's relationship with this Irish woman, but there can be no question that the relationship inspired the future associate justice to write marvelously warm, personal, and philosophical letters. To acquire these letters from Lady Castletown's descendants, it was necessary to visit them in Northern

Ireland during the worst of the Irish disturbances in the 1960s. I originally offered the complete correspondence of letters from Holmes to Lady Castletown but after transcripts were found could find no client for the complete collection. The individual letters were then offered and sold rapidly to a number of collectors. Today, one of these letters frequently sells for more than the price of the entire collection.

Charles Evans Hughes, an associate justice from 1910 to 1916, held various other offices before his appointment as chief justice in 1930, a position he held until 1941. Letters and documents by him are common, particularly as secretary of state but also as justice, and the prices are quite modest.

One of the most popular names in American legal history of this period was not a member of the Supreme Court but a lawyer noted for his defense of many unpopular causes. **Clarence Darrow**'s fame and popularity far exceeds that of many justices; material signed by him, once quite readily available, has become much scarcer in recent years. When available, Darrow's books, *Crime, Its Cause and Treatment* and *The Story of My Life,* signed by him, are excellent additions to a legal collection.

The first Jewish member of the Supreme Court, **Louis D. Brandeis**, was appointed in 1916; he is very popular with collectors of both legal history and Judaica. Letters by Brandeis are usually available. **Benjamin Cardozo** served only six years on the Court but was an influential member. He published several important books, and occasionally one of these is available with an inscription by him. One of the most liberal members of the Court was appointed by Franklin D. Roosevelt in 1939—**Felix Frankfurter**, founder of the American Civil Liberties Union. Frankfurter's letters are relatively available, and he is popular with collectors. **Frederick M. Vinson**, Truman's secretary of the treasury, briefly served as chief justice. The scarcity of his letters is tempered by less demand, and they are fairly inexpensive. Material signed by **Earl Warren**, whose Court has greatly influenced modern

Charles Evans Hughes

Clarence Darrow

Louis D. Brandeis

Benjamin Cardozo

Felix Frankfurter

Frederick M. Vinson

Earl Warren

American life, is very common, particularly since he signed many letters and photographs as governor of California.

During the middle of the twentieth century, many enterprising collectors asked the justices jointly and individually to sign souvenir pieces such as opinions, first day covers, and photographs, and these are frequently available.

15

GENERAL AMERICANA

This chapter discusses the many interesting figures in American history who have not been included in the chapters above. In some cases, these people participated in the previously discussed events but are best known for accomplishments and activities outside these areas.

Alexander Hamilton is such a person. He is most noted for his contributions to the *Federalist* and for the ideas he developed as first secretary of the treasury. He was killed at the relatively young age of forty-nine, and were it not for the official letters and documents as well as envelopes signed as free franks while he was secretary of the treasury, his autograph material would be very rare. A letter signed by him is scarce but usually available. The demand for Hamilton's material from collectors interested in both history and finance, as well as Hamilton himself, is very strong.

Aaron Burr tied in the vote for the presidency in 1800 with Thomas Jefferson, and the election was decided by Congress in favor of Jefferson. Burr became his vice president. A controversy between Burr and Hamilton led to their famous duel in which Hamilton was mortally wounded; Burr was later charged with treason (and acquitted) for his role in conspiring to seize territory from Spanish America and creating a new republic in the Southwest. Burr's letters can usually be found, normally dealing with legal affairs, but are not common; checks filled in and signed by him are frequently encountered.

DeWitt Clinton, mayor of New York City and later governor of New York, is noted for promoting the Erie Canal and the western immigration it made possible. His letters and documents are commonly available and not expensive. Material signed by **Henry**

Alexander Hamilton

Aaron Burr

DeWitt Clinton

Henry Clay

John C. Calhoun

Daniel Webster

Stephen A. Douglas

Horace Greeley

Stephen Decatur

Oliver Hazard Perry

Matthew C. Perry

Clay, one of the most important political leaders of the early nineteenth century who did not become president (he was the Whig candidate twice), is also generally available in the form of legal documents. (The University of Kentucky has acquired most of the Clay letters offered in recent decades.) Letters of **John C. Calhoun** are scarcer than those of Clay or **Daniel Webster**, but with a little patience they can be found and at a relatively low cost. Letters of Webster, like those of Clay, have been collected by institutions. He did, however, write many letters as a lawyer and political leader, and examples are readily located.

Stephen A. Douglas, "the Little Giant," is most known for his debates with Lincoln when they both ran for the Senate. His letters have been extensively collected by the Illinois Historical Library, but documents do occasionally come onto the market and are reasonably priced. **Horace Greeley**, editor of the *New York Tribune,* is famous for his advice, "Go west young man and grow up in the country." His letters are frequently offered. His handwriting is among the worst of any writer of any period.

Earlier in the nineteenth century, another noted American was killed in a duel. **Stephen Decatur**, while known for his War of 1812 victories, is most remembered for his famous words, "Our country! In her intercourse with foreign nations may she always be in the right; but our country, right or wrong." Letters by Decatur, always official ones, are very rare. Another War of 1812 hero, **Oliver Hazard Perry**, was famous for another statement. In his report on his victory in the battle of Lake Erie, Perry wrote, "We have met the enemy and they are ours." His letters are only slightly less rare than Decatur's. **Matthew C. Perry** (Oliver's brother), while very active in the Mexican War, is most known for his voyage to Japan in 1852 which opened trade with that isolated country. His letters and documents were actually common until Japanese collectors entered the field, and they have acquired virtually everything that is offered. Matthew Perry's material is still not too expensive, but the strong demand will no doubt lead to higher prices.

A half century later, Admiral **George Dewey** had the dubious distinction of defeating the Spanish fleet in Manila harbor during the Spanish-American War. Collectors have never found Dewey appealing, nor is there much interest in the Spanish-American War (except for Teddy Roosevelt's Rough Riders), and prices of his autographs reflect this lack of interest. Autograph material of Charles D. Sigsbee, the captain of the *Maine* when it was blown up in Havana harbor, one of a series of incidents that precipitated the Spanish-American War, is commonly available, but there is little demand for it. There is also little interest in the leading American generals in the First World War. **John J. Pershing** wrote many letters, and the lack of collector interest in his material is reflected in both availability and modest prices.

Recent decades have brought a keen interest in the history of black Americans. Legal documents of **Frederick Douglass**, who was born a slave but escaped and became a prominent abolitionist, are very popular with collectors. Letters of **Booker T. Washington**, the black founder of Tuskegee Institute, have become scarcer in recent years. **George Washington Carver**, the black scientist who was instrumental in promoting crop diversification among southern farmers, is rare in autograph material. Handwritten letters are what collectors are likely to find, but fewer and fewer are offered. **Martin Luther King, Jr.**, like so many modern leaders, authorized secretaries to sign his name in a manner imitating his genuine signature, and pieces, except those obtained in person, have to be examined very carefully. His autographs are rare and in great demand.

Dorothea Dix was an important reformer whose autographs have not been much collected but are

George Dewey

John J. Pershing

Frederick Douglass

Booker T. Washington

George Washington Carver

Martin Luther King, Jr.

Dorothea Dix

Susan B. Anthony

Susan B. Anthony

Clara Barton

Clara Barton

Elizabeth Cady Stanton

Elizabeth Cady Stanton

Helen Keller

Helen Keller

Mary Baker Eddy

Mary Baker Eddy

P. T. Barnum

P. T. Barnum

Alphonse Capone

Al Capone

Eliot Ness
DIRECTOR OF PUBLIC SAFETY

Eliot Ness

scarce. Examples of signatures given to admirers are more commonly seen than letters. Letters or signatures of **Clara Barton**, the founder of the American Red Cross, are somewhat scarce but generally available. **Susan B. Anthony**, America's leading suffragette, wrote many letters, but they have been collected by the University of Rochester; however, signatures and signed quotations given to admirers are available, as is an occasional letter. Autographs of her fellow suffragette, **Elizabeth Cady Stanton**, are actually scarcer, but they are in less demand and are not expensive.

Helen Keller, who was blind, deaf, and mute, captured America's heart, and her letters are fairly scarce. Many form letters asking for money are not signed by her, but sufficient genuine letters turn up to make her material generally available to collectors. Signed material of **Mary Baker Eddy**, the founder of the First Church of Christ, Scientist, is rare in all forms. The Mother Church has systematically bought everything that has come onto the market for the past several decades.

Two uniquely American personalities are **Phineas T. Barnum** and **Al Capone**. Material of Barnum, creator of "the Greatest Show on Earth," is relatively common, particularly in signed cards. He is very popular with collectors, and his letters have been aggressively collected by several institutions. Al Capone did not write letters, and anything signed by him is very rare. Equally rare is anything signed by **Eliot Ness**, the lawman who secured the evidence to convict Capone of tax evasion.

HISTORY

◆

Ancient Writing

English History

French History

European History

World War II

16

ANCIENT WRITING

Without writing there can be no culture, no communicable intelligence. Its importance cannot be overstated, though it is so basic and fundamental, its existence so accepted and understood, that it is, in fact, rarely understood at all. The history of the development of writing is extremely complex; writing systems developed in various geographic areas, most of them interrelated and having overlapping geographic and chronological boundaries.

Three writing systems are of particular interest to collectors: cuneiform, hieroglyphics, and Greek. Ancient examples of all three—written, carved, or impressed on papyrus, wood, stone, or clay—can be collected for relatively modest sums.

The most ancient system of writing that is known is cuneiform. It was invented by the Sumerians, ca. 3200–3000 B.C., and was later adopted and continued by the Assyrians and Babylonians. The Sumerians had emigrated to the southern part of Mesopotamia about 3500 B.C. and formed there, in an area between the Tigris and Euphrates rivers, the earliest known civilization. Culturally, they are the most important and best known of the ancient peoples of this time; they created an important literature as well as a complex system of law, religion, business, and administration.

Until a substantial group of clay tablets bearing cuneiform inscriptions was discovered in the latter part of the nineteenth century, little was known of the existence and civilization of the Sumerians. Excavations unearthed great quantities of their writings, principally on clay tablets [65] but also on bricks and clay cones [64].

64 Sumerian cuneiform clay cone bearing a dedication inscription of Gudea, governor of Lagash, to Ningishzida, at the building of a temple in Girsu, a section of Lagash, ca. 2130 B.C.

65 Sumerian cuneiform clay tablet, recording the disbursement of fifty-three oxen, Third Dynasty of Ur, 2049 B.C.

The earliest examples of Sumerian writing are not actually cuneiform, that is, wedge shaped, but pictographic, and they could serve only the most basic administrative functions. The Sumerians soon developed a new writing system combining ideographic and phonetic writing.

This new script was true cuneiform writing: wedge-shaped characters impressed into wet clay tablets that were then fired, the durability of which is attested by the great numbers that have survived into the twentieth century. Scribes employed a straight length of reed with a broad head as a stylus to make the impressions in the clay.

As the ideographic influence decreased and the phonetic values became predominant, many ambiguities in meaning occurred. Determinative signs were introduced to place the text within a frame of reference. These determinatives were ideograms that were already in use and also new forms to clarify particular phonetic values.

The Assyrians and Babylonians took over the Sumerians' writing system about 2500 B.C. and continued to develop it, principally from a stylistic standpoint. It became more complex with the Babylonian influence; and in the late eighteenth century B.C., under Hammurabi, it became the instrument of the classical age of Babylonian science and literature. At this time the number of cuneiform symbols was approximately six to seven hundred, consisting of six vowel sounds, ninety-seven simple syllables, approximately two hundred more complex syllables, and about three hundred ideograms.

During the ninth to seventh centuries B.C., the Assyrian kings established libraries containing tens of thousands of clay tablets concerning religion, philosophy, astronomy, mathematics, mythology, law, history, medicine, science, and histories of the campaigns and activities of the kings. Many tablets have been excavated at Nineveh, where very fine Assyrian dictionaries were also found. These were substantially larger and more comprehensive than their Babylonian counterparts. Artistically engraved tablets represented the final period of preeminence of cuneiform writing in Mesopotamia; the Aramaic nomads inundated the Tigris–Euphrates Valley beginning in the eighth century B.C. and gradually replaced cuneiform with their own alphabetical script and language.

Cuneiform still had specialized uses, such as for astronomy texts, and it was adopted by the Persians, who simplified it greatly under the influence of the Aramaic alphabet. This renaissance in Persia was short-lived, and the final cuneiform examples date from approximately A.D. 50.

Nearly all of the cuneiform examples available to collectors are from about 2000 B.C., most being dated during the period known as Ur III, the Third Dynasty, which lasted from 2113 to 2006 B.C. During this period clay tablets are the most available form [65]. They document agricultural transactions; accounts for commodities such as silver, copper, garments, beer, and bread; sacrificial offerings; rations and work assignments for harvests and weaving; and the hiring of boats. Clay cones [64] containing dedications of various buildings such as temples, palaces, and fortresses are much scarcer. Clay tablets that have been sealed within an "envelope" or outer shell that bears an inscription of the contents of the tablet inside are rarely encountered

66 Sumerian cuneiform clay tablet (front and back) with most of its clay envelope, recording the delivery of fifteen bushels of grain for the brewing of beer, 2055 B.C.

67
Sumerian cuneiform clay tablet with an impression of a cylinder seal showing two persons making an offering to a god. The inscription to the right records the assignment of various female workers to weaving tasks, Dynasty of Ur III, 2113–2006 B.C.

68
Cylindrical clay label or bulla, hollow in the center and attached to the container that notes individual transactions of cattle. The label records the expenditure of 2288 small cattle and bears a full scribal seal consisting of human figures and a cuneiform inscription, 2038–2030 B.C.

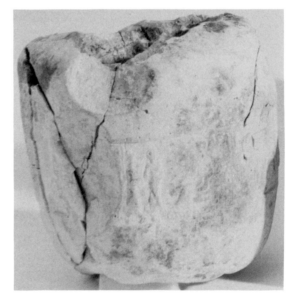

[66]. Tablets bearing impressions of cylinder seals, used by important individuals to identify themselves, are also very desirable [67]. Rarest are the circular clay "labels" that were formed to close agricultural sacks [68]. Cuneiform examples made after 2000 B.C. are much rarer. Babylonian examples are more usually cone shaped, and

dedication bricks bearing inscriptions are sometimes encountered [69]. In addition to the form bearing the cuneiform script, size, content, and condition are all factors that determine value.

69 Clay and straw brick bearing a cuneiform inscription of Nebuchadnezzar, king of Babylonia, ca. 604–562 B.C.

The Egyptian system of writing is the other most important script of the ancient Near East. Egyptian hieroglyphic writing is also the most pictorial of analytic scripts; it was used primarily for religious purposes. Hieroglyphs were carved in stone [71] and wood on temple walls, tombs, and sacred monuments; painted on pottery and wood [70]; and written on papyrus [72] and linen.

The earliest-known Egyptian hieroglyphic inscriptions are from about 3000 B.C., and it is generally believed that Egyptian writing developed in substantially the same manner as cuneiform: a pictographic system evolving into a transitional one consisting of pictographs and ideographs and finally a combination of pictographs, ideographs, and, most important, phonograms. It is believed that a phonetic system of writing was developed in the early years of the third millennium B.C. This system remained unchanged for the following thirty centuries.

The unique sacredness of hieroglyphics in their employment in ritual, funerary, and royal texts ensured their continuation in their most elaborate, intricate, and monumental form. They required considerable time and space to carve and paint, and their narrow evenness was contrary to the type of writing that was most easily and quickly written on papyrus with a brush pen. Business documents, private correspondence, and literary manuscripts were executed in hieroglyphs with difficulty. Because of their monumental and religious use, hieroglyphics carved in stone [71] and wood are the most available to collectors. Hieroglyphic manuscripts on papyrus [72], almost always of a section of the Book of the Dead, have become relatively rare. (The Book of the Dead contains prayers, hymns, and charms meant to help the soul in the afterworld.)

A script that could be executed with more facility was developed about six hundred years after hieroglyphics and existed concurrently with it. This was a cursive form of hieroglyphics, without the pictorial quality, and is known as the hieratic script.

70 Egyptian hieroglyphic inscription from the Book of the Dead, gesso-painted on wood, Ptolemaic period, 4th–2nd century B.C.

72
Fragment from the Egyptian Book of the Dead written in a cursive hieroglyphic script, Late Ramesside period, ca. 1200–1085 B.C.

71 Egyptian stele carved in limestone with a dedication in hieroglyphics to Necho in the fourteenth year of his reign by Neshor, 596 B.C.

Ligatured groups of characters were formed in the hieratic script; and in the period 2000–1790 B.C. the horizontal line, written from right to left, replaced the vertical line. Increasing cursiveness led the hieratic script to the point of servicing only as a priestly shorthand, unreadable to most; and it was superseded by a new script, although it continued to be used for religious works until the second century of the Christian era. Hieratic examples have been available in sections of the Book of the Dead written on linen [73] and very rarely, on papyrus.

73 Fragment from the Book of the Dead, written in hieratic script on linen, early Ptolemaic period, ca. 300 B.C. A drawing in the center shows the deceased, an Egyptian god, and an offering table between the two figures.

74 Section of a practice writing board, of soft wood, with four lines of a literary text written in demotic script, ca. 1st century B.C.–1st century A.D.

The demotic script [74] first appeared in the seventh century B.C. and was directly derivative from the hieratic and, therefore, the hieroglyphic. The new script showed an extraordinary degree of erosion from its predecessors. New and independent signs had resulted from the amalgamation of whole related groups of hieratic characters. Other hieratic signs were abbreviated; and while determinatives were still employed, they were used less, thus creating additional ambiguities. The extreme cursiveness of this script and its greater use of ligatures gave it an appearance

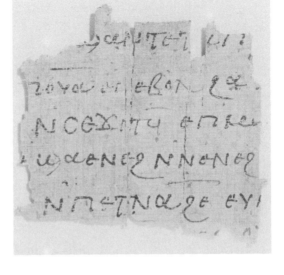

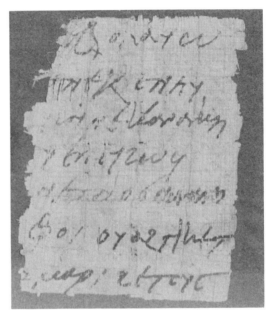

75 Example of a strong uncial script written in Coptic, giving an account of the martyrdom of Apachamoul, who was visited in prison by Christ, Upper Egypt, A.D. 550–650 (above)

76 Fragment from a literary text, written on papyrus in a widely spaced semi-uncial Coptic hand, ca. A.D. 550–650 (top right)

77 Fragment of a letter, written on papyrus in a southern Coptic dialect, in a large semi-cursive script, ca. 4th–8th century A.D. (bottom right)

unrelated to its predecessors. Its popularity in Egypt was such that it soon was the predominant script for all business and private writing, as well as for literary compositions. The Ptolemies considered demotic of greater importance than hieratic and equal in importance to hieroglyphic and Greek writing.

From a collector's viewpoint, examples of demotic script are the most difficult to obtain. Their everyday and nonreligious use meant that they were not preserved in tombs, and most examples encountered are business notes written on the back of shards (broken pieces of pottery).

After the entry of Alexander the Great into Egypt, the Greek language began to influence Egyptian writing, although the demotic continued until Christianity prevailed in Egypt. A new script emerged which employed twenty-five letters from

Greek uncial writing and seven from Egyptian demotic writing to express Egyptian sounds that did not exist in the Greek language. This new writing was Coptic [75–77]. The earliest known examples are from the third century of the Christian era. It continued in use until the ninth century, having begun to be superseded by the Arabic script after the seventh century. Examples of Coptic writing are relatively rare, and fragments with interesting content are very rare.

The Greek group of scripts is the most important to modern languages. Through its many offshoots the Greek script has provided the whole of modern Europe, the Americas, and parts of Asia with writing systems. The origin of the Greek script is in considerable dispute, but the weight of scholarly opinion is that the Greeks adapted their script from the Semites, probably in the tenth or ninth century B.C. The earliest Greek scripts, like those of the Semites, were written from right to left; they did not adopt a left-to-right method until approximately 500 B.C.

During the early centuries of Greek writing, many variations of the Greek alphabet developed. In 403 B.C., the Ionic alphabet was established as the official Greek script. The occasion for its adoption was the restoration of the democratic constitution in Athens and the rewriting of the old laws. The Ionic alphabet consisted of twenty-four letters, and it did not undergo any further basic changes.

78 Example of Greek monumental or lapidary script chiseled in stone

Greek writing did, however, undergo significant paleographic changes. Efforts to simplify the script signs continued after the adoption of the Ionian alphabet; at this time the script was known as the monumental script (or the lapidary script when effected in stone [78], or the capital script when employed in manuscripts). The simple straight lines of the monumental script were, of course, most appropriate for chiseling in stone;

and the script required the development of rounded signs when writing with a reed pen or brush. The rounding of the signs began to emerge in the earliest Greek papyri documents (ca. 300 B.C.), and eventually this rounded script developed into the uncial script, which continued in use until about A.D. 900.

Contemporary with the uncial script, a cursive script developed for unofficial or everyday use. Frequently encountered in papyri manuscripts, the cursive script is characterized by the joining of the individual letters, in contrast with their isolation in the uncial script. Abbreviations also developed more with cursive writing as speed was emphasized in its execution.

There are excellent examples of Greek writing from the ancient world that are occasionally offered for sale. Greek inscriptions carved in stone and Greek manuscript fragments on papyrus are occasionally encountered [79]; a papyrus fragment of any size or content is very rare.

The Greek system of writing gave birth to the early Italian scripts, the most important of these being that adapted to the language of the Etruscans, probably about the eighth century B.C. The Etruscans continued the development of their alphabet during the following three hundred years, when it reached its classical form of sixteen consonants. Although this script remained in use until the early part of the first century of the Christian era, it was gradually supplanted by the Latin alphabet after the Etruscans' loss of political independence to the Romans.

The Latin alphabet developed from the Etruscan, probably during the seventh century B.C. In its earliest form it contained twenty-one letters from

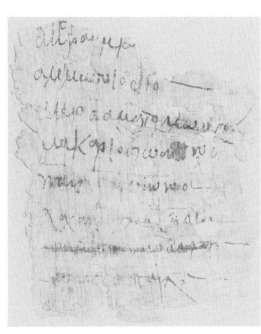

79 Papyrus fragment written in Greek script, ca. 4th–6th century A.D.

the Etruscans and, just prior to the Roman conquest of Greece, had developed into *A, B, C, D, E, F, G, H, I, K, L, M, N, O, P, Q, R, S, T, V,* and *X.* From the first century B.C., the Latin alphabet remained substantially unchanged until the additions of the letters *U, W,* and *J* in the Middle Ages. These added letters were actually differentiations from the existing letters *V* and *I.* While it remained unchanged in its characters, the Latin script did change significantly through the centuries in its writing styles.

In the first century B.C., the characteristics of Roman capital script began to develop. This script, also known as the monumental script [80], was employed in writing on

80 Roman memorial monument with a Latin inscription carved in marble

both papyri and parchment and was carved in stone. By the first or second century of the Christian era, the capital script had divided into three types: the lapidary capitals, principally employed in stone carving; book capitals, less formal in appearance than lapidary writing, being somewhat more rounded in shape; and rustic capitals, more quickly and easily written than lapidary letters but not as rounded as book capitals. Occasionally, very fine examples of Roman script, carved in stone, are available. Examples other than these monumental pieces are extremely rare.

My comments about the rarity of ancient writing have to be considered in their relative sense. Several new collectors of ancient writing would affect rarity very significantly. All ancient writing is, compared to any other collecting area, comparatively rare.

17

ENGLISH HISTORY

Throughout Europe prior to the sixteenth century, relatively few prominent individuals learned to sign their names, and England was no exception. Before the middle of the fifteenth century, virtually no one in a prominent secular position had learned to write his or her name, and documents and letters were written in the author's name by a scribe. However, from the period of medieval England, it is still possible to collect, at a relatively modest cost, documents from the reigns of monarchs back to King John. Always written on vellum, they mostly concern land transactions.

Until the end of the thirteenth century, documents were not dated. Dates can be determined by the style of handwriting (different scripts evolved over time) and also by researching the life spans of the people named in the documents, which frequently contain long lists of witnesses to the transactions. Beginning in about 1300, documents are dated more specifically, in terms of the relationship of the day to a religious holiday and to the year of the reign of the reigning monarch. Dating medieval documents requires a considerable amount of research for those prior to 1300 and reference indexes for those dated later.

A collection of autograph material of the English monarchs can, theoretically, begin with something signed by **Edward IV**, but any such item is very rarely obtainable. Autographs of Edward V and **Richard III** are very unlikely to ever be offered for sale, although very occasionally documents by Richard as Duke of Gloucester do turn up. Documents of **Henry VII**, while very rare, are possible to acquire over time. Financial documents are the most likely to be found. **Henry VIII** signed many documents, and occasionally one is offered for sale, though these are becoming

Edward IV

Richard III

Henry VII

Henry VIII

Edward VI

Mary Tudor

Mary Queen of Scots

James I

Charles I

Oliver Cromwell

Richard Cromwell

Charles II

increasingly difficult to find. (Collectors beware: Henry VIII used a wooden stamp to sign many routine documents, and these, to the unknowledgeable, can be very deceiving. Such stamps were also used by Edward VI, Mary I, James I [and his wife], Edward VII, and George V.) Signed material of the next two monarchs, **Edward VI** and **Mary Tudor**, is extremely rare. They were followed by one of the most important English monarchs, **Elizabeth I**. Documents signed by her have always been in great demand, and, though many were signed, they are increasingly difficult to find. The value of the material of both Henry VIII and Elizabeth I reflect these monarchs' great importance in history and interest to collectors.

Elizabeth's bête noire, **Mary Queen of Scots**, is very rare in letters or documents. Documents and letters of **James I** have become much more difficult to acquire, as has material of **Charles I**, though it can certainly be acquired with a little patience. Examples of **Oliver Cromwell** are rare, though documents can be found over a period of time. Much rarer is material of his son and successor, **Richard Cromwell**, who ruled England very briefly. As rulers, the Cromwells signed their documents, *Oliver P* and *Richard P,* respectively, the *P* standing for "Protector." Autograph material of **Charles II** is relatively common; many of his documents were signed while in exile before he regained the throne; they conferred commissions in his army. These are of a rather unusually small format; their size may have been necessitated by the fact that they had to be smuggled into England. Documents of **James II** can usually be found, as can those of **William III**, but examples of his queen and co-ruler, **Mary II**, are more difficult to find. Autographs of Queen **Anne** have become much scarcer in the past decade but are obtainable.

Documents of **George I** are much rarer than any of his descendants and namesakes, whose autographs are all very common. Those of **George II** are not so common. Documents of **George III** are collected because of his role in the American Revolution, and while popular with collectors, fine examples are available. His letters are not frequently seen. His son, **George IV**, was for a time regent (when George III suffered from a medical condition that affected his mind). His material is very common and collector interest is minimal and relatively uncollected except for making up sets of monarchs. Material of **William**

James II

William III

Mary II

Queen Anne

George I

George II

George IV

George III

George III, when blind

Prince Albert

William IV

Queen Victoria

Edward VII as prince

Edward VII as king

George V

Edward VIII

Wallis Simpson

Elizabeth II

IV is also very common and collector interest is minimal. The monarch who gave her name to an age, Queen **Victoria**, is another matter. Although autograph material of the queen is common, she is very popular with collectors and there is great interest in her. Her documents, usually appointments, are fairly readily found, but her letters, often written in the third person (*The Queen ...*), have become more scarce. Pieces signed by her husband, the Prince Consort **Albert**, are less common because of his early death. Victoria's son, **Edward VII**, was in late middle age by the time he finally succeeded to the throne; his autographs as king are scarce, but those as Prince of Wales are common and there has been little interest in them.

Autograph material of **George V** has been aggressively collected, which has caused his letters to be rare, though documents can usually be found. **Edward VIII** and his wife, **Wallis Simpson**, are among the best-known English personalities of modern times. Anything signed by them is in demand, and though both wrote and signed many letters and souvenir pieces, the interest in them has tended to overwhelm what is available. **George VI** is not nearly so popular with collectors, and despite his role in World War II (an important symbolic one), his material is not in significant demand. Signed material of his daughter, **Elizabeth II**, has been very popular with collectors;

George VI

146

it is mostly available in signed Christmas cards and official documents, usually pardons.

Few people have collected sets of autograph material of the prime ministers of England. Collectors have tended to concentrate on the statesmen who interest them; those prime ministers who did not have interesting careers have been of little interest among collectors. Though not prime minister (the position did not exist at the time), **William Cecil**, first baron Burghley, played an extremely important role in Elizabeth I's reign as both secretary of state and lord high treasurer. Elizabeth's other favorite was **Robert Devereux**, second earl of Essex. Documents of both are uncommon but obtainable. Much more common are documents of **Robert Walpole**, England's first prime minister (in the modern definition of the position). Financial documents signed by him are fairly readily available, and collector interest in his material is slight. Of more interest are letters and documents of **William Pitt**, the Elder (the earl of Chatham) and the Younger. Both played prominent roles in British history, but pieces signed by them are not particularly expensive and can be readily found.

Of much greater interest to collectors is material of **Benjamin Disraeli** (later earl of Beaconsfield), perhaps the most important of Queen Victoria's prime ministers and a significant novelist. His autographs are very actively collected and can be very difficult to find even in routine letters and documents concerning government affairs. Many of these are signed *D* for Disraeli or *B* for Beaconsfield. **William E. Gladstone** was another of Victoria's prominent prime ministers. His autographs are much less collected than those of Disraeli, and both availability and price reflect this lack of interest. Material of **Henry Palmerston** and Sir **Robert Peel**, other Victorian prime ministers, is even more available and less expensive, with minimal collector interest. It is not until the First World War that another prime minister has interested collectors—**David Lloyd George**, who led England during the Great War and the Versailles negotiations. His

William Cecil

Robert Devereux

William Pitt, the Elder

Robert Walpole

Pitt, the Younger

Benjamin Disraeli

William E. Gladstone

Henry Palmerston

Sir Robert Peel

David Lloyd George

Winston S. Churchill

John Churchill, duke of Marlborough

Sarah Churchill

William Bligh

Horatio Nelson

Nelson & Bronte

material is collected, but it is neither rare nor expensive.

The Englishman whose autograph material is most collected and who is one of the most popular figures in the modern history of Western civilization is **Winston Churchill**. His long life span (he was sixty-five years old when he became prime minister in 1940) led to the creation of many letters and souvenir autographs, but the demand for Churchill autograph material (along with that of Napoleon) is almost without parallel. Unfortunately his letters are almost always of a routine nature; letters revealing or discussing important matters are extremely rare. Of more interest are his signed photographs, because these portraits reveal so much of the character of one of the greatest Englishmen of all time.

Churchill's ancestor, **John Churchill**, the duke of Marlborough, was the English commander in chief during the War of the Spanish Succession. His victory at the Battle of Blenheim resulted in personal rewards and subsequently led to the building of his extraordinary residence in Oxfordshire, Blenheim Palace. Autograph material of Marlborough is not readily available these days, and it has been very actively collected. His wife, **Sarah Churchill**, a favorite of Queen Anne, was very influential during Anne's reign. Financial documents signed by her are very scarce but can be acquired with patience.

A later naval leader had a very different career. **William Bligh** was captain of the *Bounty* and the subject of the mutiny led by Fletcher Christian; his autographs are very rare but obtainable in time.

England's greatest naval legend, **Horatio Nelson**, has always been extremely popular with collectors, and there is great demand for his letters and documents. Despite his relatively brief life, he wrote many letters and documents, and because of his fame both during and after his death, they have been preserved. Fine examples are offered with some frequency, and they find a ready market. There are several variations of Nelson's signature. The earliest version is his full

148

signature, *Horatio Nelson,* signed with his right hand. After he lost his right arm in battle at Santa Cruz on July 25, 1797, he immediately began signing with his left hand. In 1798, when he was made Baron Nelson of the Nile, he signed his name *Nelson.* The following year he was given an additional honor, Duke of Bronte, and thereafter signed letters and documents *Nelson & Bronte.* There has always been great collector interest in Nelson's mistress as well. Autograph material of **Emma Hamilton** is rare in all forms, though occasionally it is possible to find an example.

Nelson's counterpart on land, the Duke of **Wellington**, was born Arthur Wesley. He signed himself as such until May 1798 when he changed his name to Wellesley, taking the name of his father, Garrett Wellesley. In 1809, he became Viscount Wellington and then Duke of Wellington. Wellington lived for many years after his famous victory over Napoleon at Waterloo, and his later letters are commonly available. Wartime letters are much scarcer. His early letters prior to the Napoleonic Wars are also rare. Many of Wellington's later letters are written in the third person (*The Duke of Wellington . . .*), and virtually all are rather difficult to decipher. (Later letters that are more legible are frequently written by his secretary who skillfully imitated his handwriting.)

Autograph material of **Daniel O'Connell**, the Irish nationalist leader of the early part of the nineteenth century, is quite scarce. The same is true of **Charles S. Parnell**, his counterpart during the last half of the nineteenth century. In the early part of the twentieth century, Irish nationalism was taken further by the Irish rebel, **Roger Casement**, who was hanged in 1916. Letters by him are very rare and in equal demand.

In a very different area is **Robert Baden-Powell**, founder of the Boy Scout movement. His letters, though not common, can generally be found. The same is true of the founder of the Salvation Army,

Emma Hamilton

Wellington

Daniel O'Connell

Charles S. Parnell

Roger Casement

Robert Baden-Powell

149

William Booth

William Booth

William Booth, whose material is more commonly seen in signed photographs than in letters. Material of **Edith Cavell**, the British nurse shot by the Germans in World War I for helping soldiers to escape, is rare, though it is possible to acquire something signed by her.

E. Cavell

Edith Cavell

18

FRENCH HISTORY

81 French charter from the reign of Louix IX recording a grant by Guillermus de La mayra to the church of Maria de Insula in Arverto, dated May 4, 1247

Letters and documents concerning French history are generally more available than pieces of comparable importance in American or English history. This is the result of several factors. Historically, French institutions waited for families to make gifts of papers and did not actively pursue them; as a result, after World War II there were significant collections in private hands. Immediately after the war, many American collectors seized the opportunity to acquire major collections without any competition from French collectors, who, generally impoverished from the war years, were out of the market. From the late 1940s through the late 1970s, Americans acquired many major collections of French letters and documents, and today many of the important pieces and collections being offered for sale are coming from these American collectors.

Charles VII

Louis XI

Charles VIII

Louis XII

Francis I

Henry II

The French National Archives, realizing that so much material had been exported, established the strictest export control laws for historical letters and documents (export licenses are difficult and very time consuming to obtain). At auction the French National Archives has the right (which it exercises very frequently) to "preempt the sale" after the auction has taken place and take important pieces for the Archives. This is not a rare or unusual occurrence; it can happen many times in one sale. The Archives has accomplished its goal to reduce drastically the export of historical letters and documents.

If a collector is interested in a specific area of French history, one that is not of general international interest, he may have an opportunity to acquire interesting pieces that may not occur again. Many collectors have been drawn to both French historical and literary letters and documents, because they are the last areas of collecting in the field of Western culture where it is still possible to acquire important pieces. The major names and areas of interest that have international appeal are well collected, but as of this writing, it is still not too late to form a very interesting collection in other areas.

Prior to the late fifteenth century, leading personalities in France, as in other countries, did not sign their names; scribes were employed for this purpose. Medieval history can, however, be represented by documents from the reigns of the medieval kings; these interesting legal documents, written on vellum and dating from the twelfth century onward, usually concern land transactions and are relatively inexpensive [81, p. 151].

A collection of documents of French kings can begin with **Charles VII** (1422–1461), but there are many rarities, though they are not nearly as expensive as those of their English counterparts. Autographs of **Louis XI**, **Charles VIII**, and **Louis XII** are all very rare. Documents of **Francis I**, one of the most important monarchs of the Renaissance, are surprisingly available at relatively reasonable sums. Documents of **Henry II** are actually much rarer than his years on the throne would indicate, but those of his queen, **Catherine de Médicis**, can generally be acquired, and there is much more popular interest in her. Autographs of **Francis II**, king from 1559 to 1560, are very rare. Letters and documents of **Charles IX** can generally be acquired, as can documents of **Henry III** and **Henry IV**.

Marie de Médicis, queen of Henry IV, was regent for her son, **Louis XIII**, and like the letters and documents of Catherine de Médicis, those of Marie are very popularly collected. Examples of Louis XIII are collected mainly to complete sets of kings. **Cardinal de Richelieu**, Marie de Médicis' close adviser, had great influence over her. His autograph material can be collected but has become increasingly difficult to find. Collectors must be aware that Louis XIV, Louis XV, and Louis XVI all authorized secretaries to sign letters and documents for them and that many of these secretaries imitated their monarchs' signatures very well. Theoretically, they drew a line from the secretarial signatures down to their own at the bottom of the documents or letters, but in many cases they failed to do this (the presence of such a line, however, does not always mean that the secretary has signed it). All letters and documents not bearing a second signature are

Catherine de Médicis

Francis II

Charles IX

Henry III

Henry IV

Marie de Médicis

Cardinal de Richelieu

Louis XIII

Louis XIV

Louis XV

Madame du Pompadour

Madame du Barry

Louis XVI

Marie Antoinette

suspect (it would appear that officials at the time were also frustrated with the royal habit of secretarial signatures and did not accept documents without the second signature). When the king himself signed, the signature is usually written to the left of the secretarial signature, and in many cases, the word *bon* is added in his hand. Marie Antoinette, whose secretaries signed many of her financial documents in her name, frequently added *payez* in her own hand, then signed her name below the notation.

Of the Louis, **Louis XIV** is by far the most important. During his reign he cleverly and ruthlessly made himself the most powerful figure in France, and France the most important country in Europe. There is a very strong demand among French collectors for material of Louis XIV—particularly letters, which are much sought after. **Louis XV** is a much less interesting monarch, but his genuine letters and documents are, again, not commonly available. His mistress, **Madame du Pompadour**, greatly influenced his policies and French history of the period; her autograph material is much rarer. Pompadour's personal letters (almost always unsigned) have been aggressively collected by a number of serious collectors in recent and past decades, and a collector would be very fortunate to find anything at all in her handwriting. Material of her successor, **Madame du Barry**, is more available, usually in the form of signed receipts. Du Barry's documents are very popular with collectors in many countries, and her autographs are increasingly hard to find.

Louis XVI, the well-meaning but ineffective king who led France into the Revolution, can generally be found in the form of official documents, usually concerning finance, signed by secretaries but bearing his genuine signature under the word *bon*. Interest in his material is primarily because of his role in the American and French revolutions; there is little interest in him as a person. This is certainly not true of **Marie Antoinette**, his queen, in whom there is great interest. Many of her documents were signed for her, and genuine ones sometimes can be distinguished by

154

the second, genuine signature. Demand for these is very strong, and it can frequently take considerable time to find an example. Her personal letters were never signed and are extremely rare.

Maximilien Robespierre, one of the greatest leaders of the French Revolution, is found in signed documents that are quite rare though obtainable. Part of his rarity stems from his death at an early age in 1794, a death that marked the end of the Reign of Terror. Autograph material of Robespierre's colleague at the beginning of the Revolution, **Georges Danton**, is equally rare though also obtainable with patience. Danton became more moderate in his views and began to oppose Robespierre; he was himself executed in 1794, just before Robespierre's death at the guillotine. The man who gave his name to this symbol of the French Revolution was **Joseph-Ignace Guillotin**, a French physician who was a proponent of humane capital punishment and championed the beheading device that bears his name. His autographs are very rare but do, very infrequently, come onto the market. **Comte de Mirabeau**, the great orator of the early years of the French Revolution whose untimely death left many might-have-beens about its outcome, is relatively rare in signed pieces and is more frequently encountered in drafts of letters.

Napoleon Bonaparte is one of the most popularly collected personalities from any period, country, or field. He took personal control of all military and political affairs and as a result, signed large numbers of letters, endorsed many reports, and signed many documents. Many are now in institutions, but the collector can still obtain very fine examples of this extraordinary figure in Western history. His handwritten letters from any period are extremely rare and virtually unobtainable.

The body of Napoleon's earliest letters is nearly always in the hand of a secretary but signed by him with the name, *Buonaparte,* the rarest form of his signature, though this increases the value only slightly. More common is his signature, *Bonaparte,* and some of the letter sheets he used while general in chief of the

Maximilien Robespierre

Georges Danton

Joseph-Ignace Guillotin

Comte de Mirabeau

Napoleon, signed *Buonaparte*

Napoleon, signed *Bonaparte*

155

Napoleon, signed *Np*

Napoleon, signed *Napol*

Josephine

Josephine, signed *Lapagerie Bonaparte*

Marie Louise

Napoleon II

Charles Maurice Talleyrand

army of Italy and later as first consul are extremely attractive, with engraved vignettes at the top. In 1804, Napoleon crowned himself emperor and began using the name Napoleon but very rarely signed it in full; he most commonly signed it *Np* and *Nap,* less commonly, *Napol.* Napoleon never allowed secretaries to sign his letters, though some documents were signed for him with the name *Bonaparte.*

Napoleonic material is also available in the form of endorsements signed on reports to him. Some of these, though very few, are in his handwriting, usually consisting of a line or two, and are almost illegible. Endorsements are usually signed *Np.* The rarest Napoleon items are dated from St. Helena, his final exile, and are extremely rare. Pieces from his first exile, the island of Elba, are rare, and letters from Russia are also rare, with those from Moscow being the rarest and most desirable date line for collectors.

Autograph material of **Josephine,** Napoleon's first wife, is very popularly collected by those specializing in her material alone as well as those collecting in the field of French history and those collecting autographs from the age of Napoleon. Letters signed *Josephine* are more desirable and valuable than those signed *Lapagerie Bonaparte,* an earlier signature combining her maiden and married names. Letters of Napoleon's second wife, **Marie Louise,** are much more commonly available, more because of less collector interest in her than lack of availability. Her letters are certainly as rare as Josephine's, particularly while married to Napoleon. Her later letters are more likely to be encountered.

Napoleon II, the duc de Reichstadt, was named successor on the abdication of his father, Napoleon I, but the Allies refused to accept him. His material is extremely rare, and the only possible example a collector can obtain is a page written in his hand from his school notebook. **Charles Maurice Talleyrand,** Napoleon's minister of foreign affairs, demonstrated his skills at

156

diplomacy by playing a leading role in the restoration of the Bourbons at the downfall of Napoleon. His material is very popular with collectors, particularly several who have specialized in collecting his letters, but an official signed letter can usually be found. **Louis XVIII** wrote many letters from exile during the French Revolution and Napoleon's rule, and most of these are in his hand and signed *Louis Xavier Stanislas*. In 1815, he was put on the throne of France; he died in 1824. His letters are scarce but can generally be obtained. Nearly half a century later France was again dominated by a Napoleon—the nephew of Napoleon I, the son of Napoleon's brother, Louis, king of Holland. Louis Napoleon, who became dictator of France, proclaimed himself to be **Napoleon III** and ruled France with his queen, **Eugenie**. His letters and official documents, together with hers, are generally available and popular with collectors.

Toward the end of the nineteenth century, France was shaken by the trial of **Alfred Dreyfus**, who was falsely condemned in 1894 of treason based on forged evidence. Sentenced to Devil's Island, off the coast of South America, Dreyfus remained there until he was given a new trial, spurred in part by the efforts of Émile Zola. Eventually, evidence of the false charges overcame the anti-Semitism that had influenced the case and Dreyfus was set free. His letters are occasionally available and popularly collected.

France provided three collected leaders during the First World War, one of whom continued to serve throughout the Second World War. **Joseph Joffre** was commander in chief of the Allied armies in France and planned and directed the battle of Marne, which stopped the German advance on Paris; Marshal **Ferdinand Foch** was the supreme commander in 1918. The autographs of both Joffre and Foch are generally available at reasonable prices. Also available, as there is no significant collector interest, is autograph material of **Philip Pétain**. He was the hero of Verdun who was chosen by the Germans to head the puppet Vichy government in World War II.

Louis XVIII,
signed *Louis Stanislas Xavier*

Napoleon III

Eugenie

Alfred Dreyfus

Joseph Joffre

Ferdinand Foch

Philip Pétain

Charles de Gaulle

Of much greater interest, both in France and in other countries, is autograph material of **Charles de Gaulle**. This difficult leader was, nevertheless, the only Frenchman who made a claim to leadership in the dark days of 1940, and he was very important to the Allied cause in organizing and influencing the French resistance. De Gaulle material written during the war is the rarest and most desirable, particularly when he first arrived in London and began organizing support among the other Frenchmen who had escaped. Later letters and documents signed as president of France are more available but are still not common.

19

EUROPEAN HISTORY

Letters and documents of the leading personalities of many European countries can also be collected. Because of the limitations of space here, I will discuss only those that American collectors most frequently seek.

One of the most important figures of the sixteenth century was the Holy Roman emperor, **Charles V**. He reigned over an area encompassing modern Germany and also ruled Spain as King Charles I. Documents signed by him, either as the Holy Roman emperor or king of Spain, are rare but can be found. Very rarely, one with interesting content may appear.

In Germanic history, **Frederick II** of Prussia, known as Frederick the Great, is one of the most important figures of the eighteenth century. Highly literate, Frederick gathered to his court the most artistic and brilliant people he could find. Militarily he was no less accomplished; he expanded Prussia's influence over the rest of Europe. His letters and documents are generally available to collectors.

A century later, **Otto von Bismarck**, "the Iron Chancellor," became the first chancellor of the German Empire. The Prussian leader triumphed in the Franco-Prussian War and signed many documents and official letters that are popularly collected.

Kaiser **Wilhelm**, the emperor of Germany during the First World War, was forced to abdicate and was exiled to Holland. Official documents signed by him are more common than those of Bismarck (perhaps his huge signature is indicative of the ego that led Germany into World War I). Autographs of Wilhelm's military commander in World War I, **Erich**

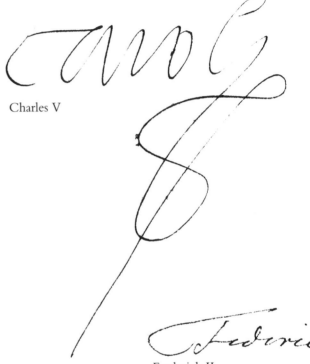

Charles V

Frederick II

Otto von Bismarck

Wilhelm II

Erich von Ludendorff

Paul von Hindenburg

Mata Hari

Maria Theresa

Metternich

Giuseppe Garibaldi

Isabella I

Ferdinand V of Castile,
Ferdinand II of Aragon

von Ludendorff, are only slightly more scarce; they can usually be found on military documents. The same is true of **Paul von Hindenburg**, the World War I hero who became the second president of the Weimar Republic. He was forced to name Adolf Hitler chancellor, and on Hindenberg's death, Hitler fully took the reins of power. Ornate calligraphic documents signed by Hindenburg, like those of Wilhelm, are usually available.

During the First World War, Germany's most famous spy was **Mata Hari**, the Dutch dancer who was caught by the French and executed by a firing squad. Her letters, occasionally available, are rare and very desirable.

In Austria, **Maria Theresa** was perhaps one of the most important leaders of her age, the eighteenth century; fortunately for collectors, she left many official ornate documents bearing her signature. Autograph material of the Austrian statesman **Metternich**, whose diplomacy dominated the Congress of Vienna in 1815 when the Napoleonic empire was broken up, is obtainable but scarce.

The Italian military and political leader **Giuseppe Garibaldi** had a long and multinational career, being exiled from his Italian homeland at various times as his military fortunes waned. With all of his struggles came a need for financial support for his causes, and he wrote many letters asking for funds. Fine examples are usually available.

Collectors are always very surprised that a document of **Isabella I** of Spain, the patron of Columbus, can be obtained. This is the result of the discovery many decades ago of a cache of her documents addressed to her chamberlain and their dispersal among collectors. Today they are occasionally offered. Documents signed by her husband and joint sovereign, **Ferdinand V** of

160

Castile, are much rarer and less frequently encountered. (Spanish monarchs signed their documents *Yo el Rey,* I the King, or *Yo la Reyna,* I the Queen.) **Philip II** generated many letters and documents as king of Spain during the crucial years of conflict with England, and they are obtainable at this time.

Peter the Great of Russia reorganized his country's government and military establishments and built up its commerce. Letters and documents by this important leader of seventeenth- and eighteenth-century Russia, though quite rare, can be found. Less rare though certainly scarce and in demand are letters and documents of **Catherine the Great**. Occasionally, an ornate calligraphic example is found, but most are official letters or documents in her capacity as czarina of Russia.

More than a century later, **Nicholas II** and his czarina, **Alexandra**, were murdered during the Communist Revolution. Their autograph material is much rarer, partly because of their early deaths and also because it has been avidly collected. Autograph material of the leader of the revolution, **Vladimir Lenin**, is very rare. His autographs were very aggressively collected by Armand Hammer who presented his acquisitions

Philip II

Peter I

Catherine II

Nicholas II

Alexandra

Vladimir Lenin

Joseph Stalin

to the Russian government and various Russian leaders. Lenin material today, were it to come onto the market, would not have the ready market that Hammer provided, but its rarity would cause it to fetch a high price nevertheless. Autograph material of **Joseph Stalin** has always been very rare as well, though not in as much demand as Lenin's. With the political changes in Russia now taking place, I do think it possible that material of Stalin may begin to be offered. At this time collectors can mainly hope to

Leon Trotsky

Mikhail Gorbachev

acquire an autograph given at one of the allied conferences. Stalin's early victim, **Leon Trotsky**, who was banished from Russia by Stalin in 1929 and murdered in exile eleven years later, is much more available in letters, though they are quite scarce. The most popular Russian of modern times is **Mikhail Gorbachev**. Genuinely signed pieces by the leader who ended the cold war are rare but obtainable.

20

WORLD WAR II

Collecting letters and documents of World War II can be particularly satisfying, because the events and personalities are so close to our own time that few of us were not affected by it. It may also have been the last great world event in which individuals made the difference between victory and defeat, in which individual leadership was the deciding factor in many battles and ingenuity and cleverness could turn the tide.

Generally, autograph material of most of the leading figures in World War II is available. There are, of course, many exceptions. George Patton, for example, did not write many letters during the war and apparently was not asked to sign very many souvenir pieces for soldiers. His death at the end of the war also meant that he, unlike nearly all the other American generals, did not go on to another career during which many letters were created. The military leadership just below the top commanders were sometimes asked to sign souvenir pieces during the war, but autograph material of these generals, whose names were not well known in postwar years, are harder to locate although not expensive when found.

The reason nearly all wartime letters are of a general or souvenir nature is that, unlike the Civil War, soldiers of all ranks were forbidden to write about military events or keep diaries. Censorship was very strict, and even Eisenhower's letters to his wife during the war were censored—although in his case, Ike did it himself.

World War II can be said to have begun with the signing of the Versailles Treaty, which ended World War I. From a collecting standpoint, however, many World War II collections start with the beginnings of the Nazi party in Germany. Historical letters and documents of nearly all of the leading personalities of the Third Reich can be obtained. Their availability is due, in large part, to the very widespread practice of souvenir hunting among the American soldiers entering Germany in the spring of 1945. Offices were ransacked everywhere and any letters bearing the Nazi swastika were brought home, along with daggers, guns, flags, and everything else that was thought of as a war trophy. (This practice was not limited to the enlisted men; General Bedell Smith, Eisenhower's chief of staff, carried as his personal side arm a captured German Lugar pistol.)

Documents of **Adolf Hitler** are generally available in official orders, more commonly before the war but also occasionally during the war years. Many of the ornate promotions and awards are not signed by Hitler but bear a lithographed signature of incredibly good quality. These documents require a very careful examination under magnification to determine if they are genuinely signed. Hitler also sent out routine letters acknowledging birthday wishes and Christmas greetings, and these bear excellent lithographed signatures as well. Letters and signed photographs of Hitler are much rarer than documents.

The Hitler diaries made the subject of Hitler forgeries well known, but the forgeries that may confront the collector, in addition to the official lithographed ones, can be extremely well executed. A supply of blank sheets of Hitler's official and personal stationery became available when soldiers took them from each of the Führer's offices. With a typewriter of the period and a knowledge of the German language and procedures, a forger could, without too much difficulty, prepare a very genuine-looking typewritten letter. The problem lies in forging the signature. Many collectors, when everything else looks genuine, pay little attention to the signature and are duped. Anything of a souvenir nature purported to be signed by Hitler should also be examined very closely. Pieces bearing Hitler's handwriting, in addition to his signature, are not only very rare but very unusual as well. Hitler did not like writing by hand, and such an example requires very careful examination.

Adolf Hitler

Letters and documents of Hitler's early confidant, **Rudolf Hess**, are rarely encountered. Hess's role in the Nazi party lessened in the 1930s, resulting in the creation of fewer letters and documents, and his imprisonment in England after his flight in May 1941 brought an end to his letter writing (except to his family). **Hermann Göring**, the World War I fighter ace, joined Hitler's cause very early. Letters and documents by him are somewhat scarce, mostly because they have been actively collected, but examples can usually be found. The first leader of the SA, **Ernst Röhm**, is another matter. Fearing the rising power of Röhm and wanting to mollify others, Hitler charged Röhm and all his cohorts with conspiracy to overthrow him and had them executed in the purge of June 1934. Letters and documents of Röhm are very scarce.

Letters of the Führer's private secretary, the ever-present **Martin Bormann**, are the most common of the leaders of the Third Reich who did not survive the war or the Nuremberg trials. His typewritten letters and orders carrying out Hitler's wishes are normally available. Letters of **Joseph Goebbels**, the minister of propaganda and the evil genius who focused the energy of a nation of desperate people to bring such horror on the world, are slightly scarcer than Göring's. They are not rare, but they are not always available.

Albert Speer, Hitler's architect and wartime minister of armaments and war production, is scarce in autograph material from wartime but common from the period after his release from Spandau prison in 1966. Speer's memoirs, one of the most remarkable books about the war (if not the most remarkable), prompted many people to write to him, and he was eager to answer their letters. He frequently sent signed photographs and signed souvenir copies of excerpts of his book. Speer's willingness to express guilt for the horrors of the Third Reich made him an acceptable correspondent to many.

Joachim von Ribbentrop, Hitler's ambassador to England in the 1930s, also held many other posts and served as minister of foreign affairs during the war. Letters and documents of

Rudolf Hess

Hermann Göring

Ernst Röhm

Martin Bormann

Joseph Goebbels

Albert Speer

Joachim von Ribbentrop

Heinrich Himmler

Heil Hitler!

Reinhard Heydrich

Adolf Eichmann

Wilhelm Keitel

Alfred Jodl

Albert Kesselring

Erwin Rommel

Ribbentrop, who was executed after the Nuremberg trials, are somewhat scarce. The same is true of the leader of the SS, **Heinrich Himmler**, who committed suicide in May 1945 after his capture by the British. Autograph material of Himmler is very popular with collectors, illustrating humankind's fascination with evil. Some have likened his unusual signature to a series of bayonet points. Assassination took the life of one of Himmler's most ruthless henchmen, **Reinhard Heydrich**, and consequently material signed by him is rare, although occasionally available. One of the greatest rarities of the Third Reich is material of Himmler's subordinate, **Adolf Eichmann**. Extremely few documents of this administrator of the Holocaust have survived.

Field Marshal **Wilhelm Keitel** was superseded by Hitler as commander of the armed forces, but as the Führer's deputy, he did sign many documents, and like **Alfred Jodl**, chief of staff of the German army, his letters and documents are scarce. **Albert Kesselring**, commander of the German forces in Italy, survived the war and the Nuremberg trials (his death sentence was commuted to life imprisonment, but he was freed in 1952). His family letters from Spandau are rarely offered on the market, but letters from the brief period between his release and natural death are occasionally offered. Wartime letters are much scarcer.

Of the Third Reich's military commanders, none have fascinated those on both sides of the war as much as **Erwin Rommel**. Considered by most to be Germany's best field commander, and not to have been

166

more than a nominal Nazi, Rommel is one of the war's most popular figures for collectors. His letters and documents from almost any period are rare, particularly those from Africa. Occasionally, a handwritten postcard to his wife will appear on the market, usually written during the 1930s. Rommel's commander on the western front, **Gerd von Rundstedt**, is not nearly so popular among collectors, and his autograph material is rarely available, except in postcards sent home to his wife. These postcards were recently discovered and when absorbed into collections, will once again put Rundstedt into a rarer category.

Hitler's successor as Führer, Admiral **Karl Dönitz**, signed Germany's surrender in May 1945. He survived the Nuremberg trials and a ten-year sentence in Spandau prison and carried on correspondences with many people. Like Speer, Dönitz was willing to sign copies of surrender documents and excerpts from his books as well as many photographs.

It is not an exaggeration to say that France's World War II effort was represented by one man—**Charles de Gaulle** (resistance leader Jean Moulin, an outstanding hero, is unobtainable in autograph material). De Gaulle's letters and documents are collected by French collectors as well as by collectors in other countries. Wartime autograph material of de Gaulle is very rare and usually consists of letters written from London early in the war. Later letters written during his political career and documents signed as president of France are more frequently available. Beware of notes without correspondents' names which de Gaulle sent to acknowledge greetings; these appear to be handwritten by him, but a quick examination with a magnifying glass will show that they are printed.

Wartime autograph material of **Benito Mussolini**, at one time Hitler's mentor, is rare. Letters and signed photographs from the early years of the Fascist party are more commonly available. His popularity with collectors is not comparable with the personalities of the Third Reich.

Ort und Straße genau angeben
Gerd von Rundstedt

Karl Dönitz

Charles de Gaulle

Benito Mussolini

Neville Chamberlain

Winston S. Churchill

Claude Auchinleck

Bernard Montgomery

The man some may perhaps consider partly responsible for World War II, **Neville Chamberlain**, has been for the most part ignored by collectors. His letters and signed photographs are encountered but find a market only among those collecting all the personalities of the war—the good, the evil, and the incompetent.

His successor, **Winston Spencer Churchill**, is, along with Napoleon, the most popular historical figure in the field of collecting historical letters and documents. Churchill's appeal cannot be overstated. Everything concerning him continues to fascinate and engross new generations. The fact that his career as Britain's wartime leader began when he was sixty-five years old inspires all of us. Churchill's letters, though in great demand, are usually available; he lived a very long life, and everyone saved the letters of the "greatest Englishman who ever lived." Unfortunately, his letters contain none of the fire and emotion of his speeches, and a letter discussing policy would be extremely rare. Perhaps of more interest are his signed photographs, particularly the wartime ones, which evoke all the feeling of the leader who brought England to "her finest hour." Churchill freely gave his signature when asked, but he also had a deceptive series of handwritten notes printed for distribution on those occasions when the burden of his correspondence became overwhelming. Churchill's letters, signatures, and signed photographs are frequently available.

Claude Auchinleck, commander in chief in Africa, was one of the first "victims" of the new prime minister's "action today" policy. He was fired by Churchill for not being bold enough and reassigned to command in India. His letters are collectable though not particularly common, and there is no great demand for them. Churchill's handpicked successor as leader in Africa, **Bernard Montgomery**, is relatively common in letters and signed photographs of the postwar period and occasionally is available in wartime pieces. There is a reasonably strong demand for material by

Montgomery because he was an important wartime commander. His letters reflect Churchill's remark that Montgomery was "impossible in defeat and insufferable in victory."

Much scarcer is material of **Louis Mountbatten**; early in the war he was commander of Britain's commandos and later was appointed supreme allied commander of Southeast Asia. Mountbatten's career has recently been questioned in a biography and there has been little collector interest in him. Viscount **Alanbrooke** was Churchill's chairman of the Imperial General Staff; his material is also not common but is not particularly collected except by those seeking letters of all the major figures of the war.

Russia's actions in World War II, at first despicable with the Hitler–Stalin pact and the division of Poland, were later, militarily, incredible. Autograph material of Russia's military leaders very rarely appears on the market. Anything signed by the outstanding Russian military strategist with whom Stalin was literally forced to share leadership, Marshall **Georgi Zhukov**, is extremely rare (after the war, Zhukov was consigned to oblivion by the no longer grateful Stalin). **Joseph Stalin** himself, a mass murderer on the scale of Hitler, is extremely rare in letters and very rare in documents. Several signed souvenir pieces obtained at the various allied conferences such as Potsdam or Yalta have appeared on the market but are very rare.

Autograph material of the leader of wartime Japan, Emperor **Hirohito**, have come onto the market since his death. Before then virtually nothing signed by him appeared, but since then sentimentality has begun to fade, and signed photographs and official letters and documents, while still rare, have been offered. The emperor, who was spared prosecution and certain execution primarily by Douglas MacArthur, lived a very long life, and anyone receiving a personally signed letter or document was certain to preserve it. Autographs of his wartime prime minister, **Hideki Tojo**, hanged at the end of the war, are rarely available.

Louis Mountbatten

Viscount Alanbrooke

Georgi Zhukov

Joseph Stalin

Hirohito   Hideki Tojo

Chiang Kai-Shek [signature]

Chiang
Kai-Shek

Mao Tse-Tung [signature]

Mao Tse-Tung

Franklin D. Roosevelt [signature]

Franklin D. Roosevelt

George C. Marshall [signature]

George C. Marshall

Dwight D. Eisenhower [signature]

Dwight D. Eisenhower

Japan's enemy in mainland China was **Chiang Kai-shek**. While his autographs of war date are very rare, they are much less rare after his retreat to Taiwan. He was very aware that American public opinion was vital to his claim to represent the Chinese, and the generalissimo routinely answered letters from American admirers, as did his wife. Anything signed by the leaders of the Communist forces led by **Mao Tse-tung** is virtually unobtainable.

Winston Churchill's reaction to the "day that will live in infamy"—December 7, 1941—was that he then knew the Allies would win with America's entry into the war. His relationship with Franklin D. Roosevelt was an important factor in securing the aid that England had been receiving and would be the decisive factor in focusing on the European rather than the Pacific theater.

Franklin D. Roosevelt material is relatively common. Beginning with his election to the New York State senate and appointment as assistant secretary of the navy, and continuing through a long political career that included the governorship of New York, FDR wrote many letters that are available from all periods. However, letters with interesting content, or concerning World War II, are very rare. Roosevelt's chief of staff of the army, **George C. Marshall**, who later served as secretary of state and originated the Marshall Plan, is generally available in letters, but these very rarely have interesting content.

Dwight D. Eisenhower, commander of Allied forces first in Africa and then in Europe, would be extremely rare in wartime letters discussing the war were it not for a small but extraordinary group of letters that he wrote to his wife during the war. These letters, the only handwritten letters of war date by Eisenhower, have revealed great feelings and thoughts and are among the best letters by any military leader or president. Now dispersed among private collections, letters from this small group will undoubtedly come onto the market in the future and will create great interest among collectors. Other wartime letters by Eisenhower were, if of a general nature, composed by an assistant but genuinely signed by Eisenhower. Ike also inscribed many photographs during World War II, and from a collector's as well as military historian's standpoint, Eisenhower remains very popular. The demand for Eisenhower's letters and signed photographs is greater than for autograph material of any other Allied leader except Churchill.

Eisenhower's counterpart in the Pacific theater (though he would never have agreed to such a comparison), **Douglas MacArthur**, also signed many routine letters and photographs, and again, letters of importance are very rare. The demand for MacArthur material, while quite strong in the United States, is much stronger in Japan where he is seen as the founder of modern Japan, having liberated the present generation and created equal opportunity for all Japanese. Another of MacArthur's rivals (who wasn't!) was **Chester W. Nimitz**, commander of the Pacific fleet. His autographs are much scarcer than those of MacArthur, but interest among collectors is limited to the United States. Autograph material of the other naval commander in the Pacific theater, **William F. Halsey**, is also relatively scarce.

In Europe, the commander of the army and the air force, **H. H. "Hap" Arnold**, wrote many letters, but they are not common. Of the American ground commanders of World War II, none evoke the emotional reaction and popularity of **George S. Patton**. Autograph material of Patton, next to that of Eisenhower, is the most popular among collectors and there is little material to choose from. Envelopes bearing his signature as "Censor" are the most available, but even these examples are not frequently found. Letters and documents are rare, and collectors seeking material by him should be careful not to let pieces pass by.

Patton's onetime subordinate and, after the Normandy invasion, his commander, **Omar N. Bradley**, never attracted or sought the public adulation that Patton did,

Douglas MacArthur

Chester W. Nimitz

Very truly yours,

William F. Halsey

H. H. ARNOLD
Commanding General, Army Air Forces

H. H. "Hap" Arnold

George S. Patton

Omar N. Bradley

Mark Clark

and this is reflected in the interest of collectors. Bradley lived a long life and wrote many letters that are readily available. The same is true of **Mark Clark**, the American commander in Italy. As the head of a military academy after the war, Clark freely answered all inquiries and requests for autographs.

It is interesting and satisfying to conclude a chronologically arranged World War II collection with autograph material relating to the Nuremberg trials. According to the guards who have brought material to me for sale, the Nazi prisoners were delighted to be asked for their autographs, but collecting them was strictly forbidden by the Allied Command. Nevertheless, many guards asked prisoners to autograph books, and although relatively rare and very desirable, they do come up for sale. It is a fitting way to "end" the war in one's own collection.

ARTS AND LETTERS

◆

Music

Art

American Literature

English Literature

French Literature

European Literature

The Performing Arts

21

MUSIC

The world of letters, documents, manuscripts, signed printed scores, and signed photographs relating to music is the most international of all the fields of autograph collecting. Musical notation is the same the world over; there is no language barrier, and almost every culture listens to the music of the Western world. The great composers are equally well known in New York, Tokyo, Paris, Berlin, or Moscow; collectors everywhere seek to possess something by the geniuses who have made the music that enriches our lives.

Many collectors in the field of music are composers or performers themselves. More than in any other field, those who are creating or performing today are interested in those who did so in the past. Joan Sutherland and her husband, Richard Bonynge, have been among the most active collectors, along with another major popular opera singer, several contemporary composers, and several of the most popular modern singers. Jerome Kern, the composer of *Showboat*, once remarked that he made more money when he sold his collection of manuscripts and books than he had from all his musical creations.

In the field of music, the collector might be offered a letter, less likely a document, perhaps a working manuscript; that is, a sketch or finished manuscript that is part of the composing process, or a musical quotation written out by the composer and signed by him for an admirer. Composers also signed printed music scores, and later in the nineteenth century, they signed photographs as well.

Anything in the hand of **Johann Sebastian Bach** is extremely rare and very rarely offered for sale. Letters of **Wolfgang Amadeus Mozart** are virtually unobtainable. The most likely example a collector

Johann Sebastian Bach

Wolfgang A. Mozart

Joseph Haydn

Ludwig van Beethoven

Beethoven,
signed in German script

Carl Maria von Weber

Franz Schubert

Vincenzo Bellini

Frédéric Chopin

might be offered is a page of music in Mozart's hand, and the price will reflect the enormous international popularity of the Austrian composer and the great rarity created by his early death. Autograph material of Mozart's friend and fellow Austrian, **Joseph Haydn**, is not in as much demand, nor is it quite as rare, although his autograph music is extremely rare. Haydn's letters are very rare and command substantial prices, and the most affordable example a collector may find is a printed score signed by him, probably while he was on one of his two English tours. **Ludwig van Beethoven** is another musical giant whose letters and manuscripts have been avidly sought by collectors and institutions virtually since his lifetime. Beethoven's letters and manuscripts are not as rare as Mozart's, but the demand is just as great, and collectors will be very fortunate if they can acquire anything in his hand for their collection. Letters and documents of Beethoven are more likely to be found than manuscript musical sketches.

Autograph material of a leading creator of German romanticism in music, **Carl Maria von Weber**, when compared to those composers we have been discussing, is relatively available. Documents signed by him, though rare, are more frequently encountered than his letters, and musical manuscripts are extremely rare. Handwritten examples of the Austrian composer **Franz Schubert** are again extremely rare and in great demand. A collector will very rarely find a musical page or letter but is more likely to locate a printed musical score bearing his initials. Autograph material of **Vincenzo Bellini**, the Italian opera composer, is more likely to be encountered in the form of a musical manuscript page than in anything bearing his signature. Manuscripts are rare, while his letters are very rare.

Frédéric Chopin's early death at the age of thirty-nine contributes to the rarity of his letters and manuscripts, which, like those of many other composers, have been collected by institutional libraries and museums for decades. There is always a great demand for anything in his handwriting. Musical manuscript pages are extremely rare, and the collector has a better chance of finding a note or letter, frequently signed with his initials or paraph (a flourish at the end of a signature, used originally as a safeguard against forgery). Autograph material of the innovative composer and great violin virtuoso of the age, **Nicolo Paganini**, is, like Bellini's, more available than that of Bach, Mozart, or Beethoven; but again, it is much rarer than material of the major composers of the latter half of the nineteenth century. Despite its rarity, the more limited appeal of Paganini's work compared to the other great composers of his age makes his letters and notes less costly when found.

Giaocchino Rossini's long life and great popularity have made his letters much less rare than those of his fellow Italian operatic composer, Bellini. Rossini's letters are more available than the letters of the other composers thus far considered, and letters, documents, and even musical quotations written out and signed by him can be found. Autograph examples of his contemporary, **Gaetano Donizetti**, are scarcer, but the collector can expect to be able to acquire a letter. Musical manuscript pages are rarer but not impossible to obtain.

Robert Schumann, one of the greatest of the romantic composers, went insane at the age of forty-four. Before being forced into musical inactivity, his genius had produced remarkable music, and his autograph material is very popular with collectors. While occasionally available, his letters are rare, any mentioning music very rare. **Clara Schumann**, his wife and interpreter of his music, was an outstanding virtuoso pianist in her own right. Her letters are scarce though not especially costly. **Felix Mendelssohn** is another composer whose life span was relatively short; he died at the age of thirty-eight. His considerable output of musical works led to great popularity in his lifetime, and he carried on many lengthy correspondences. The interest of collectors in past decades has resulted in most of these letters being acquired by institutions, and Mendelssohn material, once fairly common in letters,

Nicolo Paganini

Giaocchino Rossini

Gaetano Donizetti

Robert Schumann

Clara Schumann

Felix Mendelssohn

Franz Liszt

Richard Wagner

Johannes Brahms

Johann Strauss the Younger

Johann Strauss the Elder

is now much more difficult to obtain. Occasionally, letters written by Mendelssohn in his fluent English are encountered; musical manuscripts are very rare.

Franz Liszt, who enjoyed a long life and great popularity, wrote many letters, providing the modern collector with the opportunity to obtain fine examples at reasonable prices. Autograph musical manuscript pages of Liszt can also, on occasion, be found, as can signed photographs, though both are much rarer than his letters. Signed autograph musical quotations are much rarer than one would expect.

Of greater creative diversity, with a long life span, and enormous contemporary and modern popularity is **Richard Wagner**. Similar to the letters and manuscripts of the composers of the early part of the nineteenth century, those of Wagner have been in great demand among institutional collectors and museums since his lifetime, but the sale of one library's collection a few years ago has made material available for the present time, and the collector of today can usually locate an appealing piece for his collection. Musical manuscript pages are, however, very rare, as are signed musical quotations. Almost equally rare are his signed photographs or signed printed scores.

Autograph material of Wagner's contemporary, **Johannes Brahms**, is much scarcer, and if it were not for the correspondence with his publisher, Fritz Simrock, letters of Brahms would be much more difficult to obtain than they presently are. Anything other than a postcard to Simrock is rarely found, and autograph musical pages or signed musical quotations are extremely rare.

The autographs of **Johann Strauss the younger**, popularly known as "the Waltz King," are not nearly as common as one might imagine. While very popular in his lifetime and in the decades since, his letters and signed photographs are scarcer than those of many of his contemporaries. Musical quotations are rare. **Johann Strauss the elder,** also wrote dance music for his Austrian audiences; but his autograph material is in much less demand than that of his more famous son.

Hector Berlioz, the most important of the French romantics, falls into the category of important composers whose letters can usually be obtained but whose musical manuscripts and musical quotations are very rare. A social letter, perhaps concerning a concert, is the most frequently encountered. Letters of Berlioz's contemporary, **Georges Bizet**, are much rarer because of his early death. The author of *Carmen* is very popular among collectors, and his letters are difficult to find. Another French composer of this period, **Jacques Offenbach**, was for many years readily available in letters and musical manuscripts, and although modern collectors have taken most of the material from the market, examples are still commonly available. Brief musical sketches in Offenbach's handwriting are occasionally found. Another French contemporary is the operatic composer **Charles Gounod** of *Faust* fame. Once very common, his letters have also become more scarce, although not as scarce as Offenbach's, and they are easily found. Letters and manuscripts of **César Franck** are both less common and less popular than those of his contemporaries.

The collecting situation of the great Italian operatic composer, **Giuseppe Verdi**, is similar to that of Wagner: he had great popularity during his lifetime and the years since, lived a long life, and has always been very popular among collectors. Letters, generally of a social nature, are frequently available; those with musical content very rarely found. Signed musical quotations are rare and very much in demand, as are signed photographs.

Hector Berlioz

Georges Bizet

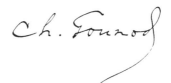
Jacques Offenbach

Charles Gounod

César Franck

Giuseppe Verdi

Peter Tchaikovsky

The great and popular Russian composer of this epoch, **Peter Tchaikovsky**, whose ballets are still

Signature of Tchaikovsky in Russian script

Nikolai Rimsky-Korsakov signature

Nikolai Rimsky-Korsakov

Anton Dvorák signature

Anton Dvorák

Edvard Grieg signature

Edvard Grieg

Hugo Wolf signature

Hugo Wolf

William S. Gilbert signature

William S. Gilbert

Arthur Sullivan signature

Arthur Sullivan

Gustav Mahler signature

Gustav Mahler

Jules Massenet signature

Jules Massenet

among the most popular in the world, is very rare in letters as well as in signed musical quotations and signed photographs. Letters and musical manuscripts of his Russian contemporary, **Nikolai Rimsky-Korsakov**, are rarer still but in less demand. The Bohemian composer, **Anton Dvorák**, is only slightly less rare in letters and equally rare in signed musical quotations.

Letters of **Edvard Grieg**, Norway's most important composer in the latter part of the nineteenth century, are usually available, and occasionally signed musical quotations are offered. Autographs of **Hugo Wolf**, the Austrian author of over three hundred German lieder and other works, are much rarer.

In England, in the late nineteenth century, lyricist **William S. Gilbert** and composer **Arthur Sullivan** were composing comic operas that are performed and sung to this day. Autograph material of Gilbert is the scarcer of the two, but both are generally available in letters, although letters of musical interest are almost never seen. They were avidly collected years ago; many are now in the Pierpont Morgan Library.

At the turn of the century, **Gustav Mahler**'s music was very popular, and his popularity has endured, causing his letters to be quite scarce although occasionally obtainable. **Jules Massenet** is one of the most available composers in letters and in signed musical quotations, frequently from *Manon*. Much scarcer are letters of his contemporary and fellow Frenchman, **Claude Debussy**, which have been very heavily collected. Most of his letters are in institutional libraries, although usually one can be acquired (early letters are signed *A.C. Debussy,* his first name being Achille). Musical quotations signed are very rare.

Claude Debussy signature

Claude Debussy

Debussy, signed A Debussy signature

Debussy,
signed *A Debussy*

Letters and musical quotations of his contemporary, the French composer **Camille Saint-Saëns**, are much more common. In recent decades many of his letters were collected by an American university library, but a sufficient number are on the market to satisfy the demands of collectors. Much less available and more in the category of Debussy's are letters of **Maurice Ravel**, perhaps most noted for his work, *Boléro*. Musical quotations signed are rare, and on very rare occasions one from *Boléro* may be found.

The Italian operatic composer of *I Pagliacci,* **Ruggiero Leoncavallo**, lived a long life and enjoyed great popularity. He wrote many letters that are more readily available than those of most other operatic composers. Vastly more popular in contemporary operatic performances and among collectors is **Giacomo Puccini**. His long life span and his enormous popularity both during his lifetime and the decades since have ensured that his letters would be saved. Puccini's admirers have very actively collected his letters, and it is now rare to find letters with the emotional or musical content that were available a few years ago. Puccini, more than any other major composer, also wrote out and signed musical manuscript quotations, sometimes from *La Bohème;* while scarce and in great demand, these can be found. Musical sketches are very rare, while signed photographs are likely to be frequently available.

Meanwhile, in England, **Edward Elgar** was writing his very popular music, including the march, *Pomp and Circumstance*. Elgar's letters are generally available, but signed musical quotations and photographs are rare. The Polish pianist and composer, **Ignace Paderewski**, who after World War I became Poland's prime minister for ten months, was very popular with the public. He performed extensively and gave numerous autographs to admirers. Frequently these were signed photographs that are today usually available. Letters and manuscripts of **Béla Bartók**, the Hungarian composer who fled to

Camille Saint-Saëns

Maurice Ravel

Ruggiero Leoncavallo

Giacomo Puccini

Edward Elgar

Ignace Paderewski

Béla Bartók

Franz Lehár

Richard Strauss

Sergei Rachmaninoff

Rachmaninoff's
signature in
Russian script

Arnold Schönberg

Pietro Mascagni

Jean Sibelius

Igor Stravinsky

the United States, are much less common and have been seriously collected by an institutional library. Letters can be found, but they are scarce; manuscripts are very rare. The situation is quite different with **Franz Lehár**, Bartók's fellow Hungarian, whose operettas have been enormously popular. Letters are frequently available, though not in any quantity, and signed photographs are relatively common. It is also possible to find printed musical scores signed by Lehár.

Letters of the Russian pianist and composer **Sergei Rachmaninoff** would be much rarer were it not for those he wrote while on tours, during which he also signed programs for admirers. He remains popular today, and the modern collector will usually be able to acquire a fine example signed by him. Rachmaninoff's contemporary, **Arnold Schönberg**, emigrated to the United States from his native Austria just before World War II. His autograph material is uncommon, but it is popularly collected and therefore generally unavailable.

Richard Strauss's popularity has suffered because of his strong pro-Nazi sympathies (he was president of the Reich's music department), though in recent years many more collectors have sought his material. His letters are available, and collectors can usually find musical quotations signed by him. The Italian composer **Pietro Mascagni** is not as popular with collectors as his musical accomplishments would seem to warrant. Letters are relatively common and not particularly expensive. Autographs of the composer of Finland's national anthem, *Finlandia*, **Jean Sibelius**, would be rare were it not for one correspondence carried on with an American which has been dispersed among collectors. Besides these typewritten letters very little material is offered.

Autograph material of the great Russian-American composer, **Igor Stravinsky**, is rare except for signatures and social notes, which are scarce. Signed

Sigmund Romberg

Sigmund Romberg

Dmitri Shostakovich

Dmitri Shostakovich

photographs are also uncommon, and musical manuscripts are very rare. Stravinsky donated many of his papers to the Library of Congress, and after his death and a change in the tax laws, his heirs sold the bulk of the papers to the Sacher Institute in Switzerland. **Dimitri Shostakovich** did not venture out of the Soviet Union frequently enough to write many letters or sign souvenir autographs. His material is rarely encountered but is not at present in significant demand among collectors.

Sigmund Romberg, the composer of light operas such as the *Student Prince,* is usually found in souvenir autographs—signatures or signed programs. His letters are not common. The Austrian émigré to the United States, **Fritz Kreisler**, gave many autographs during his violin concerts and these are always available. **Jascha Heifetz**, whose name is associated with musical perfection, is the Russian-born American who is probably the greatest violinist of all time. His souvenir-type signatures are usually available.

In England, **Ralph Vaughan Williams** helped to revive serious music written by native composers. Collectors can usually obtain his letters that are not in great popular demand. **Benjamin Britten**, probably the most outstanding modern English composer, is very popular among collectors, and his letters, frequently available, sell quite quickly.

Letters and musical quotations of the American composer **Edward MacDowell** are rare; they find a steady demand among a few specialist collectors. Much rarer are autographs of another American composer, **Charles Ives**, who, though not especially well

Fritz Kreisler

Jascha Heifetz

Ralph Vaughan Williams

Benjamin Britten

Edward MacDowell

Charles Ives

Aaron Copland

John Philip Sousa

Victor Herbert

George M. Cohan

George Gershwin

Jerome Kern

known, has always been a musician's musician. Anything in his hand is very rare. Far better known is **Aaron Copland**, who obligingly signed anything sent to him by fans and whose letters, currently not common, are likely to become so when his correspondents die and pass them down through families.

In the early twentieth century, **John Philip Sousa**'s music was among America's most popular. While his letters are rarely found (they have been actively collected by the Library of Congress), signed musical quotations, signatures, and signed photographs can be found. Autographs of his contemporary, **Victor Herbert**, are much scarcer but in much less demand. Unsigned autograph musical sketches appear occasionally, and signed musical quotations are frequently found. **George M. Cohan**'s letters are invariably written in pencil, and those to friends are signed *George M.* His autograph material is scarce and very popular. Signed programs can be found, but anything relating to his many popular shows and songs is very rare.

George Gershwin's popularity has soared in recent years, partly because of the discovery in Secaucus, New Jersey, of a cache of his unpublished manuscripts. These manuscripts, mislabeled more than sixty years ago, were only recently discovered in a Warner Brothers warehouse; they are now in the Library of Congress. They have enabled modern performers to stage Gershwin revivals with music unheard since the composer's lifetime. Autograph examples of Gershwin are usually available in signatures and occasionally in signed checks. Signed musical quotations and photographs are rare, and letters with musical content are very rare. The Library of Congress has for decades very aggressively purchased most of the Gershwin letters and manuscripts offered. Signed copies of his printed compositions are occasionally seen, and their prices reflect Gershwin's great popularity.

Many of **Jerome Kern**'s original manuscripts were found with the Gershwin manuscripts in the Warner

Brothers warehouse. These have also gone to the Library of Congress, and their discovery and availability have led to new recordings of many works, including the first complete performance of *Showboat*. Kern's letters are scarce, as are his musical quotations. The demand among collectors for material signed by him is only slightly less than that for Gershwin.

Cole Porter's autograph material is also very scarce and the demand for it very great. Most commonly found are signatures or signed photographs; letters are rare, and musical quotations are very rare. Autographs of **Irving Berlin**, despite his very long life, are not as common as his popularity might indicate. His letters are frequently available, along with signed copies of his printed scores, and there is a strong collector interest in his material. Autograph material of **Richard Rodgers**, the composer of many Broadway musicals, is still relatively inexpensive, compared to his importance and the interest of collectors. **Leonard Bernstein**, less prolific in popular music, generally signed pieces sent to him, but these signed pieces are not actually as common as one would imagine. There is strong collector interest in him. His own papers, like those of nearly all American composers, are in an institution.

Commonly available are autographs of **W. C. Handy**, father of the blues and composer of St. Louis Blues. He readily signed pieces sent to him, particularly musical scores. **Hoagy Carmichael**'s popularity as a songwriter continues to be very strong, and the pieces

Cole Porter

Irving Berlin

Richard Rodgers

Leonard Bernstein

W.C. Handy

Hoagy Carmichael

"Fats" Waller

Thomas "Fats" Waller

Duke Ellington

he signed for admirers find ready collectors. **Duke Ellington**'s papers have now been acquired by the Smithsonian Institution and the Library of Congress, but many pieces signed for fans do come onto the market; signatures and signed photographs are the most frequently available. All types of autograph material of **Thomas "Fats" Waller**, composer of such pieces as "Ain't Misbehavin'," are much rarer.

22

ART

For several years in the 1980s it appeared that letters, documents, and manuscripts of artists would become impossible for collectors to obtain. The Getty Museum began to acquire everything that was offered for sale in this field—buying literally everything written by artists of all periods and all cultures. Just as abruptly as they began collecting, they stopped. During these several years they acquired every dealer's inventory of artists' letters as well as all of the new material coming onto the market. Fortunately for collectors and dealers, they had not begun to pursue private collections and correspondences, and as these have come onto the market, collectors have had good opportunities to acquire material that the Getty, had they continued their acquisitions program for a few more years, would have added to their archives. Art is a very popular field among collectors from many countries, and there is a fairly direct relationship between the importance and quality of an artist's work and popularity and the value of his or her letters and documents (adjusted by the factor of the actual rarity of the autograph material).

Autograph material of Renaissance artists, such as **Michelangelo**, the Italian painter and sculptor whose influence on Western art is unparalleled, is virtually unobtainable. While it is possible that something signed by **Raphael** or **Peter Paul Rubens** could be offered for sale, it would be a very rare opportunity. This is generally true for important artists up to the end of the eighteenth century.

In England during the late eighteenth century, art was dominated by the great portrait painters. Autograph material of **Thomas Gainsborough**, known for many portraits, including *The Blue Boy*, is rarely available. Even a brief receipt is rare. Letters and

Michelangelo

Raphael

Peter Paul Rubens

Thomas Gainsborough

187

Joshua Reynolds

Sir Thomas Lawrence

Benjamin West

John Constable

J. M. W. Turner

George Cruikshank

John Leech   *William Holman Hunt*

John Millais

Dante Gabriel Rossetti

Edward Burne-Jones

documents of **Joshua Reynolds**, Gainsborough's contemporary and fellow portrait painter, is only slightly less rare but is occasionally seen in unsigned manuscript notes. Collectors have been much less interested in their contemporary, **Sir Thomas Lawrence**, also noted for his portraits. His letters are much more available and much less costly.

Benjamin West, the American who gained fame in London with his historical scenes, is not frequently seen in autograph material, although collector interest is not on the same level as that for Gainsborough and Reynolds. When pieces do appear, they are much less expensive.

The early nineteenth century saw the emergence of two of England's most important artists—**John Constable**, who greatly influenced French artists later in the century, and his contemporary, **J. M. W. Turner**. Constable's letters are rarely seen, and a number of collectors specialize in him. Turner's letters are only slightly less rare, and again many collectors have developed collections focusing on him.

Many of the popular artists of the 1830s and later were illustrators of the great literary works of their time. Letters of **George Cruikshank** are relatively common, and small sketches by him can still be found without difficulty. Cruikshank's illustrations for Charles Dickens's *Oliver Twist* and *Sketches by Boz*, however, are impossible to acquire. **John Leech** also illustrated several of Dickens's works, and he is similarly available in letters and occasionally in more complete sketches.

The mid-nineteenth century in England saw the development of the Pre-Raphaelite movement whose leaders include **William Holman Hunt, John Millais, Dante Gabriel Rossetti, Edward Burne-**

Jones, and **William Morris**. Their letters are fairly scarce though obtainable. Letters of Morris and Burne-Jones, in particular, have been collected by specialists in these artists who influenced the Arts and Crafts movement and revolutionized Victorian tastes.

Toward the end of the nineteenth century, **Kate Greenaway** illustrated her own children's books, and her charming sketches have been much sought after. A number of her sketches were distributed with the publication of a book about her which contained an original sketch in each copy. Her letters are scarce and not as frequently seen as one might imagine; the University of Southern Mississippi has actively collected both letters and drawings and has amassed much of what she wrote and drew. Autograph material of her fellow authors and illustrators of children's books, Randolph Caldecott and **Beatrix Potter**, has also been systematically collected and is rarely seen for sale. Autograph material of Greenaway's successor, **Arthur Rackham**, has also been intensely collected, and his letters are now quite scarce, those incorporating drawings rarely seen.

James A. McNeill Whistler was one of the most important artists of his day, and his letters have also been actively collected by a major American library and another in England. His letters, though not common, can be obtained by collectors. Some of his letters and notes are signed with his "butterfly" signature. Whistler's nemesis was the English art critic **John Ruskin**. In 1877, Whistler had sued Ruskin for libel over the critic's attack on *Nocturne in Black and Gold: The Falling Rocket*. He won the case but received damages of only a farthing and consequently was bankrupted by court costs. Ruskin's letters are much more available and less costly than Whistler's.

The twentieth-century sculptor **Henry Moore** has been very popular as an artist, and consequently with collectors. He signed souvenir pieces for admirers, and it is usually possible to obtain a signed photograph of one of his abstract sculptures.

The work of the early twentieth-century Norwegian painter, **Edvard Munch**, cannot leave a viewer

William Morris

Kate Greenaway

Beatrix Potter

Arthur Rackham

James A. McNeill Whistler and his butterfly signature

John Ruskin

Henry Moore

Edvard Munch

John Trumbull

Charles Wilson Peale

Rembrandt Peale

John James Audubon

Thomas Nast

Augustus Saint-Gaudens

Daniel Chester French

Maxfield Parrish

unaffected, and this has resulted in a strong interest among collectors. His letters are both rare and in great demand. Letters are obtainable, but patience may be needed before one turns up.

In America, **John Trumbull**, known for his large historical paintings, was one of the country's first popular artists. Trumbull's letters can be acquired but have been very popular with collectors and are not common. Autograph material of **Charles Wilson Peale**, the fashionable portrait painter of the middle colonies at the time, is very rare, and his letters are infrequently seen. Signed material of his brother, **Rembrandt Peale**, has also been so actively collected that it is rare as well. An artist of the early nineteenth century whose reputation and works have retained their importance to the present day is **John James Audubon**. Anything signed by him is rare, based almost equally on the rarity of the material and demand for it. Nevertheless, with patience, pieces can be found.

Later in the nineteenth century **Thomas Nast** became an important artist with his illustrations, particularly his political cartoons that were, in large part, responsible for bringing down the corrupt regime of Boss Tweed in New York City. Nast relentlessly drew satirical cartoons of Tweed that provide social commentary of the day. Original drawings for his cartoons are rare but occasionally seen, and his letters have been collected by a New York library to the point where they are rarely seen on the market. Souvenir sketches or signed checks do, however, appear once in a while.

In the field of sculpture, **Augustus Saint-Gaudens** was the foremost sculptor of the late nineteenth century, and most of his letters have been collected by a university library. Letters, when available, are not particularly expensive. **Daniel Chester French**, another important sculptor of the turn of the century who did the statue of Lincoln for the Lincoln Memorial in Washington, D.C., is frequently available in letters that are also reasonably priced.

Maxfield Parrish, probably best known as an illustrator, has also interested many collectors, but letters can usually be found. In contrast, **Winslow Homer**, an important artist of genre scenes, seascapes, and landscapes, is very rare in letters and documents. Autograph material of **John Singer Sargent**, known especially for his elegant portraits of the early twentieth century, has been actively collected by institutions, although his letters are generally available. They rival those of the Duke of Wellington in being difficult to decipher.

The American West has been the setting of many literary works and perhaps more works of art. One of the most successful and popular western artists, **Albert Bierstadt**, whose landscapes are a part of American culture, is rare in letters, though signed cards can often be found. Autograph material of George Caleb Bingham is very rarely seen, and that of **George Catlin** is only slight less rare. The first great artist to portray the lives of cowboys and Indians, **Frederic Remington**, has been very popular with collectors. Letters of the sculptor, painter, and illustrator are rare, but usually an example can be acquired. Signed material of his contemporary, **Charles M. Russell**, is much rarer.

Autograph material of most members of the Hudson River school has been actively collected by institutions, and their letters rarely are offered. The artistic image of the First World War is that of the poster of Uncle Sam created by **James Montgomery Flagg**. Flagg's letters and drawings have been somewhat neglected by collectors, and fine examples, including original drawings, can be found at reasonable prices. Much less identifiable by many is the work of one of the foremost impressionists in America, **Childe Hassam**. His letters are rare, though they do not attract as much interest from collectors as some of his contemporaries. The leading folk artist of the twentieth century, **Grandma Moses**, can be acquired in signed Christmas cards but rarely in signed notes, and letters are almost never seen.

Winslow Homer

John Singer Sargent

Albert Bierstadt

George Catlin

Frederic Remington

Charles M. Russell

Childe Hassam

James Montgomery Flagg

Grandma Moses

Edward Hopper

Edward Hopper

N. C. Wyeth

N. C. Wyeth

Andrew Wyeth

Andrew Wyeth

Norman Rockwell

Norman Rockwell

Georgia O'Keeffe

Georgia O'Keeffe

Walt Disney

Walt Disney

Diego Rivera

Diego Rivera

Christopher Wren

Christopher Wren

Letters of the realist painter **Edward Hopper** are virtually unobtainable. **N. C. Wyeth**, the successful illustrator and mural painter of the mid-nineteenth century, is most known for his illustrations of Robert Louis Stevenson's novels, _Treasure Island_ and _Kidnapped_. His letters are quite rare, and very few pieces signed by him are encountered. Letters of his son, **Andrew Wyeth**, the noted painter of precise and detailed landscapes, interiors, and figures, are rarely seen, though a letter occasionally turns up. Much more common is autograph material of **Norman Rockwell** who answered, seemingly, every letter written to him. While interest in Rockwell material is strong, there is an ample supply at this time. **Georgia O'Keeffe**, a leading American artist of the the twentieth century, is rarely seen in letters and is only available in the form of a signed endorsement on the verso of a photograph. The endorsements, recording her transactions with her dealer, were recently discovered, and when dispersed into collections, she will again be rare in all forms.

Walt Disney used several studio artists to "sign" his name when people asked for autographs. These examples are written without his characteristic flourishes and resemble the signatures seen in Disney cartoons. Nevertheless, genuine material signed by him can be collected and is very popular. Disney would readily sign autograph albums for those he encountered in person. His letters are scarce and signed cels from his cartoons are rare; both can be acquired, but usually not immediately.

South of the border, in Mexico, **Diego Rivera** was the leading painter of the twentieth century. His letters are uncommon, but there has not been a great demand, and availability and prices reflect this lack of interest.

Architecture is a very popularly collected field, though there are few architects whose letters are available. The most important English architect whose documents can be collected is **Christopher Wren**, known for many buildings, most notably St. Paul's Cathedral. His documents are rare and in demand, and an interested collector should not let one pass by.

America's first professional architect, **Charles Bulfinch**, primarily designed government buildings. Although signed documents of Bulfinch are rare, there has not been much collector interest in him, and the documents are therefore reasonably priced when available. There is much more interest in the autograph material of **Stanford White**, who designed many of the great buildings of the late nineteenth century. His letters have been rarely seen, and until a small group was found a few years ago, virtually nothing had appeared for sale. Letters and documents of the great landscape architect of this period, **Frederick Law Olmsted**, are also quite rare though not necessarily very expensive. He designed most of the great parks in the eastern United States as well as private estates and university campuses. **Frank Lloyd Wright** is the architect whose autographs are the most sought after. Though he wrote many letters, they have been very actively collected for many years and can be difficult to find. Signed books are occasionally available and immediately attract the interest of many collectors.

For many collectors, France has been the leading center for the development of expression in art. As is the case in England, letters of French artists begin to be collectable in the late eighteenth century. Autographs of **Jacques Louis David**, court painter to Napoleon and founder of neoclassicism, can usually be collected in documents, though these are not common. Documents of the great sculptor of the age, one of the greatest of any age, **Jean A. Houdon**, can be obtained, but only with patience. Very few are offered, and an interested collector should not let one go by.

Jean-Auguste-Dominique Ingres, a leader among the classicists, is frequently seen in social letters, as is **Eugène Delacroix**, who anticipated the impressionists with his romantic style. This is not true of the great caricaturist, **Honoré Daumier**, whose autographs are very rare.

Charles Bulfinch

Stanford White

Frederick Law Olmstead

Frank Lloyd Wright

Jacques Louis David

Jean A. Houdon

J. A. D. Ingres

Eugène Delacroix

Honoré Daumier

J. F. Millet *G. Courbet*

Gustave Courbet

Jean François Millet

C. Corot

Jean B. C. Corot

Ed. Manet

Edouard Manet

Claude Monet

Claude Monet

Renoir

Pierre Auguste Renoir

Degas

Edgar Degas

C. Pissarro

Camille Pissaro

Mary Cassatt

Mary Cassatt

Vincent van Gogh

Vincent Van Gogh

Tout sommeille - même l'abuse
Dans l'enivrement des parfums
Et la couleur devient exquise
Dans la puissance des tons bruns

Autograph manuscript of Van Gogh

H. de T. Lautrec

Henri Toulouse-Lautrec

The genre and landscape painter of the Barbizon school, **Jean François Millet**, is difficult to find in letters or documents, as is his contemporary and leader of the realist movement, **Gustave Courbet**, though autograph material of both is possible to acquire. **Jean B. C. Corot**, a leader of the Barbizon school, anticipated the later impressionists, and his letters appear to be more available at this time than those of Millet or Courbet.

Letters of **Edouard Manet**, the originator and leader of impressionism, are much rarer and in more demand. They are much less frequently seen now than in past years, and if it were not for a group of rent documents signed by him his autograph would be very difficult to acquire. **Claude Monet**, however, wrote a great many letters, and though very popular and in much demand, fine examples can usually be collected. Autograph material of another leader among the impressionists, **Pierre Auguste Renoir**, is rarer than Monet's and not always available. **Camille Pissaro**'s letters have been more available, in part because he has been less popular than Monet or Renoir. **Edgar Degas**'s letters are much rarer, and in recent years they have appeared less and less frequently. **Mary Cassatt**, the American artist who painted and exhibited with the French impressionists, was very popular on both sides of the Atlantic. This is reflected in the interest of today's collectors, and her letters are infrequently seen.

One of the greatest autograph rarities of the modern European artists is material of **Vincent van Gogh**. His letters are virtually unobtainable, and the only example of his handwriting that is possible to obtain is a poem or fragment of a manuscript, often biblical. These are extremely rare. Autograph material of the great chronicler of Parisian nightlife, **Henri Toulouse-Lautrec**, is now very rare. A

Paul Gauguin

Paul Gauguin

New York collector with great foresight built the greatest collection of Toulouse-Lautrec letters and has now sold it to a Japanese museum. Letters are now rarely seen, and there are always a number of collectors seeking them. Also very rare is any autograph material of **Paul Gauguin**, the leading French painter of the post-impressionist period. In part because of his isolation in Tahiti, very few letters of this important painter have surfaced, and he has been actively collected by several libraries. Rarer still are letters of **Paul Cézanne**, a founder of modern painting. Autograph material of Georges Seurat, the creator of pointillism, is unobtainable.

Much more common is autograph material of **Auguste Rodin**, the leading sculptor of realism; his letters are almost always available, though they have become scarcer in recent years. **Pablo Picasso**, one of the greatest artists of the twentieth century, lived a long life and wrote many letters and documents. Many of these are already in institutional collections, and his letters are now rarely seen. More available are signatures he gave admirers. Signed prints of his works (not signed limited editions, but prints signed for admirers) are occasionally available. Autographs of his fellow founder of cubism, **Georges Braque**, are scarcer, though not nearly as popular, and are slightly less valued by collectors.

The Spanish cubist painter, **Joan Miró**, who later turned to surrealism, signed many prints of his work, and it is chiefly in this form that his autographs are available. **Marc Chagall** based many of his works on Russian village life and Jewish folklore, and signed prints of these works are readily available. These are not the limited editions manufactured for collectors but rather commercially produced prints that Chagall was happy to sign. The autographs of **Henri Matisse**, a leading fauvist painter and sculptor, are much rarer,

Paul Cézanne

Auguste Rodin

Pablo Picasso

Georges Braque

Joan Miró

Marc Chagall

Henri Matisse

Maurice Utrillo [signature]

Maurice Utrillo

Raoul Dufy [signature]

Raoul Dufy

Georges Rouault [signature]

Georges Rouault

Salvador Dali [signature]

Salvador Dali

Alberto Giacometti [signature]

Alberto Giacometti

Calder [signature]

Alexander Calder

but letters can usually, though not immediately, be found. The same is true of **Raoul Dufy**, whose bright and colorful works did much to popularize fauvism. Letters of Dufy, however, are generally less valued by collectors than those of Matisse. Letters of **Maurice Utrillo**, famous for his Parisian street scenes, is in the same category; they are not rare but not necessarily readily available. **Georges Rouault** is yet another artist whose autograph material can be collected but it is frequently not available. **Salvador Dali**, the Spanish surrealist, like Chagall, was happy to sign prints of his works for collectors. I recall collectors telling me that they waited outside the St. Regis Hotel in New York where Dali lived and prevailed on him to sign batches of prints when he came out. Today, these have found a strong market with collectors at a time when many of the signed limited editions have been brought into question. Letters by Dali are very rare. **Alberto Giacometti** is quite rare in letters, and collectors are always seeking examples by this interesting sculptor.

Autograph material of **Alexander "Sandy" Calder**, the creator of mobiles, is occasionally available when a group of letters is found, but generally Calder material does not create as much interest as that of most of the other artists we have discussed.

23

AMERICAN LITERATURE

Letters and manuscripts in the field of American literature have been very aggressively and systematically collected by a number of institutional libraries. Many of these collections were originally formed by private collectors and either given to institutions or purchased by them. The largest collection of American literature ever formed is that of Clifton Waller Barrett, which he gave to the University of Virginia. The magnitude and importance of the Barrett collection are almost beyond comprehension in terms of today's market, and it is difficult for me to recall the days when an average monthly sale to Barrett would comprise hundreds of letters and manuscripts. Another literary collection formed in the early 1960s was that of DeCoursey Fales, which he gave to New York University. Fales, who collected letters and manuscripts of many of the authors Barrett did not specialize in, was also able to acquire authors' letters and manuscripts in great quantities. It was not uncommon for an invoice to Barrett or Fales to be ten to twelve pages long, each page listing about fifty individual pieces.

During the 1960s, the money available for university research collections greatly increased as the enrollments of graduate schools soared, and university libraries started programs to collect papers of authors that other institutions had not focused on. (There were, however, many rivalries and many authors' papers are split among several institutions.) This was also the decade when the Humanities Research Center at the University of Texas was built. The center formed an extraordinary collection of literary papers, focusing on authors born after 1850, in the most systematic and aggressive manner possible, seeking all the papers of every major and minor author of modern times. They contracted with many authors to buy all of their own papers and then contacted everyone with whom the authors corresponded in order to obtain those letters as well. The Humanities Research Center, now renamed the Harry Ransom Humanities Research Center, is a monument to foresight.

The 1960s was also a time when living authors could take a full tax deduction for the fair market value of their own papers, and virtually everyone who had published a few books had university libraries pursuing them. All of this explains why literary manuscripts are virtually nonexistent on the market and why correspondences and series of letters are also very rarely available, even those of minor authors.

Yet it is still possible to collect the letters of many leading authors in American literature. Cutbacks in university budgets have prevented these institutions from continuing their aggressive acquisition of material, and new items that are found today almost always find homes in private collections.

The first American novelist to gain an international reputation was **Charles Brockden Brown**, whose Gothic romances in the late eighteenth century secured him a place in literary history, if not literary taste. His letters are extremely rare and virtually unobtainable. Another writer who achieved international recognition was **Noah Webster**, whose *Compendious Dictionary of the English Language* was first published in 1806. His autograph material is rare in anything but signatures, and even these are not often available.

One of America's early poets, **Francis Scott Key**, was principally a lawyer, and he was in the right place at the right time to write *The Star-Spangled Banner* as British shells were fired at Fort McHenry during the War of 1812. His legal letters and documents are scarce but available. **Washington Irving** gained a great national and international reputation in the 1820s for his short stories, essays, and novels. His letters have been very popularly collected by institutions, and, although not common, examples can be found. It is also possible to acquire an original page of the manu-

Charles Brockden Brown

Noah Webster

Francis Scott Key

Washington Irving

script of the *History of the Life and Voyages of Christopher Columbus*; the complete manuscript was broken up and sold individually many decades ago.

Letters of **James Fenimore Cooper**, who was the first popular novelist to use the American frontier as a setting for his literature, in, for example, *The Deerslayer,* have also been very popularly collected by institutions but can be obtained by collectors today, although he is most commonly available in signed checks. Autograph material of **Nathaniel Hawthorne** has been very aggressively collected by institutions and private collectors. Hawthorne's letters are very rare and hardly ever offered for sale. Fortunately, the author of *The Scarlet Letter* and *The House of Seven Gables* also served as the American consul in Liverpool, and documents signed by him in that capacity do come onto the market. Autographs of **Edgar Allan Poe**, who lived a brief life (forty years), are among the greatest rarities in the American literary field. The author of *The Raven* was not well known in his lifetime, and very aggressive collecting by Richard Gimbel has resulted in Poe letters being almost unobtainable.

Another major author whose autograph material is very rare and in great demand is **Henry David Thoreau**. His letters are almost never seen, and the only autograph material available has been manuscript pages that were sold to collectors around the turn of the century. He is very popular, especially since his principal work, *Walden,* is even more relevant today than when he wrote it in 1854. Letters of Thoreau's friend, **Ralph Waldo Emerson**, the transcendental essayist and poet, are much more available but almost exclusively concern social affairs. Letters of substance were acquired long ago by institutions.

Herman Melville is an excellent example of a writer who was not well recognized in his lifetime and whose letters became very rare after his death. Melville's autographs, in fact, border on being uncollectable. His masterpiece, *Moby Dick,* was not appreciated by readers until generations later, and therefore there was no

James Fenimore Cooper

Nathaniel Hawthorne

Edgar Allan Poe

Henry David Thoreau

Ralph Waldo Emerson

Herman Melville

Harriet Beecher Stowe

Julia Ward Howe

My country, 'tis of thee,
Sweet land of liberty,
Of thee I sing;
Land where my fathers died,
Land of the pilgrims' pride,
From every mountain side
Let freedom ring;
S. F. Smith.

Samuel Francis Smith,
signed handwritten transcript of "America"

Walt Whitman

Henry Wadsworth Longfellow

John Greenleaf Whittier

Oliver Wendell Holmes

Emily Dickinson

interest in his genius until decades after his death. **Harriet Beecher Stowe**, however, was very well known for her novel, _Uncle Tom's Cabin_ (first published in 1851), and signed many cards, quotations, and letters. Her autograph material is very popular but can almost always be found in the form of signed cards.

Letters of the author of one of America's most popular songs, **Julia Ward Howe**, are generally common, but quotations from her very famous creation, "The Battle Hymn of the Republic," are rare. Letters of another author of a patriotic song, **Samuel Francis Smith**, are about as common, but excerpts from his famous work, "My Country, 'Tis of Thee," are scarce and popular with collectors.

The letters and manuscripts of **Walt Whitman**, the author of _Leaves of Grass_ (1855), have been very extensively collected by Charles Feinberg (whose collection is now at the Library of Congress) and by Waller Barrett. Whitman letters are very rare and anything signed by him infrequently seen. Signed photographs are the most frequently encountered. Autograph material of **Henry Wadsworth Longfellow**, one of the most popular poets of his day, is very common in signatures but has become scarce in letters. His papers have been very extensively collected by institutions and individuals. Autograph material of **John Greenleaf Whittier** has also been extensively collected, particularly because of his Quaker beliefs. Ordinary letters and signatures are available, but important letters are not, as these have been collected by institutions. **Oliver Wendell Holmes**, a physician who became known as a writer after the publication of _The Autocrat at the Breakfast Table_ (1858), is very common in social letters, rare in letters on medical subjects, and scarce in quotations from his poems.

Among the rarest American literary autographs are those of **Emily Dickinson** who led a reclusive life, publishing only seven poems during her lifetime (six volumes were published posthumously). Anything in her hand (notes and letters are usually unsigned) is extremely rare. Material of **Louisa May Alcott**, author of *Little Women* (1868), was scarce and has now become rare because of a specialist collector who has been acquiring all of the letters offered. Signature cards and occasionally pages of manuscripts are infrequently offered.

Eugene Field is known as the author of many children's verses, such as "Little Boy Blue." His autograph material is fairly common though it is not in the category of the autograph material of Oliver Wendell Holmes. **Horatio Alger** has become a part of American folklore, and his name is familiar from his enormously popular boys' books, over one hundred of which were written. Alger's autographs are rare; signatures can be found, but letters are very infrequently seen. Another turn-of-the-century author who was enormously popular but whose autograph material is very rare is **William Sydney Porter**, who wrote under the name O. Henry. Letters are very infrequently offered; more available are manuscript pages from one of his short stories, but these have become rare as well.

Samuel L. Clemens, who used the pseudonym Mark Twain, is the most popular author of the late nineteenth and early twentieth century, both with the general public and with collectors. He gave many signature cards to admirers (signed with both names) and wrote many letters, but they have been very aggressively collected by many institutions and private collectors. Letters are generally available, as are signatures, and signed photographs are very rare. Also rare are pages from original manuscripts, several of which Clemens broke up and distributed in editions of his books. Autograph material of **Stephen Crane**, author of *The Red Badge of Courage,* is extremely rare, and anything in his hand is nearly unobtainable. He died before the age of thirty.

Lafcadio Hearn was an American writer who moved to Japan at age thirty and subsequently became a Japanese citizen. His material has been aggressively collected by the Japanese and is very rarely seen on the

Louisa May Alcott

Eugene Field   Horatio Alger

Variant signatures of William Sydney Porter

Samuel L. Clemens

Stephen Crane

Lafcadio Hearn

Henry James

Edith Wharton

Jack London

Upton Sinclair

Theodore Dreiser

Cordially,

Edgar Rice Burroughs

Hart Crane

F. Scott Fitzgerald

American market. Autograph material of **Henry James**, an American who spent most of his life in Europe, is much more common, but it has also been aggressively acquired by many collectors. While social letters may be found, frequently of almost unbelievable length, letters with any other content are rare.

Edith Wharton's novels reflect a great sense of their period, painting a very poignant picture of the lifestyles she portrayed. Her sensitivity to the psychology of the society about which she wrote was exemplified in _Age of Innocence,_ always a popular novel but more recently a very successful movie. Although interest in Wharton has always been very strong, her letters are obtainable but less and less frequently seen.

The chronicler of the Klondike gold rush, **Jack London**, is best known for his novel _The Call of the Wild._ His autograph can generally be found only in signed checks; occasionally a letter or signed photograph will be offered, but these are rare, and he is very popular with collectors.

Upton Sinclair wrote one of the most enduring works of the muckrakers, _The Jungle,_ published in 1906. He lived to ninety years of age (I was amazed to meet him at a reception at Indiana University in the 1960s), and his letters are very common, although those with literary content find an immediate market with libraries. Autograph material of **Theodore Dreiser**, who published _Sister Carrie_ in 1911, is generally available in social and business letters but not in significant literary letters. The latter are very rarely seen. Autographs of the creator of Tarzan, **Edgar Rice Burroughs**, are also generally available but are not common. His autograph material is very popular with collectors.

Hart Crane did not live past the age of thirty-three, and his autographs are very rarely seen. **F. Scott Fitzgerald** also had a brief life (forty-four years), and his letters are quite scarce though they can be found. Autograph material of the chronicler of the Jazz Age is very popular with collectors, and anything referring to _The Great Gatsby_ would be very rare.

Ernest Hemingway's letters have been aggressively collected by many institutions and private collectors, but many are still available today from correspondences that have recently turned up. Hemingway was also asked for autographs when people met him, frequently in a bar, and these are occasionally available; the most appropriate, for his personality, are those written on bar coasters or bullfight programs. Hemingway's checks also infrequently appear for sale.

Though his works were very popular, particularly in motion picture versions, **Dashiell Hammett** was far less well known during his lifetime. Autographs of the creator of *The Maltese Falcon* and *The Thin Man* are rarely seen. Slightly more available is material of **Raymond Chandler**, the creator of Philip Marlowe and such masterpieces as *Farewell My Lovely*. A series of letters concerning his finances and taxes was sold some years ago, but if it were not for this group, his letters would be very rare. **Zane Grey** is one of the most important novelists of the American West, and his autograph material is generally available in some form, usually letters, signed checks, or photographs.

Autograph material of **Edna St. Vincent Millay** is much rarer and hardly ever seen on the market. Letters of **H. L. Mencken**, however, a master of wit and satire in both his articles and letters, are frequently seen. **Henry Miller** also wrote many letters. While Miller's papers have been extensively collected by institutions, material of this pioneer writer on sexual themes (*Tropic of Cancer* and *Tropic of Capricorn*) can usually be found in letters written late in his life.

Margaret Mitchell wrote one of America's most famous novels, but she was struck and killed by a car before she could write a sequel. *Gone With the Wind* captured the imagination of the country, and it continues to fascinate the public. Mitchell's material is very popular among collectors, and her typewritten letters find an immediate market. **Thomas Wolfe**, author of *Look Homeward, Angel,* also died quite young, and anything written by him is rare.

Ernest Hemingway

Dashiell Hammett

Raymond Chandler

Zane Grey

Edna St. Vincent Millay

H. L. Mencken

Henry Miller

Margaret Mitchell

Thomas Wolfe

Eugene O'Neill

Ezra Pound

Gertrude Stein

John Steinbeck

William Faulkner

J. D. Salinger

William Carlos Williams

Tennessee Williams

Carl Sandburg

Eugene O'Neill, one of the most prominent American playwrights of his time, wrote few letters; they are very scarce but can be found. **Ezra Pound** was a very influential writer who clouded his literary reputation with broadcasts made from Italy in support of Mussolini's Fascist regime. His letters are scarce but generally available, if not easily comprehended. **Gertrude Stein** also spent the war years in Europe, and her autograph material is scarcer than Pound's and has been more collected by institutions. However, it can usually be found without much difficulty.

Autograph material of the chronicler of America's Great Depression of the 1930s, **John Steinbeck**, can most easily be found in signed cards, but letters also come onto the market. Many have been and continue to be acquired by institutions, but the persistent collector can find a fine example for his collection. The same is not true of **William Faulkner**, whose letters are very rare, as is anything other than a signed book. Despite his long life, extremely few letters ever are offered for sale. A similar situation exists with the autograph material of **J. D. Salinger**; anything signed by him is very rare. Material of **William Carlos Williams** is much less rare and in much less demand, except for important literary letters.

Tennessee Williams's pre-eminence as a playwright has made him a very popular personality with collectors. Although his autograph material is not usually available (the University of Texas has his papers) except in signed programs, letters can be found over time. Anything relating to _Cat on a Hot Tin Roof_ or _A Street Car Named Desire,_ such as a program, is very rare. The autograph material of **Carl Sandburg**, noted for his poetry and biography of Lincoln, has

Robert Frost

Langston Hughes

MUSETTE PUBLISHERS • NEW YORK

found much less interest among collectors and is quite commonly available. Also common at one time, but now collected by many people, is material of **Robert Frost**. This great poet of New England subjects has a large following, a situation that makes his interesting autograph examples somewhat hard to find.

As a black writer, **Langston Hughes** has a large following, and his autograph material is generally available. **Truman Capote** was a pioneer of the nonfiction novel, most notably *In Cold Blood*. His material is extremely popular with collectors and not as readily available as his very public life would suggest.

Truman Capote

24

ENGLISH LITERATURE

Francis Bacon

John Locke

Daniel DeFoe

Jonathan Swift

Alexander Pope

Henry Fielding

Samuel Johnson

English literature was the most popular area of American collecting in the early decades of the twentieth century, and many major collectors, most notably Henry E. Huntington, established very important research libraries containing extensive archival collections. With relatively few exceptions, all major manuscripts in English literature are in English and American institutions. Nevertheless, there are still letters available, at varying degrees of frequency, of most of the major English authors; even though institutions kept buying aggressively until a decade or so ago, more recently discovered letters have gone into private collections.

One of the earliest major writers whose documents are possible to acquire is **Francis Bacon**, the philosopher and author. While extremely rare, examples can be obtained over time if one is patient. Autograph material of **John Locke**, the philosopher and author of *An Essay Concerning Human Understanding,* is also very rare; but letters can, on infrequent occasions, be acquired.

Documents of the novelist **Daniel DeFoe**, author of *Robinson Crusoe,* are extremely rare, as are those of **Jonathan Swift**, author of *Gulliver's Travels.* Documents and letters of the poet **Alexander Pope**, who wrote *The Rape of the Lock,* are more available than those of any of the authors above, but they are still only rarely offered for sale. When something does appear, it is usually in the form of a partly printed signed document. Autographs of **Henry Fielding**, author of *Tom Jones,* are extremely rare. Only a few pieces signed by him have been offered in recent decades. Letters of **Samuel Johnson** have been actively collected, and virtually all letters are now in permanent collections. His biographer, **James Boswell**, is only slightly less rare in letters, but Boswell material is definitely more obtainable than that of Johnson.

The national poet of Scotland, **Robert Burns**, is very rare in letters or documents and extremely rare in manuscripts (refer to my book on forgery detection for a complete discussion of the forgeries of Burns). Autograph material of **John Keats**, the poet who died at the age of twenty-six, is virtually uncollectable. The appearance on the market of anything in his handwriting, even a few lines from a letter, is extremely rare. Letters or documents of **Lord Byron**, who outlived Keats by only a few years, is more available, but almost all of his letters and manuscripts are already in institutional libraries. Nevertheless, it is possible over time to acquire a piece in his handwriting. Documents of **Percy Bysshe Shelley**, one of the great romantic poets, are occasionally available although they are certainly rare. Shelley letters, very infrequently offered for sale, are also very rare.

Sir Walter Scott, the great novelist of the period, can be found in letters, and although many have been collected by institutions, they are much more readily available than those of any previously discussed author. Collectors should be aware of the proficiency of "Antique" Smith in forging Scott's letters (see my book on forgery detection). Letters of **William Wordsworth**, the great romantic poet of this period, are much scarcer and much less frequently offered than Scott's letters. Many of his letters were written and signed for him by his wife, Mary, whose handwriting resembled his.

Autograph material, including signatures, of either Emily Brontë, the author of *Wuthering Heights,* or her sister, **Charlotte Brontë**, author of *Jane Eyre,* is very rare. Collectors desiring material of the Brontë sisters should act immediately if they are offered any opportunity to acquire a piece in their handwriting. Letters of **Thomas De Quincey**, author of *Confessions of an English Opium Eater,* are rare; for a time it was possible

James Boswell

Robert Burns

John Keats

Lord Byron

Percy Bysshe Shelley

Sir Walter Scott

William Wordsworth

Charlotte Brontë

Thomas De Quincey

Charles Dickens

Robert Browning

Elizabeth Barrett Browning

William Makepeace Thackeray

Thomas Carlyle

Alfred Lord Tennyson

Gerard Manley Hopkins

to acquire extracts of articles and drafts of letters, but these seem to have been almost completely absorbed into institutional collections.

The literary giant of the age, **Charles Dickens**, was so well known in his lifetime and the decades after his death that everyone saved his letters and the souvenir signatures he gave to his readers and admirers. His material has been very aggressively collected by institutions, and he is one of the most popularly collected personalities of Western literature. His letters are, however, generally available; and on rare occasions, a letter mentioning one of his major works may be found.

Robert Browning was one of the most popular poets of the century, and his letters have been very systematically collected for decades by the Baylor University Library. Other letters do come onto the market and can be obtained, though Baylor's collecting has made all of the letters of this poet scarce. Autograph material of his wife, **Elizabeth Barrett Browning**, author of *Sonnets from the Portuguese,* is much rarer; her letters, written in her delicate calligraphy, are rarely seen on the market.

Autograph material of **William Makepeace Thackeray** is much more available, and in recent years fewer collectors have been interested in this once very popularly collected author. A letter with important content would, however, be a real rarity on the market, and it would command immediate interest. Autograph material of **Thomas Carlyle**, the great historian and essayist, has also been very much collected in the past, and few letters are seen today. Short notes signed by him are more commonly available.

Autograph material of the poet laureate of much of the second half of the nineteenth century, **Alfred Lord Tennyson**, is also generally available in social and business letters but very rarely in letters concerning his poetry. Signed checks are also commonly available. At the opposite end of the rarity and popularity scale are letters of **Gerard Manley Hopkins**, a Jesuit priest who wrote extraordinarily fine poems. All but some immature verses and original Latin poems were published posthumously. Letters by him are extremely rare. Autograph material of the creator of *Treasure Island*, **Robert Louis Stevenson**, has been actively collected by several institutions, and today few letters are seen on the market. Documents do, however, turn up, and they can be acquired by collectors. **Charles L. Dodgson**, the Oxford mathematician who created the great children's classics *Alice's Adventures in Wonderland* and *Through the Looking Glass,* wrote under the pen name Lewis Carroll. Dodgson's letters concerning university matters are much more common than those dealing with literary matters, but neither are common. Most charming, and rare, are those written to little girls, giving a glimpse into the writing that culminated in his famous children's books.

Toward the end of the nineteenth century, **Oscar Wilde**'s conviction and imprisonment were the talk of the time, and the tragedy that befell the Irish poet and dramatist must have contributed to his shortened life span. Letters of the author of *The Importance of Being Earnest* are occasionally available but very popular with collectors, and brief social notes are the only pieces seen, virtually all other letters having been already acquired by institutions. The later nineteenth century also saw **Wilkie Collins** emerge as one of the finest of mystery writers. His letters are scarce but available.

In the last decade of the nineteenth century, Sir **Arthur Conan Doyle** began one of the most extraordinary detective series ever conceived, centering around the fictional character, Sherlock Holmes of Baker Street. Doyle's letters are scarce, and any mentioning Holmes would be exceedingly rare. Also of great interest to collectors are those letters concerning psychic phenomena, a subject that interested Doyle later in his life. Doyle's secretary made a conscious effort to imitate her employer's signature, and his letters must be examined with care for this reason.

Rupert Brooke, a poet extraordinaire killed in the trench warfare of World War I, was symbolic of the

Robert Louis Stevenson

Charles L. Dodgson

Lewis Carroll,
Dodgson's pen name

Oscar Wilde

Wilkie Collins

Sir Arthur Conan Doyle

Rupert Brooke

A. E. Housman

Rudyard Kipling

George Bernard Shaw

John Galsworthy

Joseph Conrad

Thomas Hardy

D. H. Lawrence

destruction of an entire generation of young English and French men. His letters, frequently written on postal cards, are rarely seen. A poet who enjoyed a more normal life span, **A. E. Housman,** author of *A Shropshire Lad,* is frequently available in letters, though (like virtually everyone of the period) his autograph material has been heavily collected.

One of the most popular writers of the early twentieth century, **Rudyard Kipling,** is well known for a poem that includes the line "If you can keep your head when all about you are losing theirs. . . ." Typewritten letters, generally available, are quite popular with collectors. Kipling enjoyed a large public following, and he signed many cards for admirers.

George Bernard Shaw seems to have produced more writing—in all forms—than any other writer in the twentieth century. Shaw's letters are rarely dull; they are brief and concise and sometimes very sarcastic or outright nasty. Most are written on postal cards, where only a few sentences are needed to convey an idea that would take Henry James or Marcel Proust ten or twelve pages to articulate. Shaw material is enormously popular with both institutional and private collectors because of his literary importance and the enticing content of his notes and letters. A selection of pieces is usually available for collectors.

Letters of **John Galsworthy,** the creator of the *Forsyte Saga* trilogy, are barely collected today except for important ones. In his day, Galsworthy's material was extremely popular, like that of Arnold Bennett, and its decline in popularity is an important lesson for collectors concerned with future value.

Joseph Conrad, who capitalized on his background of life at sea for the setting of such novels as *Victory* and *Lord Jim,* is scarce in letters. They have been aggressively collected and are increasingly less frequently seen. Letters of **Thomas Hardy,** author of *Far from the Madding Crowd,* have also become quite scarce because of the interest of many specialist collectors.

One of the most controversial English writers of the early twentieth century, **D. H. Lawrence,** is obtainable but rare in autograph material. Letters of this novelist, who explored the role of sex in human affairs (notably in *Sons and Lovers*), have been very actively collected, particularly by the University of Texas, and few ever come onto the market. The same is true of **T. E. Lawrence**, author of *The Seven Pillars of Wisdom,* a book that describes his role in leading the Arab revolt against the Turks. Letters of Lawrence (later known as T. E. Shaw) are rare, and virtually all of the more important ones are in institutional or private collections. The letters of **James Joyce**, who explored consciousness in *Ulysses* and *Finnegans Wake,* are also largely in institutional collections, and they are very rarely offered for sale.

The letters of **Virginia Woolf** provide relief for collectors as they can be more readily found, though they are scarce and a great number are signed with her first name or initial only. Material of the creator of fantastic science fiction romances, **H. G. Wells**, has also been actively collected by institutions, but many letters are still found, and they are generally available at reasonable prices. Autograph material of **John Masefield**, England's poet laureate from 1930 to 1967, is much more common; it has generally been neglected by institutional and private collectors. While letters concerning his main topic, the sea, are not commonly seen, others are available at very reasonable prices. This is not the case with the Irish poet and dramatist, **William Butler Yeats**, whose letters are much more in demand; many of them have been collected by institutions, including Emory University in Atlanta.

Max Beerbohm, the important critic and caricaturist, is generally available in letters but not in caricatures. Letters of **George Orwell**, the author of the classic novels *1984* and *Animal Farm,* are much rarer. Orwell had a relatively brief life, and his letters, always typewritten, are not often seen for sale. This is not the situation with **E. M. Forster**, author of *A Passage to India*, who is commonly available in handwritten letters. **Somerset Maugham**'s letters are

T. E. Lawrence

T. E. Lawrence,
signed T. E. Shaw

James Joyce

Virginia Woolf

H. G. Wells

John Masefield

William Butler Yeats

Max Beerbohm

George Orwell

E. M. Forster

William Somerset Maugham

P. G. Wodehouse

T. S. Eliot

Dylan Thomas

Robert Graves

Brendan Behan

Samuel Beckett

Dorothy L. Sayers

Agatha Christie

Ian Fleming

also commonly available, but these usually only discuss social and business affairs. Letters of the author of *Of Human Bondage* have been actively collected, but his long life resulted in many examples that survive today. Also relatively available are letters of the humorist **P. G. Wodehouse**.

T. S. Eliot, an American expatriate who moved to London, is usually available in letters concerning the affairs of Faber & Faber, the publishing house where he worked as an editor and of which he was a partner. Autograph examples of **Dylan Thomas**, the Welsh poet, are much scarcer than those of Eliot; he is only seen in handwritten letters, almost always having something to do with his work. His early death at the age of forty-one and the interest of institutions in collecting his papers have certainly made them more difficult to obtain than those of his contemporaries. A poet who enjoyed a much longer life was **Robert Graves**, and his letters, though actively collected as well, can usually be found. **Brendan Behan**'s situation is more similar to Dylan Thomas's; both had short lives, and like Thomas's autographs, those of the author of *Borstal Boy* are rare in letters or anything else signed by him. **Samuel Beckett**, who lived into his eighties, was the Irish critic and playwright whose writings on existential philosophical thought made an important contribution to twentieth century literature. He wrote many notes and brief letters that are usually available.

The great English tradition of mystery writing, begun by Wilkie Collins and brought to its height by Doyle, was continued by **Dorothy Sayers**, whose letters, while they can be found, are not common, and by **Agatha Christie**, whose material is both more available (in signed cards) and in much more demand. Christie's letters, when available, rapidly disappear into collections. **Ian Fleming**, who worked for the British secret service in World War II, used his experiences to create the most popular modern spy series. Fleming's central character, James Bond, has become a part of modern culture, but his letters, unfortunately, have become a part of very few collections; they are surprisingly rare.

212

25

FRENCH LITERATURE

French literature, like French history, offers many collecting opportunities not available in American and English literature. It is still possible to assemble a collection of interesting letters by many French authors, and even manuscripts can occasionally be found. Many major private French collections were formed in the United States after World War II, but American institutions (with some exceptions, such as Harvard) did not focus on French literature when funds were available. These French collections, when offered for sale, have found their primary market among American private collectors, with the result that collectors have opportunities each time a collection is offered. (Similar material offered in France faces strict export controls and preemption by the French government.)

Nevertheless, seventeenth-century French literature is virtually uncollectable. Examples of Jean Molière and Jean Racine are unobtainable, while those of the Marquise de Sévigné and Jacques Bossuet are nearly so. Documents of **Jean de La Fontaine**, author of the famous *Fables,* are extremely rare.

In the eighteenth century, the Age of Enlightenment influenced intellectual thinking in literature, philosophy, art, and politics, and literary output had a particularly philosophical aspect. Four writers dominated this period of rationalization: Denis Diderot, Montesquieu, Jean Jacques Rousseau, and François Voltaire. **Diderot** and the others who collaborated with him on his *Encyclopédie* (notably Jean d'Alembert) created one of the most noteworthy works of French literary history. Diderot's letters are very rare, and he very rarely signed any of them. Those of d'Alembert are more readily found but are certainly not common. Letters of **Montesquieu** are usually in the form of unsigned drafts, and even these are now rarely seen for sale.

Jean de La Fontaine

Denis Diderot

Montesquieu

Jean Jacques Rousseau

François Voltaire

Marquis de Sade

Comte de Mirabeau

Caron de Beaumarchais

François de Chateaubriand

Alphonse de Lamartine

Victor Hugo

Rousseau's letters and documents are very rare, but his autograph material can be obtained in the form of a manuscript page, a group of which was broken up and sold individually some time ago. One of these pages represents an excellent example of an otherwise extremely rare autograph. **Voltaire**'s long life and many involvements led to many letters, but many European libraries have collected them for decades, and his material is not common, though a fine example can sometimes be acquired.

One of the late eighteenth century's more colorful literary figures was the **Marquis de Sade**, whose own personal life was virtually chronicled in his works. His erotic novel, *Justine,* published in 1791, described activities that became known by a term derived from the author's own name, sadism. De Sade's letters, again, usually unsigned, are rare but obtainable; signed ones are very rare. Another interesting figure was the **Comte de Mirabeau**, the great orator of the French Revolution. Mirabeau's autograph material can be found with some patience. Documents or letters of **Caron de Beaumarchais**, author of *The Barber of Seville* (which inspired Rossini) and *The Marriage of Figaro* (which inspired Mozart), are very rare in anything literary but can be found in letters relating to his financial work for King Louis XVI.

Nineteenth-century French literature begins to offer many more collecting opportunities. The early years are dominated by the romantic movement, two of the authors of this period being **François de Chateaubriand** and **Alphonse de Lamartine**. They held government positions and created many letters and documents, although their letters concerning literature are rarely seen. Neither of these is expensive or generally difficult to locate.

Perhaps the most important writer of the mid-nineteenth century, and a leader of the romantic movement, was **Victor Hugo**. Banished from France in 1851 by Napoleon III (he returned from exile in 1870), Hugo wrote many of the most important works of the time, including the still very popular work *Les*

Misérables. His letters are usually available, but those with literary content are rare. Manuscript fragments, mostly notes, can also sometimes be found. Hugo's contemporary, **Alexandre Dumas père**, was both a novelist and playwright. Many of his works have also continued to be popular, including *The Count of Monte Cristo* and *The Three Musketeers*. Dumas material is frequently available in letters and also in short manuscripts of articles written for various publications. His son, known as **Dumas fils**, was also a playwright and novelist, and his material is more common and in less demand.

The greatest novelist of the period and one of the founders of realism in novels, **Honoré de Balzac**, is in tremendous demand, particularly in France, and his letters, while many were written, are very difficult to find. Anything mentioning his masterpiece, *La Comédie Humaine,* would be extremely rare. Autograph material of another important romantic novelist of the earlier nineteenth century, **Stendhal** (pseudonym, of Marie Henri Beyle), is not in as much demand as that of Balzac but is, in fact, much rarer and very infrequently seen. One of the most interesting novelists of the mid-century, **George Sand**, is much more available in letters. Noted for her individual, personal style as well as her writing, Sand carried on extensive correspondences, and while very popular among collectors in many countries, her letters can usually be found without difficulty. **Gustav Flaubert**, the pioneer of realism most noted for his first novel, *Madame Bovary*, is rare in letters, but they can still be found. Manuscripts are occasionally offered, but these are frequently notes from the works of others rather than ideas and thoughts that are his own.

Later in the century **Émile Zola** founded naturalism in French literature, and he is also very actively collected because of his role in the Alfred Dreyfus affair. Dreyfus's letter to a newspaper prompted Zola to write *J'Accuse,* one of the most famous journalistic attacks of all time; it resulted in Zola's flight from France and exile in England. Zola's letters have been actively collected

Alexandre Dumas père

Alexandre Dumas fils

Honoré de Balzac

Stendhal

George Sand

Gustav Flaubert

Émile Zola

Guy de Maupassant [signature]

GUY DE MAUPASSANT   Guy de Maupassant

Jules Verne [signature]

Jules Verne

Baudelaire [signature]

Charles Baudelaire

P. Verlaine [signature]

Paul Verlaine

Paul Valéry [signature]

Paul Valery

Rimbaud [signature]

Arthur Rimbaud

Marcel Proust [signature]

Marcel Proust

André Gide [signature]

André Gide

by many, including Brown University, but they can still be found. Letters of **Guy de Maupassant**, the extraordinary short story writer, are harder to find. His relatively brief life span contributed to this (he was born in 1840 and died in 1893). Another very popular author of the period was **Jules Verne**, who played a leading role in creating the genre of science fiction writing with such works as *Voyage to the Center of the Earth* and *Around the World in Eighty Days*. His letters, never common, have been aggressively collected by French and other European collectors and are now very difficult to find.

Turning from novels to poetry, there is the giant of the age, **Charles Baudelaire**. His volume of verse, *Les Fleurs du Mal,* established his reputation among scholars and readers, and his material is in great demand among collectors. Occasionally, his letters mention his translation into French of Edgar Allen Poe's works, but anything in his hand is, today, very much prized. **Paul Verlaine**, a little later in the nineteenth century, was a leading poet among the symbolists; he was followed by **Paul Valery**. Material of both poets is becoming more difficult to acquire but can still be found. Impossible to obtain is material of **Arthur Rimbaud**, the symbolist poet who died at the age of thirty-seven. I have had only one document by this important poet.

Twentieth-century French literature can be considered to begin with the extraordinary writer of novels and letters, **Marcel Proust**. His masterpiece, *A Remembrance of Times Past,* gives great insight into the complex man, as do his letters. Proust certainly wrote many letters in his relatively brief life span, from 1871 to 1922, but they have been very aggressively collected by many institutions and collectors over the years, including the University of Illinois, and are now very difficult to find. His letters can be interesting, but Proust can also take six pages to discuss why he may or may not want to come to dinner and still not reach a decision! **André Gide** is another important writer of the early part of the twentieth century, and his letters are much more available, though there has always been considerable demand among collectors for them. Letters of **Paul Claudel** are much scarcer but in less demand; and letters of **Romain Rolland** are both more common and in less demand, resulting in unusual opportunities for collectors interested in this significant writer of the earlier twentieth century. **Anatole France** is another important writer of the early twentieth century whose material is relatively common and available. It has not been as avidly collected as the quality of his literature might warrant.

Surrealism is one of the most interesting literary movements of any period. **André Breton** was one of its leaders; he was the author of the dictionary *Manifeste du Surréalisme*, which defined the movement. His letters, appreciated by a relatively small group of collectors, are not as rare as they may be in the future. Much rarer is material of **Guillaume Apollinaire**, an important poet of the early twentieth century associated with the surrealists. Despite the rarity of his letters, the lack of popular interest has resulted in his letters being very reasonably priced, considering his importance.

Autograph material of **Jean Cocteau** is another matter. Cocteau's fairly long life and the fame that he sustained throughout his career resulted in many letters and brief manuscripts, but his popularity has put much of this material into permanent collections. Nevertheless, examples are usually available, and the collector should have a fine selection to choose from. Cocteau's sketches, however, are rare, particularly those of the profile for which he became famous. Between the wars, **Sidonie Gabrielle Colette** was one of the most popular French authors. Her popularity continues to this day, and her letters, while generally available, sell quite readily. **André Malraux** is usually available in routine letters but very rarely in letters of literary significance. Another very important modern French writer, **Albert Camus**, is rare in letters and manuscript fragments. Neither are commonly found, though it is certainly possible to collect material by them.

Paul Claudel

Romain Rolland

Anatole France

André Breton

Guillaume Apollinaire

Jean Cocteau

Sidonie Gabrielle Colette

André Malraux

Albert Camus

217

Jean Paul Sartre

Simone de Beauvoir

Modern French literature evolved into existentialism, a movement founded and enunciated by **Jean Paul Sartre**, whose letters are rare and whose autograph is most likely to be available in an original manuscript page. Sartre parted with many of his drafts of important works, and in the 1960s these were frequently broken up into individual pages for collectors. Autograph material of this important French writer was for some time undervalued because his political views at the time of the Vietnam War were not shared by many collectors, but in recent years he has been seen in a more literary context, and his manuscripts are now rare. Sartre's collaborator in literature and life, **Simone de Beauvoir**, is noted for her work, _The Second Sex_. Her letters are scarcer than Sartre's, and—although they are not in great demand at this time—they may become more difficult to find in the future.

26

EUROPEAN LITERATURE

Letters and documents of many of the interesting and popular authors of the nineteenth and twentieth centuries from other European countries can be collected as well. Failure to include an author here does not mean that his material cannot be collected; an arbitrary line had to be drawn, and I have focused on those who are most inquired about.

Collecting letters and documents of the major figures of German literature and philosophy has always been very popular in the United States as well as in Europe. The German heritage of many successful Americans has certainly played a part in this interest, but of greater importance is the fact that Germany has produced many great writers and philosophers.

Germany's own interest in her literature has always been very strong, and it has never been stronger than in recent decades. During the nineteenth century, major autograph dealers flourished in Germany, ensuring the preservation of letters and documents by making the public aware of their value (Goethe himself was a very active autograph collector). German institutions have always avidly collected the papers of their national writers and, with the exception of the period of the Third Reich and the postwar years, continue to do so. The interest within Germany for letters of authors not as well known outside the country is very strong, and material of these authors is much more commonly offered by German dealers. The major figures, however, have an international following among both readers and collectors.

The eighteenth-century philosopher, **Immanuel Kant**, is the first of the major German philosophers whose documents collectors have a chance of obtaining. His position as a professor at Königsberg caused

Immanuel Kant

Friedrich von Schiller

Johann Wolfgang von Goethe

G. W. F. Hegel

Arthur Schopenhauer

Henri Heine

Heinrich Heine

Wilhelm Grimm

Jacob Grimm

Karl Marx

him to sign various university documents relating to students, and while quite rare, these do infrequently appear. The same is not true with the playwright and poet **Friedrich von Schiller**, whose autographs are extremely rare in any form. (He was also forged in the nineteenth century, and these fabrications are extremely well done; anything purported to be signed by Schiller must be examined with the knowledge that the forgeries are almost always contemporary and the handwriting extremely well accomplished.)

The giant of the age, **Johann Wolfgang von Goethe**, was a true Renaissance man with interests in many fields. These interests led him to write many letters and documents, but they have been very avidly collected both by institutional libraries and private collectors, and the demand for his material is very strong. Pieces signed by him are certainly obtainable, and the prices reflect the international competition for them. (Goethe also signed printed broadsides of his poems that, when offered, are very popular with collectors.) A letter signed with his initial, *G,* as was sometimes his custom, will generally bring less than one signed *Goethe* if the content is similar. **Georg Wilhelm Friedrich Hegel** continued the tradition of philosophical writing, and his letters are extremely rare. However, like Kant at Königsberg, Hegel at Jena University signed various school documents, which makes it possible to obtain his autograph. Both collecting and reading **Arthur Schopenhauer** can lead to pessimism. Letters or notes by him are rare and very infrequently seen.

The poet **Heinrich Heine** probably produced many letters during his lifetime, but nearly all of them seem to have been collected by German institutions, and they are now rarely encountered. Autographs of the authors of *Grimm's Fairy Tales,* the brothers **Jacob** and **Wilhelm Grimm**, are more common but still not readily found. Letters with literary content are very rare.

One German philosophical writer whose material may become more common is **Karl Marx**. For many years, Armand Hammer acquired everything of Marx's that was offered and made gifts of the letters and manuscripts to the Soviets. Without Hammer's aggressive collecting and with the lack of a following for Marx's philosophy, new material coming onto the market may find a substantially reduced collector interest. **Friedrich Nietzsche** is another of the great philosophers whose autographs have been very actively collected by German institutions and private collectors. His letters and documents are very rare.

Autograph material of the poet **Rainer Maria Rilke** is also very avidly collected, though letters are obtainable. (Many of Auguste Rodin's letters are in Rilke's handwriting; Rilke served for years as Rodin's secretary and wrote the text of many of the sculptor's letters.) Also very popularly collected and sometimes obtainable are autographs of **Erich Maria Remarque**, author of *All Quiet on the Western Front.* Autograph material of the Austrian writer **Franz Kafka**, chronicler of the anxieties and alienation of twentieth-century Western society, is extremely rare. One of the major literary figures whose letters and manuscripts are more available is **Hermann Hesse**, who left Germany and became a Swiss citizen. His novels with the theme of man in search of spiritual fulfillment have created a great interest among collectors, particularly in Japan where he is perhaps most popular. Broadsides of his poems signed by him also appear for sale. Another major writer whose autographs are actively collected is **Thomas Mann**, who fled Nazi Germany for the United States in 1938. Letters with literary content are rare and find an immediate market, but a sufficient number of others dealing with minor literary or other affairs are offered to make his autograph material usually available. Autograph material of **Bertolt Brecht**, the German playwright and poet, is much rarer than his career and life would indicate. Very few pieces turn up, and they command appropriate prices.

Russia has produced a number of very important authors in the nineteenth and twentieth centuries.

Friedrich Nietzsche

Rainer Maria Rilke

sincerely yours,

Erich Maria Remarque

Franz Kafka

Hermann Hesse

Thomas Mann

Bertolt Brecht

(signature)
Fyodor Dostoyevsky

(signature)
Aleksandr Pushkin

(signature)

(signature)
Variant signatures of Ivan Turgenev

(signature)
Leo Tolstoy

(signature)
Tolstoy's signature in Russian script

(signature)
Boris Pasternak

(signature)
Niccolò Machiavelli

(signature)
Anton Chekhov

(signature)
Maxim Gorky

Four of the greatest writers of the nineteenth century, **Anton Chekhov**, **Fyodor Dostoyevsky**, Nikolay Gogol, and **Aleksandr Pushkin**, are virtually unobtainable in autograph material, and any opportunity to obtain something signed by any of them is indeed an event. Only slightly less rare are letters of **Maxim Gorky**, the writer who was very involved with Bolshevik politics. Letters of **Ivan Turgenev**, who left Russia and lived in various European capitals, are much more available than letters of his countrymen.

In the twentieth century, autograph material of **Leo Tolstoy**, author of _War and Peace_ and _Anna Karenina_, seems common by comparison; while letters are generally available, demand for them has also been very strong. Material of **Boris Pasternak**, most famous for his novel _Dr. Zhivago_, is very scarce but can be found. His letters are usually very cautiously written and reveal little of himself and his thoughts.

Autograph material of the great Italian writers of the sixteenth century is virtually impossible to obtain. Several times in the past few decades pieces by **Niccolò Machiavelli**, whose name has been synonymous with the intrigues described in _The Prince_, have appeared for sale. They are extremely rare, and an example may not again be offered for decades. At the other end of the chronological spectrum and rarity

222

Gabriel D'Annunzio

scale is material of **Gabriel D'Annunzio**. The decadent poet wrote large numbers of very flowery letters that are readily available today. Interest in D'Annunzio is almost, at this time, overwhelmed by the number of letters he wrote.

Among the major authors of Scandinavian literature, **Hans Christian Andersen**, the Danish writer of fairy tales, is scarce but usually available in letters. Letters or documents of the Norwegian dramatist **Henrik Ibsen** are scarcer. Autographs of Ibsen, like those of Andersen, are popularly collected, but examples can usually be obtained.

Hans Christian Andersen

Andersen's signature in German script

Henrik Ibsen

27

THE PERFORMING ARTS

David Garrick

David Garrick

Henry Irving

Henry Irving

John Wilkes Booth

John Wilkes Booth

Edwin Booth

Edwin Booth

P. T. Barnum

P. T. Barnum

Jenny Lind

Jenny Lind

During the past decade, the interest of collectors in the performing arts of the eighteenth and nineteenth centuries has declined, but many new collectors have specialized in twentieth-century performers. Undoubtedly, the availability of these more recent performers' talents on video and sound recordings has made the difference, while a decline in interest in the earlier performers may in part be because their performances can only be experienced in books. Several institutional theater collections have acquired many of the major eighteenth- and nineteenth-century private collections, and there seems to be very little material available on the market and few collectors seeking it.

Letters and documents of **David Garrick**, the English producer, dramatist, and actor, have usually been the starting point for a collection of theatrical material. Today, Garrick's autographs are very rarely seen. Later in the nineteenth century, **Henry Irving** is the dominant figure, and his letters, of which there are many, are readily available at modest cost.

In the United States, the Booth family was most prominent. Material of **John Wilkes Booth**, the assassin of Abraham Lincoln, is very rare, but that of his brother, **Edwin Booth**, is much more commonly seen. Letters are frequently available; signed photographs can less often be acquired.

The major showman of the nineteenth century, **Phineas T. Barnum**, is generally available in signed cards and letters. Barnum's letters in particular have been actively collected by several institutions and many private collectors. **Jenny Lind**, the Swedish soprano who was brought to America by Barnum, is also popular, though certainly less so than Barnum. Her autograph material can usually be found at reasonable

Sarah Bernhardt (signature)

Sarah Bernhardt

prices, particularly if a letter is signed with her married name, _Jenny Goldschmidt,_ which is considered less desirable among collectors.

Sarah Bernhardt was one of the most popular actresses for decades, and her letters and signed photographs were saved by almost everyone who received them. While she is still quite popular, signed pieces by her are usually available. Somewhat less common is material of Bernhardt's contemporary, the Italian actress **Eleanora Duse**. Very popular with collectors is autograph material of another contemporary, the British actress **Lillie Langtry**, whose letters have become scarce because of her popularity. As with material of Jenny Lind, it is more desirable to have a letter signed _Lillie Langtry_ than one with her married name.

In the field of dance, the early part of the twentieth century saw the rapid emergence and almost equally rapid disappearance of the incomparable **Waslaw Nijinsky**, who performed with **Sergei Diaghilev**'s Ballet Russe. Autographs of Nijinsky, who went insane in 1919, are very rare, and those of Diaghilev are also very rarely available. Material of **Anna Pavlova** is much more frequently seen, almost always in signed photographs of the ballerina in performance or signed album pages. Examples of **Isadora Duncan** are much rarer and are only seen in letters.

Anna Pavlova (signature)

Anna Pavlova

Comedy has always been very popular with audiences and collectors, and in the earlier part of the twentieth century several comedians were particularly prominent. **Stan Laurel** and **Oliver Hardy** jointly signed many photographs for fans, and these, though

Eleanora Duse (signature)

Eleanora Duse

Lillie Langtry (signature)

Lillie Langtry

Waslaw Nijinsky (signature)

Waslaw Nijinsky

Sergei Diaghilev (signature)

Sergei Diaghilev

Isadora Duncan (signature)

Isadora Duncan

Stan Laurel (signature)

Stan Laurel

Oliver Hardy (signature)

Oliver Hardy

Bud Abbott and Lou Costello

Groucho, Chico, Harpo, and Zeppo Marx

W. C. Fields

Will Rogers

Lucille Ball

Harry Houdini

D. W. Griffith

somewhat scarce, can be found today. Much less frequently seen are signed photographs, as indeed anything of **Bud Abbott** and **Lou Costello**. **W. C. Fields** is also very popular with collectors; his material is rare in letters and very scarce in signatures (beware of secretarial ones). The **Marx Brothers** (Chico, Harpo, Groucho, and Zeppo) are very rarely seen in signed photographs or letters bearing all four of their signatures. Examples of individual signatures can be found. Autograph material of **Will Rogers** has been in considerable demand. Signatures on cards are almost the only form found, and they are scarce. Letters are rare, and signed photographs are very rare (nearly all bear a printed signature). Of more recent times, **Lucille Ball** has been highly regarded by fans and collectors. Photographs signed _Love Lucy_ are of very doubtful authenticity, but legal documents or signatures in albums are usually genuine and always popular.

In the field of magic, **Harry Houdini** stands out as the greatest magician of the era. His autograph material is as popular now with collectors as he was popular with his audiences. Houdini's letters and signed photographs have been in great demand and have become difficult to find. Anything at all signed by Houdini is now scarce, particularly his books.

The person considered the single most important figure in the early history of American film is **D. W. Griffith**; his autographs are scarce but can be found. Collector interest is not as strong as one might imagine

Rudolph Valentino [signature]

Rudolph Valentino

for the pioneer of the monumental film, *The Birth of a Nation.*

Autograph material of motion picture stars is an area where the collector must be very cautious. Legal documents and signed album pages, almost always acquired in person, are the safest types of items to collect, whereas signed photographs are always suspect unless there is reason to establish their genuineness. It is unreasonable to believe that movie stars in the prime of their careers had the time to sign the enormous numbers of photographs that have appeared on the market. Nearly all of these were signed by secretaries in response to autograph requests. However, photographs signed after a performer has retired are frequently genuine, as are letters, and many seem to relish the attention paid to them by autograph seekers.

Rudolph Valentino, America's first great matinee idol, unfortunately set the stage both with his own popularity and with the many photographs sent to admirers that are not genuinely signed by him. Valentino's letters are also not usually genuine. **Douglas Fairbanks**, the first of the great swashbuckling heroes, did sign many photographs and autograph albums, and these are generally available as are those of his wife, "America's Sweetheart," **Mary Pickford**. The great Barrymore family is also very popular with collectors, particularly **John Barrymore**, who died at a much younger age than Ethel and Lionel. **Greta Garbo**'s autographs are the great rarity of the prewar period. Even after her death few letters have surfaced, and they have brought very high prices from collectors appreciating the onetime opportunity to obtain them. A collector is fortunate to find a signed card.

Autograph material of **Judy Garland** is scarce, in part because she has been so popularly collected. Examples of **Bela Lugosi** are scarce, as are those of

Douglas Fairbanks [signature]

Mary Pickford [signature] 1926.

John Barrymore [signature]

Greta Garbo [signature]

Judy Garland [signature]

Bela Lugosi [signature]

227

Orson Welles

Boris Karloff

Clark Gable

Vivien Leigh

Laurence Olivier

Cary Grant

Fred Astaire

Basil Rathbone

Errol Flynn

Boris Karloff, but signatures of both can be acquired. Autograph material of **Orson Welles** can usually be found, but anything concerning his masterpiece, _Citizen Kane_, is very rare. Autographs of **Clark Gable** would be much rarer if it were not for a group of signed checks found some years ago. Otherwise, only signed album pages are available. The demand for material signed by the star of _Gone With the Wind_ is very strong. This is also true of his co-star, **Vivien Leigh**, whose autographs are rarer than those of Gable. Her husband, **Laurence Olivier**, one of England's greatest actors, had such a long career, wrote many letters, and signed so many albums that his material is readily available. His autographs are very popular and will eventually be difficult to find.

Signed material of **Cary Grant** is fairly scarce and is found only in album pages. **Fred Astaire** is an example of an important performer who, in retirement, sent admirers genuinely signed photographs. His material is thus much more available to collectors. **Errol Flynn** is usually seen only in signatures, but letters do occasionally surface and are quickly bought by collectors. Material of **Basil Rathbone** can also be found, but a signed photograph as Sherlock Holmes

228

Gary Cooper

Humphrey
Bogart

Cecil B. deMille

Alfred Hitchcock

Mae West

Noel Coward

James Dean

would be very rare. Signatures of **Gary Cooper**, like those of Cary Grant, are available almost exclusively in signed album leaves. Of the popular more modern actors, autograph material of **Humphrey Bogart** is among the rarest and most desirable. His secretary signed his photographs and letters written on postcards, and genuine pieces are seen very infrequently.

Generally, material of the creators of movies are less valuable than those of the performers. This is true with **Cecil B. deMille**, producer of such spectacles as *The Ten Commandments*. DeMille's material is quite inexpensive and always available, usually in signed checks. A director who is popular with collectors is **Alfred Hitchcock**, who occasionally would sign his name and incorporate a drawing of his profile. His material is not readily available but can usually be found.

Mae West is another star who lived long enough in retirement to sign many genuine photographs and other pieces. Her material is usually available and reasonably priced. West continues to be very popular, perhaps because of the image she has come to symbolize rather than because anyone remembers her performances. The actor, playwright, and composer **Noel Coward** has always been very popular, and his signature is very distinctive. His material is commonly available; only very fine signed photographs are rare. Recently, his typewritten letters have been forged, but reliable dealers are aware of this fact. Signatures of **James Dean**, as one would expect, are very rare and in great demand from his many ardent followers. Perhaps the most famous movie star of modern times

Tommy Dorsey

Jimmy Dorsey

Glenn Miller

Enrico Caruso

Maria Callas

Louis Armstrong

Marilyn Monroe

is **Marilyn Monroe**. Many of her photographs were signed by secretaries, but album pages, personal photographs, checks, and contracts, all genuinely signed, are frequently available and command prices commensurate with her enormous popularity.

The leaders of the "Big Bands" are also popular with collectors. Material of the **Dorsey brothers**, Tommy and Jimmy, are usually available, while that of **Glenn Miller**, who was killed in World War II, is particularly popular and scarce.

In the field of opera, one of the most popular singers of all time is **Enrico Caruso**, and the interest of collectors in his material continues today. Letters are fairly common, as are signed cards; signed photographs, depending on their quality, can be relatively expensive. Caricatures drawn by the tenor are very desirable, but most desirable of all are his self-portraits. **Maria Callas** is also very popular with collectors; her material was relatively expensive even before her early death. Signed programs, photographs, and album leaves are likely to be offered, with prices reflecting their scarcity and popularity.

Louis Armstrong, also known as Satchmo, is as popular as jazz itself. He signed many album pages, and they rapidly find homes with admirers. Signed photographs are much scarcer. His material can usually be found, but demand is outpacing the number of new

Josephine Baker
Paris

Josephine Baker

Al Jolson

Al Jolson

Paul Robeson

Paul Robeson

Eddie Cantor

Eddie Cantor

Maurice Chevalier

Maurice Chevalier

Buddy Holly

Buddy
Holly

Elvis Presley

Elvis Presley

pieces being offered for sale. **Josephine Baker**, the jazz singer who became so popular in France that she adopted French citizenship, is much less common in autograph material. **Al Jolson** is very popular, and he can generally be found in signatures. **Eddie Cantor**, who started his career with the Ziegfield Follies, is likewise very popular, but fine examples of his material can usually be found. Material of **Paul Robeson**, perhaps most noted for singing "Ol' Man River," is much scarcer and also popular. **Maurice Chevalier**, the Parisian café singer who was at one time placed on the "death list" of the French resistance for continuing to entertain in Paris during the occupation, is mildly popular with collectors, and his material is generally quite common.

In the area of modern American music, **Buddy Holly**'s autograph material is very scarce because of the plane crash that took his life at an early age. In recent years his family has sold all his memorabilia, including everything from his school homework to his guitar and eyeglasses, but pieces signed by him continue to be rare and very popular. "The King," **Elvis Presley**, is

George Harrison
and Ringo Starr

enormously popular with collectors. Pieces signed for fans can generally be found, but these have a ready group of waiting collectors. The **Beatles**' popularity, like Presley's, continues to be very great. Pages signed by all four rock-and-roll singers can be found, as well as their individual signatures. Programs signed by the four are scarcer, and rarer still are the albums and genuinely signed photographs (many of these, bearing secretarial signatures, were mailed to fans). Fine examples are usually obtainable at prices reflecting their great popularity.

John Lennon and
Paul McCartney

OTHER AREAS

◆

Science

Business & Economics

Adventure & Exploration

Religion

Sports

Varia

28

SCIENCE

In the field of science, collectors have generally collected letters, documents, and manuscripts of specific individuals or those within a specific area of science, for example, medicine, rather than the entire field. Many scientists have been regarded as being among the most important people in history, and their autograph material has been very popularly collected by private collectors, libraries, and museums. Science, like music and art, is an area of great international appeal, and collectors from many countries compete for letters and documents of the same scientists.

Letters and documents of sixteenth-century scientists are virtually unobtainable. Examples of Galileo and Nicolaus Copernicus are exceedingly rare. The earliest of the great scientists whose autograph material is possible to obtain is **Isaac Newton**. Documents signed by him are very rare and less and less frequently seen. Newton's great rival, **Gottfried Wilhelm von Leibniz**, laid the foundation of integral and differential calculus. His documents and letters are much rarer than those of Newton, but they are in somewhat less popular demand.

Documents or letters of the Swedish botanist **Carolus Linnaeus**, who in the eighteenth century established modern systematic botany, are very rare but can be obtained on occasion. In the late eighteenth century, as in other fields of collecting, letters and documents of the major scientists become more available. In the field of chemistry, **Antoine Laurent Lavoisier**, the founder of modern chemistry, lived a relatively short life (it was quite literally cut short by the guillotine during the French Revolution's Reign of Terror). His documents are rare but possible to collect. Also in France, the **Montgolfier brothers**, Joseph and Jacques, were pioneering with balloons and in 1783,

Isaac Newton

Gottfried Wilhelm von Leibniz

Carolus Linnaeus

Antoine Lavoisier

Joseph Montgolfier

Jacques Montgolfier

Joseph Priestley

Humphry Davy

André Ampère

Michael Faraday

Edward Jenner

James Watt

Charles Babbage

Joseph N. Niepce

Alessandro Volta

accomplished the first manned ascent. Letters by both men are rare and infrequently seen on the market.

In England, in the field of chemistry, the clergyman **Joseph Priestley** experimented with gases and discovered oxygen. His letters concerning religion are more common than those on science but are rare nevertheless. This is not the case with **Humphry Davy**, who experimented with the physiological effects of various gases. At this time, his letters are more generally available.

Early in the nineteenth century, experiments in electricity were taking place in many countries. In Italy, **Alessandro Volta** was making great progress toward understanding this new force (the volt is named in his honor), while in France, **André Ampère** formulated the mathematical basis of electrodynamics (the amp is named after him). Letters of Volta are very rare, and he is more likely to be found in documents, while letters of Ampère are only slightly less rare. In England, **Michael Faraday** carried on important electrical experiments; his letters are generally more available and not expensive.

At the end of the eighteenth century, **Edward Jenner** developed his concept of vaccination; his letters are very rarely seen. Letters of **James Watt**, the Scottish scientist who invented the modern condensing steam engine, are also rare but are likely to be encountered over time. (Material of his son and namesake can be mistaken for that of the inventor.) One of the most interesting scientists of the early nineteenth century was **Charles Babbage**, the inventor of a calculating machine that was the forerunner of the computer. His letters are fairly rare; virtually all of them discuss social matters.

France was the setting for the invention of photography. **Joseph N. Niepce** is credited with producing the world's first photograph, and anything signed by him is very rare. Niepce's colleague, **Louis Daguerre**, who worked with Niepce until his death, continued his experiments and developed the Daguerrotype process of photography. Daguerre's material is also rare but more likely to be obtainable than anything of Niepce.

American inventiveness and ingenuity at the turn of the nineteenth century was not lacking. Its applications were based, however, more on practical needs than on theoretical applications. **Eli Whitney** invented the cotton gin to solve a serious problem in cotton processing. His letters, in strong demand from collectors, are scarce though they can be located over time. Letters or documents of **Robert Fulton** are much rarer and more expensive. Not only did Fulton invent submarines but his work with steamboats resulted in the development of the first commercially viable steamboat. His letters are rare mainly because they were aggressively acquired by several private collectors in the past who have given their collections to institutions.

In the 1830s, the artist and inventor **Samuel F. B. Morse** experimented with magnetic telegraphy and on May 24, 1844, sent the world's first message over his line between Washington and Baltimore, "What hath God wrought!" His letters are not rare, as he lived a long life and was very well known in his lifetime. Morse is very popular with collectors. Much rarer is material of the inventor of the vulcanization process, **Charles Goodyear**, whose patent for the process is the basis of the rubber manufacturing industry. Goodyear's autograph material is very rarely seen. Also very rarely seen is material of William T. G. Morton, the dentist who invented the process of using ether for surgical operations (first used on a patient in 1846). A collector desiring something of this interesting inventor should act quickly if material becomes available. In the same year, **Elias Howe** invented the sewing machine, revolutionizing an industry. His letters and documents are also very rare, though it is possible, with great patience, to obtain something signed by him. Another American inventor who responded to a need

Louis Daguerre

Eli Whitney

Robert Fulton

Samuel F. B. Morse

Charles Goodyear

Elias Howe

Richard J. Gatling

Charles Darwin

Alexander Graham Bell

Louis Pasteur

Joseph Lister

Robert Koch

Wilhelm C. Roentgen

George Eastman

was **Richard J. Gatling**, who invented the Gatling gun during the Civil War. His letters are rare, but signed cards are frequently available.

In England, **Charles Darwin** pondered one of the greatest scientific questions, the origin of life, and expressed his ideas in his provocative work, *On the Origin of Species,* published in 1859, which created a storm of controversy. His letters and manuscript pages have been very popular with collectors for decades and have been very actively collected by institutions as well. His letters are very scarce, but an example can usually be found for a collection.

Later in the century, an invention many now consider indispensable, the telephone, was developed in Boston by a teacher of deaf students, **Alexander Graham Bell**. His pioneering experiments with sound led to his receiving a patent for this fundamental invention of modern life. His letters are generally available, as are signatures on cards, though his autograph material is not as common as one might imagine, given his notoriety during and after his lifetime.

In France, **Louis Pasteur** was busily engaged in solving many problems, including those relating to the fermentation of wine and beer and threats to the French silk industry. One of his most notable discoveries was inoculation to protect both man and animals from rabies. His letters, once fairly available, have been very actively collected by many private collectors and institutions and are now difficult to find. In a similar area of scientific research, **Joseph Lister** in England realized that many of the problems of infection could be prevented and founded antiseptic surgery. Increasingly sought after in recent years, Lister's letters are still available, although increasingly less so. Letters of **Robert Koch**, the German bacteriologist of the same period, are very rarely seen. Letters and documents of **Wilhelm C. Roentgen**, the German physician who discovered X-rays in 1895, are also very rare as they have always been in great demand, particularly from collectors whose profession is radiology. Another type of film was developed by **George Eastman**, the inventor of the Kodak box camera. Eastman is found only in signed cards; letters are very rare. The late nineteenth century also saw the discovery by **Nikola Tesla** of the principle leading to alternating current machinery. Despite Tesla's long career, his letters are not common, though they are not in much demand, resulting in their being hard to find but not very expensive when they are found.

   One of the most important and popular personalities in the field of science whose autograph material is also one of the most popularly collected in the whole field of historical letters and documents is **Thomas A. Edison**. Fortunately, Edison's long life span, his instantly recognizable name, and his many business ventures led to the creation and saving of many pieces signed by him. His autograph material has always been very popularly collected, but fine examples are usually available for collectors. Most commonly seen are signatures on checks or on cards. Letters and signed photographs are scarcer. Routine business documents mainly concerning minutes of board of directors meetings have also been available but are not very popular with collectors. The electrical engineer **Charles P. Steinmetz** was overshadowed by Edison in his lifetime and in his popularity with collectors. His letters are rare, and he is more frequently encountered in signed checks. Steinmetz's autograph material is relatively inexpensive. For many years, **Guglielmo Marconi**'s name was synonymous with wireless telegraphy, and his autographs were commonly saved. Marconi is usually found in signed cards or notes, occasionally in a letter or signed photograph.

   Autograph material of **Pierre Curie**, the French chemist known for his work in radioactivity with his wife, **Marie**, is very rare in signed or unsigned letters or manuscripts. (Collectors should be aware of an excellent facsimile of a handwritten and signed letter of Curie dated May 21, 1904, which has frequently been mistaken for a genuine piece.) If the opportunity arises to acquire a Pierre Curie letter or manuscript, the collector should not let it pass by. Letters signed by his

Nikola Tesla

Thomas A. Edison

Charles Steinmetz

Guglielmo Marconi

Pierre Curie

Marie Curie

Wilbur Wright

Wilbur Wright

Orville Wright

Orville Wright

Glenn H. Curtiss

Glenn H. Curtiss

A. Einstein.

Albert Einstein

wife, Marie, the discoverer of radium, are also very rare, but they are not as rare as those of Pierre. She wrote a biography of her husband, *Pierre Curie*, of which there were one hundred limited signed copies. It is in this form that her autograph is most available.

The age of heavier-than-air aviation began with the flight of the **Wright brothers** on December 17, 1903. During the next eight years, Wilbur and Orville toured, mostly in Europe, and occasionally signed postcards at demonstrations of their airplane. Wilbur's early death in May 1912 has caused pieces signed by him to be extremely rare. Orville lived a long life and was very well known. Letters signed by him are rare, but signed envelopes are frequently available and signed checks are plentiful. Orville Wright also signed some photographs of the first flight at Kitty Hawk, and they represent a dramatic link with this momentous event. They are rare and very popular with collectors but are occasionally offered for sale. A contemporary of the Wright brothers, **Glenn H. Curtiss**, invented many aviation devices and was also very popularly known as a pilot in his day. Pieces signed by him are rare, but his material is not nearly as popular with collectors and can usually be found at reasonable prices.

No person has dominated twentieth-century science as much as **Albert Einstein**, and his autograph material is among the most popularly collected. Einstein's letters were, it seems, almost always saved by recipients, and, at the present time, it is possible to obtain letters with interesting content, though their prices reflect the great interest and competition among collectors for them. Handwritten letters are rare; typewritten ones in German are more common. Letters about science are the rarest and most desirable, followed by those concerning Jewish causes. Many letters discuss the refugee problems in the 1930s and reveal the energy Einstein expended to help fellow Jews get out of Germany. Wide variations in prices of letters reflect these differences in content. (Beware of form letters concerning atomic issues as these bear printed signatures.) Photographs signed by Einstein are rarer than his letters; signed sketches of him are much more commonly seen and not nearly as popular with collectors; and signed books are rare but are seen on occasion. Manuscripts are very rare.

Anything in the handwriting of **Robert H. Goddard**, the pioneer experimenter with rockets, is extremely rare. With great patience, it may be possible to find a piece, but a collector is very unlikely to find anything. Autograph material of one of the best-known modern rocket scientists, **Wernher von Braun**, who led the Nazi V2 rocket program and later the American space effort, is scarce but usually available. Letters of the physicist **Robert A. Millikan** can be obtained for relatively modest amounts. Letters or other pieces signed by **Niels Bohr**, the Danish physicist, are much rarer and are avidly sought after by many collectors interested in his nuclear discoveries.

In the field of medicine, Sir **William Osler**'s teachings greatly influenced medical progress, and this is reflected in the popularity of his autograph material among collectors. His letters are scarce but can usually be found. **Florence Nightingale** also had great influence on patient care and hospital reform. Her letters, at one time common, have been actively collected by several institutions and are now much less frequently seen. Letters of **Harvey Cushing**, the neurosurgeon, are also collected, especially by physicians, and though not common, a good typewritten letter signed can usually be found. A very popular person in the field of medicine is Sir **Alexander Fleming**, the Scottish bacteriologist who was one of the discoverers of penicillin. Material signed by him is rare and eagerly sought after. A signature on a card or perhaps a letter may be found, though at increasingly long intervals.

One of the most influential people of the twentieth century has been **Sigmund Freud**, and the interest of collectors in his letters has been very strong. Freud hardly ever gave signatures to admirers, but he wrote many notes and letters in his psychiatric practice.

Robert H. Goddard

Wernher von Braun

Robert A. Millikan

Niels Bohr

Sir William Osler

Florence Nightingale

Harvey Cushing

Sir Alexander Fleming

Sigmund Freud

Carl Jung

Signed photographs are very rare. The prices for Freud material reflect the content of the letters, and it is still possible to obtain a letter with interesting content. Material of **Carl Jung**, the Swiss psychologist and psychiatrist who founded analytic psychology, is also very popular and is scarcer, though in less demand than Freud material. Letters, frequently relating to patients, are occasionally offered at lower prices than comparable letters by Freud.

29

BUSINESS AND ECONOMICS

When I first started in the autograph field in the late 1950s, there was virtually no interest in business leaders and economists, but that changed some years ago, and today it is a very popular field of collecting. The Japanese interest in economics has led to the acquisition of the papers of Western economists by Japanese universities, and letters and documents of leading businessmen are very popularly collected in the United States and Japan.

Letters of **Adam Smith**, author of *Inquiry into the Nature and Causes of the Wealth of Nations,* are now very rarely encountered. The collector, if fortunate, may find a document signed by Smith as commissioner of the customhouse of Edinburgh or as a member of the senate of Glasgow University. Rarer still are letters or documents signed by **Thomas R. Malthus**, whose *Essay on the Principle of Population* gained him a place as a major economic philosopher.

In the nineteenth century, the economist **John Stuart Mill** is most noted for his work *On Liberty*. His letters have been very actively collected by both institutions and private collectors and are now infrequently found.

Autograph material of **John Maynard Keynes**, in the twentieth century, is the most available of all, but only in brief notes or letters. Like his predecessors, he has been very actively collected by Japanese libraries.

In the world of financiers the Rothschild family, founded by Meyer Amschel Rothschild at the end of the eighteenth century, is the most famous banking dynasty. Letters and documents by the founding Rothschild are very rare and examples signed by any of his five sons uncommon. Collectors must beware of routine financial documents that appear to be signed by

Adam Smith

Thomas R. Malthus

John Stuart Mill

John Maynard Keynes

Nathan Meyer Rothschild

John Jacob Astor

Cornelius Vanderbilt

Albert Gallatin

Samuel Colt

Eli Whitney

one of the sons as head of a Rothschild branch but that are actually signed in the name of the firm by a secretary. The most collectable Rothschild is **Nathan Meyer Rothschild**, whose signature appears on a bond of the Imperial Commission of the Sinking Fund. A small group of these were recently discovered; when they are dispersed into collections, the autograph material of Nathan Meyer Rothschild will again be as rare as that of his brothers.

In America, one of the first major business leaders was **John Jacob Astor**, originally a fur trader who started his business in upper New York State, then developed and extended it to the Pacific and later went into New York real estate. His autograph material is scarce in documents and rare in letters. Autographs of his descendants who administered and augmented the Astor fortune are also in demand, but they command considerably lower prices than those of the founder of the dynasty.

Cornelius Vanderbilt, known as "the Commodore," began his empire in the freight and ferry business in New York harbor. His letters and documents, like Astor's, are not common, and anything of substance is very rare. Vanderbilt's descendant and namesake developed the railroads, greatly enhancing the family fortune. His autograph material is more available, particularly in the form of railroad bonds. These ornately engraved documents signed by Vanderbilt were discovered some years ago, dispersed among collectors, and now occasionally reappear on the market.

Albert Gallatin, the brilliant financier who was secretary of the treasury under Jefferson and Madison, wrote many official Treasury Department letters that are commonly available.

Early in the nineteenth century, **Sam Colt** invented the revolver, and his firearms company developed into one of the most famous American businesses. His letters and documents, mainly concerning his business, are rare but occasionally available. Similarly, **Eli Whitney**, whose invention of the cotton gin was not profitable (because of patent infringements), developed a firearms company based on interchangeability of parts. Today his letters are rare but can also be obtained.

Letters of **George Peabody**, the American who went to London and developed a leading financial business there selling American bonds to Europeans, is relatively common and available. In later life Peabody was very involved in charitable work, and between his business correspondence and his charitable involvements, he wrote many letters that survive. Peabody's principal assistant was Junius Spencer Morgan whose son, **Pierpont Morgan**, became the leading financier at the end of the nineteenth century. Morgan's letters are rare, signed photographs very rare. However, the financier would sign cards for admirers, and he also signed various bonds that are generally available and popular with collectors.

Letters of **Jay Cooke**, the banker who helped finance the Civil War and later the Northern Pacific Railroad, are scarce though usually available. **John D. Rockefeller**'s long life did not result in his letters and documents being common. His letters do turn up, but they are in considerable demand. Early material from the decades when Rockefeller was building his empire is very rare.

Letters and documents of **Jay Gould**, whose business ventures were more concerned with stock manipulations than with the organizing or running of companies, is occasionally available either in the form of signed stock certificates or letters. James J. Hill, in many ways the complete opposite of Gould, chose to build railroads rather than speculate in their stock. Hill's letters and documents are quite scarce, and because demand is not as great as for the other railroad barons and financiers, they are more frequently available.

Much rarer is autograph material of the inventor of the McCormick reaping machine, **Cyrus H. McCormick**. Until several years ago when a group of his signed checks appeared on the market, autographs

George Peabody

Pierpont Morgan

Jay Cooke

John D. Rockefeller

Jay Gould

Cyrus H. McCormick

E Howe Jr

Elias Howe

Geo. Westinghouse

George Westinghouse

Andrew Carnegie

Andrew Carnegie

H. C. Frick

Henry Clay Frick

Hetty H R Green

Hetty Green

Mark Hopkins

Mark Hopkins

Leland Stanford

Leland Stanford

Henry Ford

Henry Ford

Harvey S Firestone

Harvey Firestone

of McCormick were among the rarest of the business leaders. Autographs of **Elias Howe**, the inventor of the sewing machine, are very rare, but it is possible, with time, to locate something signed by him.

The inventor of the railroad air brake and other railroad systems, **George Westinghouse**, also founded a company that has become a household name. His autograph material is much scarcer than one might imagine, and signed cards are the only examples a collector can realistically hope to find. **Andrew Carnegie**, in contrast, loved to be in the public eye, and his letters and other signed pieces are usually available. Anything concerning his business dealings would be very rare. Carnegie's partner and the man who received much of the bad publicity during the Homestead strike, **Henry Clay Frick**, was a relative recluse, and his letters and documents are much rarer than those of Carnegie.

Autographs of the "Witch of Wall Street," **Hetty Green**, are among the rarest in this field. Material by her is rarely seen on the market or in collections. Autograph material of the "Big Four" of late nineteenth-century business history is frequently sought by collectors. Material of **Mark Hopkins** is the most common, usually in the form of letters, followed by that of **Collis P. Huntington**, whose letters are rare but whose signed bonds are more frequently found. Material of **Leland Stanford** is rarely found in any form, and that of Charles Crocker is rarer still.

C P Huntington

Collis P. Huntington

The twentieth century saw one of the most important business ideas—the assembly line—developed by **Henry Ford**. Despite his fame and long life, material signed by Ford, while sometimes obtainable, is quite scarce. Equally scarce are autographs of the man who made the inventions and built the company that provided the tires for Ford automobiles, **Harvey S. Firestone**. Anything other than a signature on a card is rare.

In the newspaper industry, **William Randolph Hearst** was building his empire in the early part of the twentieth century. Letters by Hearst are rare and signatures scarce, though usually obtainable.

William Randolph Hearst signature

William Randolph Hearst

Andrew Mellon signature

Andrew Mellon

The financier whose letters and documents are the most common of all those considered here is **Andrew W. Mellon**. Mellon served as secretary of the treasury and in this capacity, signed a great number of official letters. Autographs of his contemporary, **J. Paul Getty**, are only available occasionally, usually a brief letter or a signature on a card.

J. Paul Getty signature

J. Paul Getty

The outstanding recluse among modern businessmen, **Howard Hughes**, is rare in all autograph forms. Letters from his days as an aviator are frequently signed by a secretary, and collectors must be wary.

Howard Hughes signature

Howard Hughes

30

ADVENTURE AND EXPLORATION

Hernando Cortés

David Livingstone

Henry M. Stanley

Richard F. Burton

Edward Whymper

Sir John Franklin

This chapter is concerned with explorers outside of the American West—those who explored the inner regions of Africa, sought out the North and South poles, and explored the limits of aviation. All were adventurers, because to some degree, they were seeking to explore as much for the adventure itself as any practical purpose. Of the early explorers of the New World, virtually no autograph material exists in private ownership. Autographs of Christopher Columbus, Hernando de Soto, Ferdinand Magellan, Vasco da Gama, and Amerigo Vespucci are unobtainable. From this era of early exploration of the New World, only the autograph of **Hernando Cortés**, the conqueror of Mexico, could possibly be obtained.

David Livingstone was and is the most well known of the African explorers; his letters have been saved by past generations and generally can be found. The man sent to find Livingstone, **Henry M. Stanley**, is also generally available in letters that are less costly than those of Livingstone. The British explorer, Sir **Richard F. Burton**, has attracted so many collectors in past generations that his letters are now rarely seen.

In 1865, **Edward Whymper** was the first to scale the Matterhorn, and his writings, which brought the Alps to the forefront as a tourist area, also made him the best-known mountaineer of the time. His letters are rare but appeal to a limited number of collectors. They can be difficult to find but inexpensive when they are found.

In the earlier part of the nineteenth century, many explorers tried to find a northwest passage that would save ships the long voyage around Cape Horn at the tip of South America. The most famous of these, Sir **John Franklin**, was lost, together with his entire expedition, in 1847. His letters were saved by the people of his generation, as his name became more and more famous as expeditions were organized to try to find him. Today his letters are usually available, as are examples by many of those who led the arctic expeditions to rescue him, such as Sir **William E. Parry**.

The quest for the North Pole was dominated by **Robert E. Peary**, and his letters are readily available today. Many mention raising funds and his writings or lectures concerning his polar expeditions. Autographs of his companion, Matthew Henson, who was less well known until the age of black history, are much rarer than Peary's. At the other end of the earth, there were those who sought to reach the South Pole. Their autographs are all still collectable, even those of the unfortunate **Robert Falcon Scott** who reached the pole just after the Norwegian **Roald Amundsen** and who died with his men on their return to base camp. Many of Scott's letters concern fund raising and lectures in conjunction with his expeditions. Amundsen's letters are scarcer, though signatures on cards are probably as available as Scott's. **Ernest H. Shackleton** was equal in fame to Scott, and while his letters and signed photographs are not common, they can generally be found. As with Scott, many of his letters concern fund raising and lectures. **Richard E. Byrd** is perhaps the best-known Antarctic explorer, and his autograph material is relatively common as his long life and many public activities have provided collectors with many fine examples.

In the field of aviation, the adventurers (as opposed to the inventors; see chapter 28 on science) were very popular in their lifetimes and signed many souvenir flight covers and cards. These were saved by future generations, and they are nearly as admired and collected today as in the past. Autographs of the early aviators who took part in the first air races are generally not collected because of their great rarity. The autograph material of many like **Louis Bleriot**, who was the first to fly the English Channel, is in demand, and pieces are frequently available. Autographs of many

William E. Parry

Robert E. Peary

Robert Falcon Scott

Roald Amundsen

Ernest H. Shackleton

Richard E. Byrd

Louis Bleriot

J. Alcock.

John W. Alcock

A Whitten Brown

Arthur Whitten Brown

Charles A. Lindbergh

Charles Lindbergh

Amelia Earhart

Amelia Earhart

Howard Hughes

Howard Hughes

Edgar Rickenbacker

Eddie Rickenbacker

Wm. Mitchell

William Mitchell

other early aviators, for example, the crew of the first airplane to cross the Atlantic Ocean, the NC4, are quite rare, and they are relatively forgotten. More popular are pieces signed by **John W. Alcock** and **Arthur Whitten Brown**, the first to fly an aircraft nonstop across the Atlantic. Material signed by these two aviators is very rare.

The impact of **Charles Lindbergh**'s first solo flight across the Atlantic in 1927 is still felt in the collecting world today. Lindbergh signed many souvenir pieces, documents, photographs, books, menus, and so on, before he withdrew from the public after the kidnapping of his son and his involvement in isolationist politics just before World War II. He is among today's most popular figures and, fortunately, fine pieces signed by him are frequently available.

Of almost equal interest is **Amelia Earhart**, whose autograph material is scarcer than Lindbergh's, particularly her letters. The most commonly available pieces are album leaves signed by her and copies of her books with presentation inscriptions. Occasionally, but rarely, signed photographs or signed envelopes carried on one of her flights are encountered.

Howard Hughes, probably more notable as an aircraft adventurer and inventor than as a businessman, is very rare in anything that is genuinely signed. Many of his letters from the 1930s and 1940s, in response to fans of his aeronautical adventures, are signed by secretaries.

Autographs of **Eddie Rickenbacker**, famous as a flying ace in World War I, are fairly common in his capacity as president of Eastern Airlines. Rickenbacker's superior in World War I, **William Mitchell**, who performed demonstrations that airplanes could sink battleships by aerial bombardment (leading to his court martial), is rare in written material and in reasonable demand.

The history of aviation contains the names of scores of pilots who made first flights, such as Dieudonné Coste and Maurice Bellonte (who made the first flight from Paris to New York), and in their day their autographs were frequently sought and therefore occasionally surface today. None are particularly expensive, or particularly collected.

31

RELIGION

The interest of collectors in the field of religion is limited to relatively few personalities—popes of the Catholic church, persons the Catholic church have designated as saints, and those who have founded various sects of the Protestant church. (Judaica, a very actively collected area, is discussed in chapter 33, "Varia.") Except for the major figures (and very few others), there is virtually no interest among collectors in other religious figures. J. Pierpont Morgan began his collection by assembling signatures and letters of Methodist and Episcopal bishops, and judging by other collections formed in the nineteenth century, this was a popular field of interest. Today, however, there is no interest whatsoever in such collections.

Collecting religious autograph material can begin with pages from medieval illuminated manuscripts. These manuscripts, generally written before the invention of printing in 1455, are sometimes exquisite examples of medieval art with their illuminated initials and borders. The most frequently encountered leaves are from the following genres:

Antiphonaries contain the choral parts of the divine office. They were designed to serve several choristers at one time and were consequently volumes with a large format. The finest examples were produced in Italy during the fourteenth and fifteenth centuries.

Books of hours, derived from the church's liturgy, were used by lay persons as personal prayer books to follow, in their own manner, the church's program of daily devotion. Although additional devotional texts could be added at the discretion of the owner, books of hours followed a certain basic outline: the calendar, sequences of the gospels, harmony of the passion, hours of the virgin, hours of the cross, hours of the holy ghost, penitential psalms and litany, office of the dead, and suffrages to various saints. The most important text was the hours of the virgin; Mary became the most popular expression of faith and devotion in the Middle Ages, and her prayer book, the book of hours, the favorite of lay persons throughout Europe. Many books of hours were executed by the finest artists of the period and were viewed among the rich as status symbols.

Breviaries contain the divine office, prayers, hymns, and other texts said by the clergy at the canonical hours of matins, lauds, prime, tierce, sext, none, vespers, and compline.

Graduals, books containing that part of the Roman Catholic liturgy chanted by the congregation, derive their name from the gradual in the Mass, a short passage from the Psalms to be said or sung right after the Epistle. They are frequently quite large as they were intended, like antiphonaries, to be used by several choristers simultaneously.

Missals, or Mass books, contain the prayers said by the priest at the altar, as well as those read or sung in connection with the offering of the Mass.

Psalters contain the 150 Psalms, the Te Deum, and other canticles, a litany of saints, and prayers. Until the fourteenth century, they formed by far the largest class of liturgical illuminated manuscripts.

The earliest autograph that we have had of a religious leader is a confirmation of privileges and possessions signed by **Alexander III** [82, below], who was pope from 1159 to 1181. His signature [1, p. 3] predates the period when educated men learned to write and consists of an elongated double *S* (an abbreviation for the word *subscripsi,* meaning I have signed), the letter *E* from the word *Ego,* and the cross in the rota (two concentric circles). Within the circle the scribe has written the names of the saints Peter

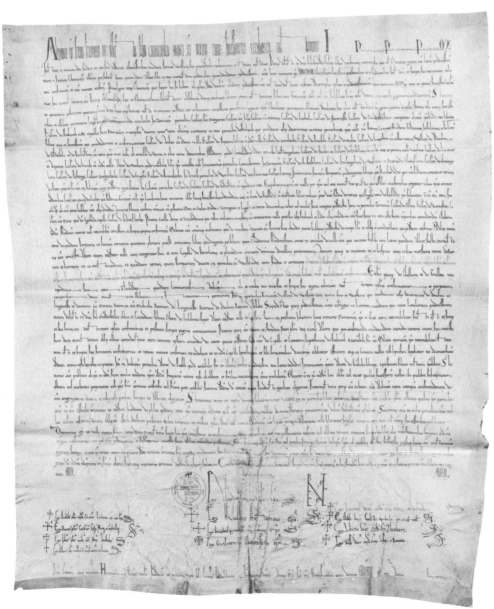

82 Greater Bull signed by Alexander III, dated May 25, 1163

Joannes XXIII

Pope John XXIII

Vre tres humble serviteur Vincens Depaul

St. Vincent de Paul

vostre tres humble serviteur francois de Sales

St. François de Sales

Most truly yours John H Card. Newman

Cardinal John Henry Newman

Martinus Luther D

Martin Luther

Calvin

John Calvin

J Wesley

John Wesley

and Paul and of the pope himself, and around the circumference, a text from the Bible, chosen by each pope and used throughout his reign. This document is witnessed by ten cardinals who have also signed the double S next to their names, which the scribe has written.

It is not until the early sixteenth century that documents signed by popes can realistically be collected. Before 1500, there is little likelihood of anything being available. Generally letters and documents of the popes become less scarce as we move toward the twentieth century, but there are many rarities, and in fact, material of the popes as a group, with modern exceptions, are relatively rare although not popularly collected. Pieces signed while pope, with the papal name, are much more desirable than pieces signed prior to the papacy. Autographs of **Pope John XXIII** are by far the most popularly collected of the modern popes.

Autograph material of Catholic saints is quite rare in general, and extremely few examples are seen. Material of **St. Vincent de Paul** and **St. François de Sales** can both be found but are extremely rare. The most sought after Catholic theologian, though neither pope nor saint, is **Cardinal John Henry Newman**, the leader of the Oxford movement. As an educator and author, Newman corresponded widely, and his letters are not rare. Infrequently, letters discussing Catholic theology surface and find a ready market.

The father of the Reformation, **Martin Luther**, wrote and signed many letters and documents, but these have been so avidly collected for centuries that few are ever encountered outside of institutional libraries or museums. Equally rare is autograph material of **John Calvin**, the French theologian and reformer who brought his own version of Protestantism to the theological academy he founded at Geneva. Letters of the founder of the Methodist church, **John Wesley**, are also rare but less so than those of Luther or Calvin. Several decades ago Wesley's letters were found with some frequency, but active collecting by institutions has removed nearly all of these from the market and his material is now rarely seen.

254

In colonial America, letters and documents of the Mather family of Congregational preachers are impossible to collect except for those of **Cotton Mather**, the grandson of the first of these fire and brimstone preachers, Richard Mather. Though rare, Cotton Mather's documents can still occasionally be found.

The powerful religious movement in America known as Mormonism was founded by **Joseph Smith** in upstate New York in 1830, with the publication of his Book of Mormon. His controversial group moved a number of times, and in one of these locations, Kirtland, Ohio, Smith served as the cashier of the Kirtland Safety Society Bank and in this capacity signed the bank's currency. Today, these notes, though scarce, provide the most available autograph examples of the founder of Mormonism. Other types of documents are very rare and letters, extremely rare. From Ohio, the Mormons moved to Missouri and then to Illinois where Smith was murdered in 1844 at the age of thirty-nine. The challenge of finding a new home for the Mormons fell to **Brigham Young** who lived a long life (he died in 1877) after leading the Mormons into the basin of the Great Salt Lake. His letters as governor are found infrequently; however, he signed many cards for admirers, and these are usually available.

Mary Baker Eddy developed a belief in spiritual healing and in 1875 published *Science and Health* explaining her spiritual and metaphysical system. During her long life she carried on extensive correspondences with her followers, but the systematic search for these letters over past decades by the church's archives has made her letters very rare. Her popularity among her followers has, in addition, created a strong demand for those letters that are found.

A collector seeking autograph material by other religious leaders who have played a lesser role is faced with a situation in which the lack of interest among collectors in the past has led to the material not being saved. If a collection of cardinals' letters, for example, could be found, the price would be modest, but it is very unlikely such a collection would have been saved.

Cotton Mather

Joseph Smith

Brigham Young

Mary Baker Eddy

32

SPORTS

Babe Ruth

Lou Gehrig

Ty Cobb

Connie Mack

Jackie Robinson

Robert T. Jones

Bill Tilden

The field of sports autographs has recently become extraordinarily popular, and prices for material by living sports heroes have reached levels that seem quite unreasonable. My involvement in autograph material in the sports field excludes that of living personalities and is limited to the classic athletes in each area. Many others are offered to collectors, but they are outside my scope.

Baseball autograph material has always been the most popular of sports areas, and **Babe Ruth**, the epitome of the sport. Ruth was very popular and happy to sign his autograph at events. Everyone saved his signature as his name was synonymous with America's pastime. These signatures, usually on album pages, are as popular today as they were when fans waited for hours outside Yankee Stadium to obtain them decades ago. Signed photographs of Babe Ruth are much scarcer (beware of examples signed by his wife for him), and baseballs signed by Ruth are eagerly sought after. (Many of these have been varnished in misguided efforts to preserve them; the varnish reduces the value.) Signatures of Ruth's teammate, **Lou Gehrig**, are virtually equal in value and are actually scarcer. As with Ruth, the most frequently available form is an album page signed. Other baseball players from its golden age include **Ty Cobb**, whose autographs are available mostly on signed checks; **Connie Mack**, available in many forms; and **Jackie Robinson**, whose popularity with collectors and autograph values are comparable to the classic players of the earlier generation.

In the field of golf, **Bobby Jones**, who dominated the sport in the 1930s, is so much in demand that any pieces we are able to find are sold almost instantly. In tennis, **Bill Tilden** is almost as popular among

Gene Tunney (signature)

Gene Tunney

collectors, and few pieces are ever available. Boxing, like baseball, attracted autograph seekers during the great years, and pages signed by **Gene Tunney** and **Jack Dempsey** are common. Signatures of the earlier heroes of boxing, **John L. Sullivan** and **James J. Corbett**, are much scarcer. **Knute Rockne**, the most famous name in football during the early years, is very scarce in autographs and difficult, though not impossible, to find.

The Olympic star who dominated the 1936 Olympic games held in Hitler's Germany, **Jesse Owens**, gave his autograph quite freely, and these are usually available today. One of the saddest stories in American sports history is that of **Jim Thorpe**, the superstar in many different sports who forfeited his Olympic medals for winning the decathlon and pentathlon because he had earlier unknowingly lost his amateur status. His autographs are very rare and much sought after by collectors.

Jesse Owens (signature)

Jesse Owens

Jack Dempsey (signature)

Jack Dempsey

John L. Sullivan (signature)

John L. Sullivan

Yours Truly Jas J. Corbett (signature)

James J. Corbett

Knute K. Rockne (signature)

Knute Rockne

Jim Thorpe (signature)

Jim Thorpe

33

VARIA

One of the most popular areas of collecting is Judaica. Many of the personalities whose letters are collected as part of a Judaica collection are discussed in other chapters concerning their particular fields of endeavor. Here, I will discuss several figures who are most known for their espousal of Jewish and Zionist causes.

Mordecai N. Noah was a journalist and eminent American Jewish leader of the first half of the nineteenth century. His letters are rare but appreciated by only very specialized collectors, and prices are relatively reasonable. Letters of **Moses Mendelssohn**, the German Jewish philosopher, are rare and in great demand. Autograph material of **Theodor Herzl**, the leading Zionist and advocate of the founding of a Jewish state in Palestine, is very popularly collected. His letters are rare, but one, over time, can be found. Letters, usually typewritten, of **Henrietta Szold**, the American Zionist leader who founded Hadassah, are not common but infrequently turn up. Letters of **Chaim Weizmann**, another Zionist leader who favored a Jewish national home in Palestine, are much rarer but can, with patience, be found. One of the most popular Israeli leaders is **David Ben-Gurion**. Material signed by him is frequently available, and his popularity has made it very desirable among collectors. Signatures, signed photographs, and letters can all be found. Occasionally, signed copies of the limited edition of his book, *Israel: A Personal History,* are offered, and they find an immediate market.

Mordecai N. Noah

Moses Mendelssohn

Theodore Herzl

Henrietta Szold

Chaim Weizmann

Signature of Ben-Gurion in Hebrew script

David Ben-Gurion

Benito Juárez

Maximilian

The leading figures in Mexican history have always been of interest to certain American collectors. Letters and documents of **Benito Juárez**, the revolutionary and statesman, are rare; few pieces are offered, though it is possible to obtain one. Autograph material of the hapless **Maximilian**, the Austrian archduke who accepted the throne as emperor of Mexico and was executed after his overthrow, is also rare but can be found. **Pancho Villa**, the revolutionary leader at the turn of the century who was basically a bandit, is rarer and more difficult to obtain in any autograph form.

In South America, **José de San Martín**, the Argentinian soldier and statesman who established independence in Chile and Peru, set the stage for **Simón Bolívar**. His material is rarely seen but possible to obtain. Autograph material of Bolívar, the Liberator of Colombia, Peru, and Bolivia, has been very actively acquired, particularly by collectors in Venezuela. Although he is the most popular South American leader, his official letters and documents can be found. Autograph material of **Antonio José de Sucre**, the liberator of Equador, and **Bernardo O'Higgins**, the revolutionary leader

Pancho Villa

José de San Martín

Simón Bolívar

Bernardo O'Higgins

Antonio José de Sucre

259

Eva Peron

and first Chilean head of state, is also very actively sought by South American collectors. Of more modern interest is material of Juan and **Eva Perón**. Juan Perón's autographs are not nearly as popular with collectors, or as rare, as those of his wife, whose letters, documents, and signed photographs are rare and in much demand.

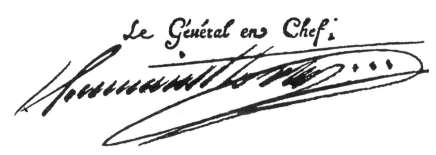
Pierre Toussaint L'Ouverture

In the Caribbean, **Pierre Toussaint L'Ouverture** led a rebellion in Haiti that freed the slaves, after which he established an independent country. His documents are rare but are occasionally offered. Material of **Henri Christophe**, who continued Toussaint L'Ouverture's leadership after the latter's death, is much scarcer and more difficult to find.

Henri Christophe

In Asia, **Sun Yat-sen**, the father of modern China, spent many years in Western Europe and wrote many letters, few of which have survived. His letters are very rare but can be found over time. Autograph material of **Mao Tse-tung**, the founder of Communist China, is virtually unobtainable, as is that of the Communist leaders led by Mao. Letters of **Zhou En-lai**, China's leader second only to Mao, are very rare but seen on occasion. Autograph material of the Vietnamese leader, **Ho Chi-minh**, who waged successful wars against both French and American forces, is very rare, with a signed piece surfacing every several years, but there is not a great demand for those that are found.

Sun Yat-sen

Mao Tse-tung

Zhou En-lai

Ho Chi-minh

One of the most popular personalities of the twentieth century is **Mohandas K. Gandhi**, who wrote many letters, but the demand for them by collectors has been extraordinarily strong, and while one is usually available, they are getting much rarer.

Mohandas K. Gandhi

Albert Schweitzer, the great musicologist who is principally known as a humanitarian, has a unique place in history. His letters and documents are scarce, particularly so since most of his correspondence was answered and signed for him by an assistant. Letters responding to "fan mail" are almost certainly not written or signed by him.

Those interested in English legal history are frequently surprised that they can, on rare occasions, obtain a piece signed by the author of *Commentaries on the Laws of England*, **Sir William Blackstone**.

Another popular area with legal history collectors is medieval indentures and deeds. After 1300, legal documents in England were dated according to the year of the reigning monarch, and occasionally fine examples bear wax seals suspended from the lower margin by vellum strips. French legal documents and deeds from even earlier times are readily available. These relics of the medieval world are relatively quite inexpensive.

Albert Schweitzer

Sir William Blackstone

BIBLIOGRAPHY

GUIDES TO COLLECTING AND OTHER USEFUL WORKS

Albrecht, Otto Edwin. *A Census of Autograph Music Manuscripts of European Composers in American Libraries.* Philadelphia: University of Pennsylvania Press, 1953. A list of 2,017 manuscripts by 571 European composers.

Appleton's Cyclopaedia of American Biography. Edited by James Grant Wilson and John Fiske. 6 volumes. New York: Appleton, 1887–1889. Contains biographical data on persons not easily found elsewhere, with facsimile signatures.

Barksdale, A. Beverly. *Composer Portraits and Autograph Scores.* Toledo, Oh.: Toledo Museum of Art, 1954. Catalog of a comprehensive exhibition.

Benjamin, Mary A. *Autographs: A Key to Collecting.* New York: Bowker, 1946; rev. ed., 1963. A standard reference work.

_____. *The Presidents: A Survey of Autograph Values.* New York: Walter R. Benjamin Autographs, 1965. A dated work on the quality, demand, and availability of presidential material through Lyndon B. Johnson.

Berkeley, Edmund, Jr., Herbert E. Klingelhofer, and Kenneth W. Rendell. *Autographs and Manuscripts: A Collector's Manual.* New York: Scribner's, 1978. The standard and most comprehensive reference work in the field.

Binns, Norman E. *An Introduction to Historical Bibliography.* London: Association of Assistant Librarians, 1962. A bibliographical guide for finding information on any aspect of American history.

Blatt, Marvin B., and Norman Schwab. *Seeing Double: The Autopen Guide.* North Babylon, N.Y.: 1986.

Books and Manuscripts From the Heineman Collection. New York: Pierpont Morgan Library, 1963.

Bordin, Ruth B., and Robert M. Warner. *The Modern Manuscript Library.* New York: Scarecrow, 1966. An introductory manual for archivists, but also helpful to collectors.

Bresslau, Harry. *Handbuch der Urkundenlehre.* 3d ed. 3 volumes. Berlin: Walter de Gruyter, 1958. The best study on early German and Italian official documents.

Brumbaugh, Thomas B. "Pursuing the Documents of Art." *Auction* 2, no. 6 (February 1969): 10-13.

Catalogue of the Famous Music Library . . . of the Late W. H. Cummings. [London: Sotheby, Wilkinson & Hodge, 1917]. Auction catalog of a great private collection bought by the Nanki Music Library in Tokyo.

Chu, Petra Ten-Doesschate. "Unsuspected Pleasures in Artists' Letters." *Apollo* 104 (October 1976): 298-305.

Croft, Peter J. *Literary Autographs: Papers Read at a Clark Library Seminar, 26th of April, 1980.* Los Angeles: Clark Memorial Library, 1983.

Deuel, Leo. *Testaments of Time: The Search for Lost Manuscripts and Records.* New York: Knopf, 1965. An account of the search for papyrus scrolls, clay tablets, and other early writing in Europe, Asia, and the Americas, with translations, facsimiles, and an excellent bibliography.

Deutsch, Otto Erich. "Collections, Private." *Grove's Dictionary of Music and Musicians.* 5th ed. New York: St. Martin's Press, 1954. II, 373-375. A seminal historical survey, through 1950.

Dictionary of American Biography. Edited by Allen Johnson et al. 11 volumes and 10 supplements. New York: Scribner's, 1928–1994. The standard reference on noted deceased Americans.

Dictionary of National Biography. Edited by Leslie Stephen and Sidney Lee. 22 volumes and 10 supplements. London: Smith, Elder and Oxford University Press, 1908. The standard reference on noted deceased Britons.

Diringer, David. *Writing.* New York: Praeger, 1962.

Draper, Lyman Copeland. *An Essay on the Autograph Collections of the Signers of the Declaration of Independence and of the Constitution.* New York: Burns, 1889. Interesting for its comments on early collecting efforts in these areas.

Duckett, Kenneth W. *Modern Manuscripts: A Practical Manual for Their Management, Care, and Use.* Nashville: American Association for State and Local History, 1975. A manual for professionals that will also interest collectors. Includes a bibliography and lists of common facsimiles and appraisers.

Eastburn, Walter N. "The Problem of Aging Signatures." *Manuscripts* 9, no. 4 (Fall 1957): 258–260.

_____. "John Morton, Changeable Signer." *Manuscripts* 12, no. 1 (Winter 1960): 12–19.

Eaton, Dorothy S., and Vincent L. Eaton. "George Washington's Handwriting." *Autograph Collectors' Journal* 4, no. 1 (Fall 1951): 20–22.

Eaton, Vincent L. "Abraham Lincoln: His Hand and Pen." *Manuscripts* 11, no. 1 (Winter 1959): 5–12.

The Elizabeth Sprague Coolidge Foundation of Autograph Musical Scores. Washington, D.C.: U.S. Government Printing Office, 1950.

Elsevier's Lexicon of Archive Terminology. Amsterdam, London, and New York: Elsevier, 1964.

An Exhibit of Music Including Manuscripts . . . Held in Washington, D.C. on December 28, 29 and 30, 1938. Washington, D.C.: U.S. Government Printing Office, 1939.

Fields, Joseph E. "Thomas Lynch, Jr. and His Autographs." *Autograph Collectors' Journal* 4, no. 1 (Fall 1951): 6–10.

_____. "The Autographs of Arthur Middleton." *Autograph Collectors' Journal* 4, no. 2 (Winter 1952): 2–18.

Freidel, Frank, and Richard K. Shoman, eds. *Harvard Guide to American History.* 2 volumes. Cambridge: Belknap, 1974.

Gaucheron, Roger, ed. *Les Lettres, Autographes, et Manuscrits de la Collection de Henri de Rothschild.* Paris: Morgan & Rahir, 1924.

Gaur, Albertine. *A History of Writing.* London: British Library, 1984.

Gerigk, Herbert. *Neue Liebe zu alten Schriften. Vom Autogrammjäger zum Autographensammler.* Stuttgart: Deutsche Verlags-Anstalt, 1974. A practical guide for collectors.

Goldbeck, Frederik, and A. Fehr. *Bibliothèque Alfred Cortot . . . catalogue.* [Argenteuil: Coulouma, 1936]. Catalog of a great private collection; only volume I published.

Gombosi, Marilyn, ed. *Catalog of the Johannes Herbst Collection.* Chapel Hill: University of North Carolina Press, 1970. Catalog of eighteenth- and early nineteenth century manuscripts of the Moravian Music Foundation in Winston-Salem, N.C.

Hamilton, Charles. *Collecting Autographs and Manuscripts.* Norman, Okla.: University of Oklahoma Press, 1961. A useful guide with anecdotes and facsimiles.

_____. *Scribblers and Scoundrels.* New York: Paul S. Eriksson, 1968. Encounters with autographs and their forgers.

Hamilton, Charles, and Diane Hamilton. *Big Name Hunting: A Beginner's Guide to Autograph Collecting.* New York: Simon & Schuster, 1973.

Jensen, Hans. *Die Schrift in Vergangenheit und Gegenwart.* Berlin: Veb Deutscher Verlag der Wissenschaften, 1958.

Jung, Hermann. *Ullstein Autographenbuch. Vom Sammeln handschriftlicher Kostbarkeiten.* Frankfurt-am-Main, 1971. An informative source on the history of autograph collecting; dated on market values.

Kallir, Rudolf F. *Autographensammler—lebenslaenglich.* Zurich: Atlantis, 1977.

King, A. Hyatt. *Some British Collectors of Music.* Cambridge: Cambridge University Press, 1963. Contains classified lists of collectors, beginning in the mid-seventeenth century.

Kinsky, Georg. *Musikhistorisches Museum von Wilhelm Heyer in Cöln.* Katalog IV: *Musik-autographen.* 4 parts in 3 volumes. Leipzig: Breitkopf & Härtel, 1910–1916. An exemplary catalog of a great collection of musical autographs.

———. *Katalog der Musikautographen Sammlung Louis Koch . . . von Scarlatti bis Stravinsky.* Stuttgart: Hoffmannsche Buchdruckerei F. Krais, 1953. Catalog of an important collection strong in German classical and Romantic music.

The Koussevitzky Music Foundation, 1942–1967. Washington, D.C.: Serge Koussevitky Foundation in the Library of Congress, 1967. Catalog of musical autographs.

Leisinger, A. H., Jr. "The Exhibit of Documents." *American Archivist* 26 (January 1963): 75–86.

Lingelbach, William E. "B. Franklin and the Art of Writing." *Autograph Collectors' Journal* 4, no. 3 (Spring 1952): 3–9.

McNeil, Donald R. *The American Collector.* Madison, Wis.: State Historical Society of Wisconsin, 1955.

The Manuscript Society. *What Is Autograph Collecting?* [Somerville, Mass.]: the Society, [1969].

Mecklenburg, Günther. *Vom Autographensammeln: Versuch einer Darstellung seines Wesens und seiner Geschichte im deutschen Sprachgebiet.* Marburg: Stargardt, 1963. A comprehensive work on significant autograph collections and collecting in Germany, Austria, and Switzerland by the most noted German dealer and auctioneer.

Moran, Hugh A. *The Alphabet and the Ancient Calendar Signs: Astrological Signs in the Origin of the Alphabet.* Palo Alto, Calif.: Pacific Books, [1953].

Munby, Alan Noel Latimer. *The Cult of the Autograph Letter in England.* London: Athlone, 1962.

Nash, Ray. "The Handwriting of the Founding Fathers." *Manuscripts* 7, no. 4 (Summer 1955): 208–213.

Nicolas, Alain. *Les Autographes.* Paris: Maisonneuve, 1988.

Ostromecki, Walter A., Jr. *The First Ladies of the United States.* Encino, Ca.: 1989.

Pfudel, Ernst. *Die Musik-Handschriften der Konigl. Ritter-Akademie zu Liegnitz.* ("Monatshefte für Musikgeschichte. Beilage. Jahrgang 18 & 21"). Leipzig: Breitkopf & Härtel, 1886–1889.

Reed, John F. "Questions and Answers." *Manuscripts* 16, no. 4 (Summer 1964): 53–54. On Washington's handwriting.

Rendell, Kenneth W. *Fundamentals of Autograph Collecting.* Somerville, Mass.: Rendell, 1972.

Ricci, Seymour de. *English Collectors of Books and Manuscripts (1530–1930) and Their Marks of Ownership.* Cambridge: Cambridge University Press, 1930, 1960.

Schang, F. C. *Visiting Cards of Celebrities.* Paris: Hazan, [1971].

_____. *Visiting Cards of Prima Donnas.* Stuart, Fla.: Southeastern, 1973.

_____. *Visiting Cards of Violinists.* [Stuart, Fla.: Southeastern, 1975].

_____. *Visiting Cards of Pianists.* New York: Patelson Music House, [1979].

_____. *Visiting Cards of Painters.* New York: Whittenborn Books, 1989.

Schmieder, Wolfgang. *Musiker–Handschriften in Drei Jahrhunderten.* Leipzig: Breitkopf & Härtel, 1939.

Scott, Henry T., and Samuel Davey. *A Guide to the Collector of Historical Documents, Literary Manuscripts and Autograph Letters.* London: Davey, 1891. Includes an index of sources to facsimiles.

_____. *Autograph Collecting: A Practical Manual for Amateurs and Historical Students.* London: Gill, 1894. A detailed manual, reflecting on collecting of the period.

Sowards, Neil. *The Handbook of Check Collecting.* Fort Wayne, Ind.: the author, 1976.

Van Patten, Nathan. *A Memorial Library of Music at Stanford University.* Stanford: Stanford University Press, 1950. A collection emphasizing association items.

Stevens, Robley D. *Enjoy Your Leisure Time: Autograph Collecting Guide.* Ann Arbor: Edwards, [1955].

Storm, Colton, and Howard Peckham. *Invitation to Book Collecting: Its Pleasures and Practices With Kindred Discussion of Manuscripts, Maps, and Prints.* New York: Bowker, 1947.

Strutz, Henry. "Autograph Cataloguer, Save That Album." *Hobbies* 80 (May 1975): 154-155. A discussion of well-known European autographs and noted collections.

Sullivan, George. *The Complete Book of Autograph Collecting.* New York: Dodd, Mead, 1971. An introductory guide with facsimiles and addresses of celebrities.

Sutherland, James, ed. *Oxford Book of Literary Anecdotes.* Oxford: Clarendon Press, 1975.

Taylor, John M. *The Autograph Collector's Checklist.* Burbank, Ca.: Manuscript Society, 1990.

Tessier, Georges. *Diplomatique royale française.* Paris: Editions Picard, 1962. The standard work on French royal documents, with facsimiles.

Versteigerung der Musikbibliothek des Herrn Dr. Werner Wolffheim. 2 volumes in 4 parts. Berlin: Breslauer & Liepmannssohn, 1928-1929. Classified catalog of a great collection.

Waters, Edward N. "The Music Collection of the Heineman Foundation." *Notes* 7 (March 1950): 181-216.

_____. *Autograph Musical Scores and Autograph Letters in the Whittall Foundation Collection.* Washington, D.C.: U.S. Government Printing Office, 1951. A descriptive catalog of musical autographs in the Library of Congress since 1951.

Williams, Robert. *Adventures of an Autograph Collector.* New York: Exposition, 1952.

Wittnebert, Al. *Signatures of the Stars.* [Hollywood, Fla.]: Universal Autograph Collectors Club, [1988].

Wolbe, Eugen. *Handbuch für Autographensammler.* Berlin: R. C. Schmidt, 1923. A dated but still useful guide.

FACSIMILES

Note: Facsimiles can also be found in many of the titles in "Forgeries," "General Works," "Memoirs," and "Periodicals."

Albrecht, Otto Edwin, Herbert Cahoon, and Douglas C. Ewing. *The Mary Flagler Cary Music Collection: Printed Books and Music, Manuscripts, Autograph Letters, Documents, Portraits.* New York: Pierpont Morgan Library, 1970.

_____. "Musical Treasures in the Morgan Library." *Notes* 18 (June 1972): 643–651.

Ammann, R. *Die Handschrift de Künstler.* Bern: H. Huben, [1953].

Autograph Letters & Manuscripts: Major Acquisitions of the Pierpont Morgan Library, 1924–1974. New York: Pierpont Morgan Library, 1974.

Bérard, Auguste Simon Louis, et al. *Isographie des hommes célèbres, ou collection de facsimile de lettres autographes et de signatures.* 4 volumes. Paris: 1828–1843; *Supplement* by Étienne Charavay, 1880. Arguably the most useful book of facsimiles of European personalities.

British Autography. A Collection of Facsimiles of the Hand Writing of Royal and Illustrious Personages, with their authentic Portraits. 3 volumes. London: J. Thane.

Brotherhead, William, ed. *The Book of the Signers: Containing Fac-simile Letters of the Signers of the Declaration of Independence.* Philadelphia: W. Brotherhead, 1861.

Cahoon, Herbert, Thomas V. Lange, and Charles A. Ryskamp. *American Literary Autographs from Washington Irving to Henry James.* New York: Dover Publications, in association with the Pierpont Morgan Library, 1977.

Camner, James, and Neale Lanigan, Jr. *Film Autographs, 1894–1941.* Camner, 1978.

Carr, Paul K. *The Autographs of President Gerald R. Ford.* [Rockville, Md.]: Universal Autograph Collectors Club, 1974.

_____. *Machine Signed Signatures.* [Washington, D.C.]: Universal Autograph Collectors Club, [1984].

_____. *From the Eisenhower Files.* Santa Monica, Ca.: Modoc Press, 1995.

Casoni, Frederick. *The Handwriting of Richard M. Nixon.* Rockville Centre, N.Y.: Universal Autograph Collectors Club, 1982.

Charavay, Étienne. *Catalogue de la précieuse collection d'autographes composant le cabinet de M. Alfred Bovet.* 3 volumes. Paris: É. Charavay, 1884–1885. One of the most important facsimile works of European material.

_____. *Inventaire des Autographes et des Documents Historiques Composant La Collection M. Benjamin Fillon.* Paris: Étienne Charavay and Frederic Naylor, 1877.

Croft, Peter J. *Autograph Poetry in the English Language.* 2 volumes. New York: McGraw-Hill, 1973. A chronological treatment from William Herbert to Dylan Thomas.

Czwiklitzer, Christophe. *Lettres Autographes de Peintres et Sculpteurs du XVe Siècle à Nos Jours.* Basel: Éditions Art, 1976.

Darvick, Herman. *Philographic Study of Jimmy Carter.* [Rockville Centre, N.Y.]: Universal Autograph Collectors Club, 1978.

Dawson, Giles Edwin, and Laetitia Kennedy-Skipton. *Elizabethan Handwriting.* New York: Norton, [1966].

Fairbank, Alfred John, and Berthold Wolpe. *Renaissance Handwriting.* London: Faber and Faber, [1960].

Friendenthall, Richard. *Letters of the Great Artists from Ghiberti to Gainsborough* and *Letters of the Great Artists from Blake to Pollock.* London: Thames and Hudson, 1963.

Geigy-Hagenback, Karl. *Album von Handschriften berühmter Persönlichkeiten vom Mittelalter bis zur Neuzeit.* 1925. A comprehensive work of facsimiles of European signatures.

Gerstenberg, Walter, and Martin Hürlimann, eds. *Musiker-handschriften.* 2 volumes. Zurich: Atlantis, 1960. Includes 152 plates of facsimiles with brief comments.

_____. *Composers' Autographs.* Translated by Ernst Roth. 2 volumes. Teaneck, N.J.: Fairleigh Dickinson University Press, 1968. Includes 140 plates of facsimiles.

Grasberger, Franz. *Die Handschriften der Meister: Berümte Werke der Tonkunst im Autograph.* Vienna: Gesellschaft der Musikfreunde, 1966. Catalog of six exhibitions, extensively illustrated with facsimiles of the holograph scores of great composers from Bach to the present day.

_____. *Kostbarkeiten der Musik.* I: *Das Lied.* Tutzing, Ger.: Hans Schneider, 1968. Contains many facsimiles of holograph songs.

Greg, Walter Wilson. *English Literary Autographs, 1550–1650.* 3 volumes. Oxford: Oxford University Press, 1925–1932. Reprint. Nendeln, Liechtenstein: Kraus Reprint, 1968.

Grieve, Hilda Elizabeth Poole. *Examples of English Handwriting, 1150–1750.* [Essex, England]: Essex Education Committee, 1974.

Hamilton, Charles. *American Autographs.* 2 volumes. Norman, Okla.: University of Oklahoma Press, 1983. The definitive selection of facsimile examples of American presidents and a wide-ranging selection of facsimiles of participants in the American Revolution, as well as illustrations of secretarial and forged signatures.

_____. *The Book of Autographs.* New York: Simon & Schuster, 1978. Contains over 5,000 prices and 1,000 facsimiles.

_____. *Leaders and Personalities of the Third Reich: Their Biographies, Portraits, and Autographs.* San Jose, Calif.: R. James Bender, 1984. A comprehensive collection of facsimiles of Third Reich personalities.

_____. *The Signature of America.* New York: Harper & Row, 1979. One of the most comprehensive books of facsimiles of signatures.

Hardy, William John. *The Handwriting of the Kings and Queens of England.* [London]: Religious Tract Society, 1893.

Hayes, Jim. *War Between the States: Autographs and Biographical Information.* James Island, So. Car.: 1989.

Hector, Leonard Charles. *The Handwriting of English Documents.* 2d ed. London: E. Arnold, 1966. A standard work.

Hürlimann, Martin. *Musiker-Handschriften: Zeugniss des Zurcher Musiklebens.* Zurich: Atlantis, 1969. Exhibition catalog with many facsimiles.

Jans, Hans Jörg, ed. *Musiker-Handschriften: Originalpartituren aus der Sammlung Dr. h. c. Paul Sacher.* Lucerne: Bärtschi & Hasler, 1973. Exhibition catalog with many facsimiles.

Jenkinson, Hilary. *Paleography and the Practical Study of the Court Hand.* Cambridge: Cambridge University Press, 1915.

Johnson, Charles. *English Court Hand, A.D. 1066 to 1500.* Oxford: Clarendon Press, 1915.

Klinkenborg, Verlyn, Herbert Cahoon, and Charles Ryskamp. *British Literary Manuscripts, Series I from 800 to 1800.* New York: Dover Publications, 1981.

Lescure, M. de. *Les autographes et le goût des autographes en France et à l'étranger.* Paris: V. Gay, 1865.

Lesure, François, and Nanie Bridgman. *Collection musicale André Meyer: Manuscrits, autographes, musique imprimée et manuscrit.* Abbéville: F. Paillart, [1960]. Contains 292 plates.

Marans, M. Wesley. *Sincerely Yours.* Boston: Little, Brown, 1983. The author's collection of autographed photos, lavishly illustrated.

Mare, A.C. de la. *The Handwriting of Italian Humanists.* Oxford: Oxford University Press, 1973.

Morrison, Alfred. *Catalogue of the Collection of Autograph Letters and Historical Documents formed between 1865 and 1882.* 6 volumes. London: Strangeways, 1883. One of the most important facsimile reference works.

Muns, J. B. *Musical Autographs: A Comparative Guide.* Berkeley, Ca.: 1989. *Supplement,* 1992.

Nash, Ray. *American Penmanship 1800–1850: A History of Writing and Bibliography of Copybooks from Jenkins to Spencer.* Worcester, Mass.: American Antiquarian Society, 1969.

Netherclift, Joseph. *Autograph Letters, Characteristic Extracts, and Signatures, From the Correspondence of Illustrious and Distinguished Women of Great Britain, From the XIVth to the XIXth Century.* [London: J. Netherclift], 1838.

[Nicolas, Alain]. *Souverains et Chefs d'État Français.* Paris: Les Neuf Muses.

Nichols, John G. *Autographs of Royal, Noble, Learned, and Remarkable Personages Conspicuous in English History.* London: J. B. Nichols, 1829.

Osley, A. S. *Scribes and Sources.* Boston: Godine, 1980.

Petti, Anthony G. *English Literary Hands From Chaucer to Dryden.* London: Edward Arnold, 1977.

Poetry, Famous Verse Manuscripts. Facsimiles of Original Manuscripts as Submitted to Poetry. [Chicago]: Poetry, 1954.

Rawlins, Ray. *Four Hundred Years of British Autographs.* London: Dent, 1970. The standard work on British autographs, with facsimiles and a bibliography.

_____. *The Guinness Book of World Autographs.* Enfield, Middlesex, Eng.: Guinness Superlatives, 1977. Contains 1,400 facsimiles arranged alphabetically.

Reese, II, Michael. *Autographs of the Confederacy.* New York: Cohasco, 1981.

Rendell, Kenneth W. *The American Frontier, from the Atlantic to the Pacific.* 3 volumes. Rendell, 1980. 1000 letters, documents, printed books, broadsides, pamphlets, maps, and other items representing virtually all major figures concerned with the exploration and crossing of the Rocky Mountains, the settlement and annexation of Texas, the California Gold

Rush, cowboys and Indians, and the settlement of the west.

_____. *The Medieval World, 800–1450.* Rendell, 1979. A comprehensive catalog of letters, documents, illuminated leaves, and manuscripts, both secular and religious, representing various aspects of life and society during the Middle Ages.

_____. *Renaissance Europe, 1450–1600.* Rendell, 1979. 270 letters, manuscripts, documents, printed books, bindings, maps, and woodcuts documenting life in Renaissance Europe and representing most of the major political and religious figures of the period.

_____. *Autograph Letters, Manuscripts, Drawings—French Artists & Authors.* Rendell, 1977. With facsimiles of signatures and manuscripts of almost all the noted French artists and authors.

Schünemann, Georg. *Musikerhandschriften von Bach bis Schumann.* Berlin and Zurich: Atlantis, 1936. Precursor of the compilations by Gerstenberg-Hürlimann, with facsimiles of musical manuscripts in the Berlin State Library.

Smith, Charles John. *Historical and Literary Curiosities, Consisting of Facsimiles of Original Documents . . .* London: Henry G. Bohn, 1840.

Stevens, Benjamin Franklin. *Facsimiles of Manuscripts in European Archives Relating to America, 1773–1783.* 24 volumes. London: Malby, 1889–1895. Reprint (25 volumes). Wilmington, Del.: Mellifont Press, 1970. Contains 2,107 facsimiles.

Strutz, Henry. "Autographs and Foreign Languages." *Hobbies* 80 (September 1975): 154-155. Discusses the correlation between autograph collecting and language learning, with facsimile signatures of European literary figures.

Tannenbaum, Samuel. A. *The Handwriting of the Renaissance.* New York: Columbia University Press, 1930. Reprint. New York: Frederick Ungar, 1967.

Taylor, John M. *From the White House Inkwell: American Presidential Autographs.* Rutland, Vt.: Charles E. Tuttle, 1968. Discusses the availability of material, with facsimiles.

Thomas, George C. *Autograph Letters and Autographs of the Signers of the Declaration of Independence.* Philadelphia: privately printed, 1908.

Thompson, H. Keith, and Henry Strutz. *Doenitz at Nuremberg: A Re-appraisal.* New York: Ambler, 1977. Contains comments on the trial by more than four hundred persons, with over three hundred of their photographs and facsimiles.

Warner, Sir George Frederick, ed. *Facsimiles of Royal, Historical, Literary and Other Autographs in the Department of Manuscripts, British Museum.* London: British Museum, 1899.

_____. *Universal Classic Manuscripts.* London and Washington, D.C.: M. W. Dunne, 1901. Contains 150 facsimiles from the British Museum's manuscript collection.

William, Henry Smith. *The History of the Art of Writing.* London: Hooper & Jackson, [1902]. Four portfolios of Oriental, classical, medieval, and modern writing, each containing two hundred facsimiles.

Winkler, Ernest William. *Manuscript Letters and Documents of Early Texians, 1821–1845.* Austin: Steck, 1937.

Winsor, Justin. *Narrative and Critical History of America.* 8 volumes. Boston and New York: Houghton Mifflin, 1884–1889. Contains many facsimiles.

Winternitz, Emanuel. *Musical Autographs From Monteverdi to Hindemith.* 2 volumes. Princeton: Princeton University Press, 1955. Reprint. New York: Dover, 1965. Commentary in Volume 1 and 196 full-page facsimiles in Volume 2.

Wright, Cyril Ernest. *English Vernacular Hands From the Twelfth to the Fifteenth Centuries.* Oxford: Clarendon Press, 1960. Contains twenty-four full-page illustrations.

FORGERIES

Baker, Jay Newton. *The Law of Disputed and Forged Documents.* Charlottesville, Va.: Michie, 1955.

Charavay, Étienne. *Faux autographes: affaire Vrain-Lucas; étude critique sur la collection vendue à M. Chel Chasles et observations sur les moyens de reconnaître les faux autographes.* Paris: J. Charavay, 1870. An exposé of the forgeries of Vrain-Lucas.

Clements, William L., Library. *Facsimiles & Forgeries: A Guide to a Timely Exhibition.* Ann Arbor, Mich.: Clements Library, 1950. A catalog that includes many better-known facsimiles.

Conway, James V. P. *Evidential Documents.* Springfield, Ill.: Charles C. Thomas, 1959.

The Diary of Jack the Ripper. Narrative by Shirley Harrison. New York: Hyperion, 1993.

Farrer, James Anson. *Literary Forgeries.* London and New York: Longmans, Green, 1907. The standard work.

Grant, Julius. *Books and Documents.* New York: Chemical Publishing, 1937.

Grebanier, Bernard D. N. *The Great Shakespeare Forgery.* New York: Norton, 1965.

Hamilton, Charles. *Great Forgers and Famous Fakes.* New York: Crown, 1980. While this work does not deal with the detection of forgeries, its numerous illustrations make it an important work in the field.

_____. *The Robot that Helped to Make a President.* New York: 1965. The first book on autopen signatures; a classic.

Harris, Robert. *Selling Hitler.* London: Faber and Faber, 1986. A detailed history of the Hitler diaries fraud inside *Stern* magazine and also at the *Sunday Times* of London.

Harrison, Wilson R. *Suspect Documents: Their Scientific Examination.* London: Sweet and Maxwell, 1958. A standard reference on forgery detection.

_____. *Forgery Detection: A Practical Guide.* New York: Praeger, 1963. A standard reference for the amateur.

Haselden, Reginald Berti. *Scientific Aids for the Study of*

Manuscripts. Oxford: Oxford University Press for the Bibliographical Society, 1935. A standard work on the use of microscopes, ultraviolet lamps, and other instruments and techniques.

Hector, Leonard Charles. *Paleography and Forgery.* York, Eng.: St. Anthony's Press, 1959.

Hilton, Ordway. *Scientific Examination of Questioned Documents.* Chicago: Callaghan, 1956.

Lindsey, Robert. *A Gathering of Saints.* New York: Simon & Schuster, 1988. The best account of the Mormon murders and fraud by the *New York Times* correspondent, considered to represent the Mormon Church in the fairest light.

Myers, Robin, and Michael Harris, eds. *Fakes and Frauds: Varieties of Deception in Print and Manuscript.* Detroit: Omnigraphics, 1989. A small but excellent general work with an important chapter by Nicholas Barker on the forgery of the *Oath of a Freeman.*

Naifeh, Steven, and Gregory White-Smith. *The Mormon Murders.* New York: 1988. Reviews of this book have heavily criticized it for being factually wrong in literally hundreds of cases. While *Salamander* staunchly defends the Mormon Church and its members and attacks everyone else, this work simply attacks everyone involved.

Rapport, Leonard. "Fakes and Facsimiles: Problems of Identification." *The American Archivist* 42, No. 1 (January 1979): 13-58.

Rendell, Kenneth W. *Forging History: The Detection of Fake Letters and Documents.* Norman, Okla.: University of Oklahoma Press, 1994.

Sillitoe, Linda, and Alan Roberts. *Salamander.* Salt Lake City: Signature Books, 1988. A lengthy account of the Mormon murders and fraud written by the reporters for the Mormon Church's newspaper and two others connected with the Church. While well-researched in some ways, this book has been heavily criticized as having been commissioned by the Mormon Church to defend its role in the case.

Tanner, Jerald. *Tracking The White Salamander.* Salt Lake City: Utah Lighthouse Ministry, [1986].

MEMOIRS

Broadley, Alexander Myrick. *Chats on Autographs.* New York: Frederick A. Stokes, [1910]. An English dealer's reminiscences, with advice and numerous facsimiles.

Charnwood, [Dorothea Mary Roby (Thorpe)], Lady. *An Autograph Collection and the Making of It.* New York: Henry Holt, [1930]. Experiences of an enthusiastic collector.

Goodspeed, Charles. *Yankee Bookseller.* Boston: Houghton Mifflin, 1937. Memoirs of the noted Boston dealer.

Gratz, Simon. *A Book About Autographs.* Philadelphia: William J. Campbell, 1920. Contains information on collecting, on European and American collections, and on forgers.

Hill, George B. *Talks About Autographs.* Boston: Houghton Mifflin, 1896. An English collector describes his collection.

Horn, J. *The Diversions of an Autograph Hunter.* London: Elliot Stock, 1894.

Joline, Adrian H. *Meditations of an Autograph Collector.* New York: Harper, 1902. A collector's memoirs.

Madigan, Thomas F. *Word Shadows of the Great.* New York: Frederick A. Stokes, 1930. Reminiscences of a great dealer.

Muir, Percival Horace. *Minding My Own Business.* London: Chatto & Windus, 1956. Memoirs of his search for manuscripts and rare printed material in Europe in the 1930s.

Osborn, James M. *Neo-philobiblon: Ruminations on Manuscript Collecting.* Austin, Texas: Humanities Research Center of the University of Texas, 1973. Memoirs of the great collector of pre-1815 British material now at Yale.

Rosenbach, Abraham S. Wolf. *Books and Bidders.* Boston: Little Brown, 1927

———. *A Book Hunter's Holiday: Adventures With Books and Manuscripts.* Boston: Houghton Mifflin, 1936. Both books are reminiscences of America's greatest collector and dealer.

Sims, George Robert. *Among My Autographs.* London: Chatto & Windus, 1904. A collector's memoirs with seventy facsimiles.

PERIODICALS

L'amateur d'autographes. Jacques-Étienne Noel Charavay et al., eds. Paris: Charavay, 1840s to date. Catalogs of this noted firm, with numerous facsimiles.

American Antiquarian. Charles De F. Burns, ed. New York: C. De F. Burns, 1869–1880. A dealer's catalogs.

American Archivist. Chicago: Society of American Archivists, 1938 to date. Contains some articles of interest to collectors.

American Book Prices Current. New York: Bowker, 1895 to date. Annual compilation of auction records for books and manuscripts with cumulative indexes.

American Clipper Monthly Catalogue of American Historical and Literary Material. Elenore Bruno, ed. Merion Station, Penn.: American Autograph Shop, 1934–1943.

Autograph Collector. Corona, Ca.: Odyssey Publications, 1986 to date.

The Book Collector. London: *The Collector,* 1952 to date. Contains articles of interest to autograph collectors.

History News. Nashville, Tenn.: American Association for State and Local History, 1941 to date. Contains some articles of interest to autograph collectors.

Manuscripts. [New York]: Manuscript Society, 1948 to date. Quarterly publication on all aspects of the autograph field.

The Month at Goodspeed's. Boston: Goodspeed's Book Shop, 1929–1969. Contains a wealth of information on autograph material, with many facsimiles.

Pen and Quill. Brooklyn, Washington, D.C.: Universal Autograph Collectors Club, 1967 to date. Contains short articles on various aspects of collecting, with addresses of celebrities and other noted personalities.

PRESERVATION AND RESTORATION

Banks, Paul N. "Matting and Framing Documents and Art Objects on Papers." *Technical Leaflet.* Chicago: Newberry Library, 1968.

Barrow, William J. *The Barrow Method of Restoring Deteriorated Documents.* Richmond, Va.: W. J. Barrow, 1966. Description of the Barrow process of deacidification and lamination.

Clapp, Anne F. *Curatorial Care of Works of Art on Paper.* New York: Nick Lyons Press, 1987. An overview of issues on preservation, with procedures for flattening, mending, and rehousing.

Cunha, George Martin, and Dorothy Grant Cunha. *Conservation of Library Materials: A Manual and Bibliography on the Care, Repair and Restoration of Library Materials.* 2 volumes. Metuchen, N.J.: Scarecrow Press, 1972. Contains an excellent bibliography

Doloff, Francis W., and Roy L. Perkinson. *How to Care for Works of Art on Paper.* Boston: Museum of Fine Arts, 1971. A pamphlet containing practical advice for the non-specialist.

Guldbeck, Per E. *The Care of Historical Collections: A Conservation Handbook for the Nonspecialist.* Nashville, Tenn.: American Association for State and Local History, 1972. Covers the care of paper and repair of simple problems.

Horton, Carolyn. *Cleaning and Preserving Bindings and Related Materials.* Chicago: American Library Association, [1969]. Contains advice on the care and handling of paper.

Kathpalia, Yash Pal. *Conservation and Restoration of Archive Materials.* Paris: UNESCO, 1973. An excellent and readable guide.

Minogue, Adelaide E. "The Repair and Preservation of Records." *Bulletin of the National Archives,* no. 5. Washington, D.C.: U.S. Government Printing Office, 1943. Dated, but advice is standard.

Ogden, Sherelyn, ed. *Preservation of Library and Archival Materials: A Manual.* 2d ed. Andover, Mass.: Northeast Document Conservation Center, 1992. A series of 37 technical leaflets on prevention of deterioration of collections that includes basic, practical information on the care of paper.

Time-Life Books. *Caring for Photographs: Display, Storage, Restoration.* New York: Time-Life Books, [1972]. A useful guide containing valuable information.

WRITING MATERIALS

Briquet, Charles Moise. *Les Filigranes.* Amsterdam: Paper Publications Society, 1968. The standard reference work on watermarks.

Carvalho, David N. *Forty Centuries of Ink, or a Chronological Narrative Concerning Ink and Its Background.* New York: Banks Law Publishing, 1904. A history of ink and writing instruments up to 1904.

Heawood, Edward. *Watermarks, Mainly of the 17th and 18th Centuries.* Hilversum, Netherlands: Paper Publications Society, 1950.

Hunter, Dard. *Old Papermaking.* [Chillicothe, Oh.: the author], 1923.

_____. *Papermaking: The History and Technique of an Ancient Craft.* New York: Knopf, 1943. A wealth of information on the subject.

_____. *Papermaking by Hand in America.* Chillicothe, Oh.: Mountain House Press, 1950.

Jahans, Gordon A. "A Brief History of Paper." *Book Collectors' Quarterly* 15 (July–September 1934): 43–58.

Labarre, E. J. *Dictionary and Encyclopedia of Paper and Papermaking.* 2d ed., rev. and enl. Amsterdam: Swets & Zeitlinger, 1952. A comprehensive guide on modern paper technology and terminology, it is weak on early papermaking.

Mitchell, Charles Ainsworth. *Inks, Their Composition and Manufacture.* 4th ed., rev. London: C. Griffin, [1937].

Nickel, Joe. *Pen, Ink and Evidence.* Lexington, Ky.: University Press of Kentucky, 1991.

Reed, Ronald. *The Nature and Making of Parchment.* Leeds, Eng.: Elmete Press, 1976.

Shorter, Alfred H. *Paper Mills and Paper Makers in England, 1495–1800.* Hilversum, Holland: Paper Publications Society, 1957. Describes individual mills.

Stevenson, Allan Henry. *Paper as Bibliographical Evidence.* London: Bibliographical Society, 1962.

Waters, Campbell Easter. *Inks.* Circular C426 of the National Bureau of Standards, U.S. Department of Commerce. Washington, D.C.: U.S. Government Printing Office, 1940. A standard work.

Weeks, Lyman Horace. *A History of Paper-Manufacturing in the United States, 1690–1916.* New York: Lockwood Trade Journal Company, 1916.

INDEX

Molière, Jean, 213 •
Monet, Claude, 194
Monroe, Elizabeth Kortright, 87
Monroe, James, 87
  land grant signed by, 77 (**57**)
  ship's passport signed by, 79 (**59**)
Monroe, Marilyn, 230
Montcalm, Marquis de, 50
Montesquieu, 213
Montgolfier, Jacques, 235–236
Montgolfier, Joseph, 235–236
Montgomery, Bernard, 168–169
Moore, Henry, 189
Morgan, J. Pierpont, 245
  collected religious autographs, 252
Morgan, John H., 68
Mormon forgeries, characteristics of
  ink in, 25
Morris, Lewis, 61, 63
Morris, Robert, 53, 60–61, 63
  corrosion of ink in signature of, 23
  (**22**)
Morris, William, 188–189
Morse, Samuel F. B., 237
Morton, John, 61, 63
Morton, William T. G., 237 •
Mosby, John S., 68
Moses, Grandma, 191
Motion picture personalities, genuine-
  ness of autographs discussed, 227
Mountbatten, Louis, 169
Mozart, Wolfgang Amadeus, 175–176
  institutional collecting of autographs
  affects rarity, 4
Munch, Edvard, 189–190
Musical autographs
  collectors of, 175
  types to collect, 175
Mussolini, Benito, 167
Napoleon I, 155–156
  secretarial signatures of, 29 (**34**), 31
Napoleon II, 156
Napoleon III, 157
Nast, Thomas, 190
Naval commissions, 73, 76 (**54**)
Nazi paper, use of, 23
Nazis. *See also* Nuremberg trials; Third
  Reich; World War II
Nebuchadnezzar (king of Babylonia),
  inscription of, 136 (**69**)
Nelson, Horatio, 148–149

Nelson, Jr., Thomas, 61, 63
Ness, Eliot, 130
Newman, Cardinal John Henry, 254
Newton, Isaac, 235
Nicholas II, 161
Niepce, Joseph N., 236–237
Nietzsche, Friedrich, 221
Nightingale, Florence, 241
Nijinsky, Waslaw, 225
Nimitz, Chester W., 171
Nixon, Richard M., 112–113
Nixon, Thelma (Pat) Ryan, 113
Noah, Mordecai H., 258
Nuremberg trials, autographs of Nazis
  who were tried, 172
Oakley, Annie, 122
O'Connell, Daniel, 149
Offenbach, Jacques, 179
O'Higgins, Bernardo, 259
O'Keeffe, Georgia, 192
Olivier, Laurence, 228
Olmsted, Frederick Law, 193
O'Neill, Eugene, 204
Orwell, George, 211
Osler, Sir William, 241
Otis, James, 51
Owens, Jesse, 257
Paca, William, 61, 63
Paderewski, Ignace, 181
Paganini, Nicolo, 177
Paine, Robert Treat, 61, 63
Paine, Thomas, 51
Palmerston, Henry, 147
Papal signature of Alexander III, 3 (**1**)
Paper, 21–23
  chemical test for dating of, 23
  color of, 22
  false aging of, 22
  forgers' acquisition of, 22
  incorrect use in forgery, 22
  Nazi stationery, use of, 23
  sizes of, 22
  types of ("laid" and "wove"), 21
  vellum, use of, 21–22
  watermarks, dating of, 21–22
Parker, Bonnie, forged signature of, 17
  (**15**)
Parker, Isaac C., 120–121
Parnell, Charles S., 149
Parrish, Maxfield, 190–191
Parry, Sir William E., 249

Pasternak, Boris, 222
Pasteur, Louis, 238
Patents, 80 (**63**)
Patton, George S., 163, 171
Pavlova, Anna, 225
Peabody, George, 245
Peale, Charles Wilson, 190
Peale, Rembrandt, 190
Peary, Robert E., 249
Peel, Sir Robert, 147
Pencils, 16, 27
Penn, John, 61, 63
Penn, William, 49
Pepperell, William, 50
Peron, Eva, 260
Peron, Juan, 260 •
Perot, Ross, public about collecting
  autographs, 7
Perry, Matthew C., 128–129
Perry, Oliver Hazard, 128
Pershing, John J., 129
Persia, cuneiform adopted and simpli-
  fied by, 134
Pétain, Philip, 157
Peter the Great, 161
Philip II, 161
Picasso, Pablo, 195
Pickering, Timothy, three-language sea
  letter signed by, 78 (**58**)
Pickett, George, 67
Pickford, Mary, 227
Pierce, Franklin, 94
Pierce, Jane Appleton, 94
Pike, Zebulon M., 118
Pitt, the Elder, William, 147
Pitt, the Younger, William, 147
Poe, Edgar Allan, 199
Polk, James K., 92
Polk, Sarah Childress, 92
Pompadour, Madame du, 154
Pope, Alexander, 206
Popes, availability of autographs of, 254
Porter, Cole, 185
Porter, David D., 70
Porter, William Sydney, 201
Postal markings, 27
Potter, Beatrix, 189
Pound, Ezra, 204
Preservation of autographs, 40–41
  acid-free storage materials, use of, 41
  albums, use of, 41